Mastering
the
Unpredictable

Landmark Books by
Meghan-Kiffer Press

DOT.CLOUD:
The 21st Century Business Platform Built on Cloud Computing

ENTERPRISE CLOUD COMPUTING:
A Strategy Guide for Business and Technology Leaders

EXTREME COMPETITION:
Innovation and the Great 21st Century Business Reformation

BUSINESS PROCESS MANAGEMENT:
The Third Wave

POWER IN THE CLOUD:
Building Information Systems at the Edge of Chaos

IT DOESN'T MATTER:
Business Processes Do

THE REAL-TIME ENTERPRISE:
Competing on Time

THE DEATH OF "E" AND THE BIRTH OF THE REAL NEW ECONOMY:
Business Models, Technologies & Strategies for the 21st Century

ENTERPRISE E-COMMERCE:
The Software Component Breakthrough
for Business-to-Business Commerce

Meghan-Kiffer Press
Tampa, Florida, USA
www.mkpress.com
Innovation at the Intersection of Business and Technology

Mastering the Unpredictable

How Adaptive Case Management Will Revolutionize the Way That Knowledge Workers Get Things Done

Keith D. Swenson

CONTRIBUTORS: Nathaniel Palmer, Jacob P. Ukelson, Tom Shepherd, John T. Matthias, Max J. Pucher, Dana Khoyi, David Hollingsworth, Frank Michael Kraft, Henk de Man, Dermot McCauley, Caffrey Lee

Meghan-Kiffer Press
Tampa, Florida, USA, www.mkpress.com
Innovation at the Intersection of Business and Technology

Publisher's Cataloging-in-Publication Data

Swenson, Keith D.
Mastering the Unpredictable: How Adaptive Case Management Will Revolutionize the
  Way That Knowledge Workers Get Things Done / Keith D. Swenson, - 1st ed.
  p. cm.
  Includes bibliographic entries and index.
  ISBN-10: 0-929652-12-6   ISBN-13: 978-0-929652-12-2
  1. Management. 2. Technological innovation. 3. Knowledge workers. 4. Case
Management. 5. Organizational effectiveness. 6. Strategic planning. 7. Organizational
change. 8. Business Process Management. 9. Workflow-Management. 10. Workflow
Management Coalition. 11. Adaptive computing systems. I. Swenson, Keith D.
II. Title

HM48.S75 2010   Library of Congress Control Number: 2010926036
303.48'33–dc22   CIP

Published by Meghan-Kiffer Press
310 East Fern Street — Suite G
Tampa, FL 33604 USA

Any product mentioned in this book may be a trademark of its company.

Meghan-Kiffer books are available at special quantity discounts for corporate education
and training use. For more information, write Special Sales, Meghan-Kiffer Press,
310 East Fern Street, Suite G, Tampa, Florida 33604, or email info@mkpress.com.

Meghan-Kiffer Press
Tampa, Florida, USA
www.mkpress.com
Innovation at the Intersection of Business and Technology

Printed in the United States of America.   SAN 249-7980
MK Printing 10 9 8 7 6 5 4 3 2 1

CONTENTS

CHAPTER 1: The Nature of Knowledge Work

This chapter introduces the concept of knowledge work and how it differs from routine work. Scientific management, from Frederick Winslow Taylor, has been at the heart of business process automation to date, but we see that it only works for predictable, repeatable processes. Knowledge work is not predictable in that way and requires a different approach. Several examples of knowledge work are presented to provide an understanding of the kind of work that is to be supported.

CHAPTER 2: What to Do When Modeling Doesn't Work

Business process management teaches that you should start with a model of the process, but it is difficult to model a process for work that does not have a predictable process in the first place. The limitation of needing to model up front is explored. An alternative is proposed for handling these emergent processes. The answer is not to attempt to make all the decisions ahead of time, but rather to put the right resources in the hands of the workers, so they can make the right decisions at the right time. The result is an approach that can still achieve the goals of understanding, visibility, and control of these emergent processes.

CHAPTER 3: Moving from Anticipation to Adaptation
41 | Tom Shepherd

Using examples of work from an insurance company, the qualities of emergent processes are examined to find that they are constantly changing. To handle this, tasks should not be rigidly fixed in an immutable process definition, but instead should be planned as the work proceeds. The planned tasks act as a guardrail to keep you from going off the road accidentally but can be changed as necessary during the work itself. This is the essence of "adaptability," which guides work and allows the plan to be modified at any time, but it does not enforce a particular pattern.

CHAPTER 4: Technology for Case Management
63 | John T. Matthias

This chapter discusses how case management systems have been marginally successful for courts in the past, and it envisions a new approach for identifying requirements and implementing systems. It presents a detailed view of the need for technology support of case management, how such systems have been constructed in the past, what possible improvements can be expected in the near future, and what one might be able to achieve with the right improvements.

CHAPTER 5: The Elements of Adaptive Case Management
89 | Max J. Pucher

Many current implementations of process and case management solutions are at odds with modern management concepts. While that applies to all workers, it is especially relevant for highly skilled knowledge workers. Motivation is achieved by empowering people to be valuable team members rather than through command-and-control-oriented process implementations. Adaptive case management sits at the center of gravity for process, content, and customer relationship management and therefore plays a key role for effective execution toward business goals. This chapter examines the requirements for the necessary technology components.

Chapter 6: Data Orientation

Business process management technology considers the process to be the focal point around which business information is organized. Knowledge work does not have a predefined process. Adaptive case management (ACM) therefore uses case data as the focal point around which processes are arranged. Using the example of an employee onboarding situation, the effects of data orientation are explored. The conclusion is that an ACM system must provide rich data representation and relationships, and in the end, the ACM system becomes a system of record for the case.

Chapter 7: Templates, Not Programs

In other parts of this book, you have seen discussions of templates. This chapter will go into some detail about what a template is. An important point is the difference between a template for an adaptive case management (ACM) solution and a process definition for a business process management (BPM) solution. Since both BPM and ACM use processes, data, forms, documents, etc., it would be easy to jump to the conclusion that an ACM solution is a lot like a BPM solution, but that is far from the truth. This chapter will explore in detail why these are so different and why this is necessary due to the inherent differences between BPM and ACM. What we will find is that a BPM solution is programmed in a very real sense because BPM addresses predictable processes. Conversely, an ACM solution cannot be programmed because the precise work pattern cannot be predicted. Instead, a template approach is used, which requires the active involvement of the case manager. We shall also see that the way a process is described in BPM and ACM is different as well because of the way that the process must be manipulated at runtime by the case manager.

CHAPTER 8: Healthcare
163 | David Hollingsworth

This chapter considers the nature of healthcare business as an archetypal example of a professional case management environment. The fundamental attributes of the care process are described, illustrating the importance of clinical knowledge as the basis for decision making and the difficulties of applying a traditional process management approach in this context, where unexpected outcomes may commonly arise. The role of the clinician within such an environment is considered as a "choreographer" of underlying clinical services, coordinating assessment and treatment delivered through a range of potential provider departments and organizations, across a range of care facilities. Potential opportunities are identified for improvement through access to integrated patient data and decision-support information, both facilitating enhanced clinical decision making. These two elements are considered key building blocks in the delivery of integrated case management within healthcare.

CHAPTER 9: Improving Knowledge Work
181 | Frank Michael Kraft

Elsewhere in this book, the challenges facing an increasing number of knowledge workers is discussed. This book is about how information technology can leverage the abilities of individual knowledge workers. This is not about individual tools; it is about a holistic approach: adaptive case management (ACM). But the approach will only work if individual knowledge workers draw immediate benefit from it. In this chapter, I argue that knowledge work will become easier, more fluent, if the right technology is provided. This is the basis for success within a network of knowledge workers, which in turn will yield the return on investment for the companies they work for. To accomplish this, the characteristics of knowledge work must be directly reflected within the information technology so that the use of such technology feels natural. I will discuss the technology needed to achieve this goal. In closing, I will sketch the full long-term potential for ACM.

CHAPTER 10: Innovation Management

As innovation work and management of innovation are extremely knowledge intensive, analysis of innovation provides a good opportunity to demonstrate adaptive case management (ACM) characteristics and to analyze and suggest practical ways of formalizing ACM, so businesspeople can share the same understanding of it and appropriate technology support can be developed. In this chapter, we will analyze and demonstrate how an ACM system, as an integral part of a broader business operations platform, can make management of innovation productive and innovation better sustainable.

CHAPTER 11: Achieving Agility

In the face of increasing global competition and rapid changes in technology, legislation, and knowledge, organizations need to overcome inertia and become agile enough to respond quickly. Organizational agility might indeed be one of the most important skills of a successful enterprise. Adaptive case management is shown to provide the right kinds of support to help an organization become more agile.

CHAPTER 12: The Next Evolution of Continuous Improvement

You've outsourced down to the core, now what? This chapter discusses how some organizations will improve business processes quantitatively, while others will make qualitative improvements with dramatically different results. A detailed example of how a new product is developed shows that this kind of work is hard to predict. Such work can be supported through the use of regular email, but the advantage of using adaptive case management is that it makes what is happening visible to everyone, allows team members to coordinate their work better, and helps new members of the team come up to speed quickly.

CHAPTER 13: Historical Perspective

This chapter presents a brief summary of the technical trends of organization support technology from the 1970s to today. While not a requirement for understanding adaptive case management (ACM), this summary is useful for those in the field to see how the other technologies fit into and ultimately helped the development of ACM. A mapping of terms used in various trends is provided to clarify how those trends fit into the status quo.

Foreword

At Forrester, we have seen interest in case management climb steadily over the last twelve months to the point that it has reached critical mass, so it's great to see a book about this very hot, albeit somewhat murky, topic add to the body of knowledge for process technology at this time. We see "case management" becoming a focal point for business-process investment in the coming months and years, even though few people really recognize the term now. Although case management is desired by businesses that buy business process management (BPM) solutions, they are unfamiliar with the term; indeed, if you say "case management" to the typical businessperson, they will likely think that it is limited for something in the legal, social work, or healthcare markets or government in general. Always on the lookout for the next new big thing in process technology, the BPM vendor community uses the term "case management" to describe this very compelling, burgeoning new market.

Recently, Craig Le Clair and I wrote the provocatively titled report "Dynamic Case Management—An Old Idea Catches New Fire" (Moore 2009). Whether it is called dynamic or adaptive case management, there are several reasons for the major uptick in interest in a new level of support that include the following:

◆ An increased need to manage the costs and risks of servicing customer requests: for example, loans, claims, and citizen benefits.

◆ A greater emphasis on automating and tracking inconsistent "incidents" that do not follow a well-defined process.

◆ New pressure on government agencies to respond quickly to a higher number of citizen requests.

◆ New demands that regulators, auditors, and litigants place on businesses to respond to external regulations.

◆ The increased use of collaboration and social media to support business processes with a high percentage of unstructured or ad hoc work.

At Forrester, we define dynamic (or adaptive) case management as a highly structured but collaborative, dynamic, and information-intensive process driven by outside events requiring incremental and progressive responses from the business domain handling the case. Examples of case folders include patient records, lawsuits, insurance claims, and contracts. The case folder for any one of these would include all of the documents, data, collaboration artifacts, policies, rules, analytics, and other information needed to process and manage the case from start to finish.

This description sounds an awful lot like enterprise content management (ECM) on steroids: ECM plus BPM plus a lot of other technology thrown into the mix that allows the case to be more dynamic and adaptive. That's a correct view of dynamic (or adaptive) case management: while it has roots in both content and process, it is enhanced by new technologies that enable dynamic, adaptive workflows to inform the design of real-world, people-oriented solutions. In fact, as the ECM market wanes and morphs into primarily compliance, records management, and eDiscovery, the ECM vendors see this new form of case management as their future—with content and process married in a tighter relationship than ever before.

Along with the anticipated wave of enthusiasm, Craig Le Clair and I see three use cases emerging in the coming years: investigative, incident management, and service request. Investigative cases include audit requests, compliance and fraud incidents, and eDiscovery needs. Incident management cases include adverse event reports, dealing with medical records, and dispute resolution. Service request cases include loan origination, claims, and customer service interactions.

To handle investigative, incident management, and service request processes, adaptive case management must go well beyond today's solutions that offer ECM plus BPM, or BPM plus ECM. Social technologies and collaboration are critical for the ad hoc and collaborative dimensions of executing case management processes. Predictive analytics and adaptive analytics are also critical for anticipating and making changes to the execution of a case. Many of these applications are actually dynamic business apps (a Forrester term), which must be capable of making changes quickly in response to events occurring within the case and in supporting the way people want to work. Many of today's case management products do not currently offer this level of design for people and are not built for constant change and adaptability.

As the technology gap becomes more acute, it will help drive innovation for truly dynamic and adaptive case management software.

As organizations continue to improve their processes using Lean, Lean Six Sigma, and BPM approaches, more organizations will renew their interest in case management. This renewed interest will come from recognition that older process-automation approaches based on mass-production concepts are not adequate in an era of people-driven processes that benefit from autonomous decision making and highly social collaborative tools. In the past, case management solutions were much more static (mimicking the mass-production processes); however, future case management solutions will be built around constant change.

Not only will the processes change, the technology will change as well. We've needed more flexibility and change in the old case management solutions for some time now, but the vendors didn't offer it. However, because software is now built on more flexible architecture, vendor solutions are much more flexible. We have service-oriented architecture (SOA), business rules, BPM, plus social media and collaboration—when all of these capabilities are added together, it allows much more flexibility for porting unstructured information in all forms: whether it's a telephone message, document, e-mail, or tweet stream.

In this new age, we've been making the following recommendations to our clients:

◆ **Set the tools aside during initial phases of the project.** Reengineer the process first; then pick the tool. The greatest value comes from thinking about the business process—the new process, not the old manual system. Focusing on the tool too early is a huge pitfall—avoid it.

◆ **Look at adaptive case management as a Lean approach for automating processes.** Adaptive case management using "design for people, build for constant change" principles is a more Lean approach than the structured, predicable, mass-production approaches often automated with BPM suites (BPMSs) that typically chunk segments of work and then flow the chunks of work down a real or imagined assembly line. Adaptive case management gives much more power and control to the knowledge worker to complete either the entire case or major sections of the case from end to end.

◆ **View case management as a dynamic business application.** Key requirements should be rooted in dynamic business apps. The application should be designed for continuous improvement, include flexipoints in the design, and be capable of evolving at the pace required for the business. The application should also be designed for people by building applications that are contextualized, individualized, seamless, visual, multimodal, social, and quick.

◆ **Take a "design-for-people" approach.** Identify which processes and people should use a case management approach. Inventory key workplaces required for types of knowledge workers and options for construction. Let usability and design skills drive process design and look broadly at how information is used to support knowledge workers. Incorporate Web 2.0 and content initiatives into your strategy.

◆ **Leverage competency centers.** Centers of excellence (COEs) help when expanding process technology to new areas. A BPM COE includes developers, business analysts, and enterprise architects, and it can be an important catalyst for looking at processes in a new light, help evangelize business process improvement within the organization, and help the organization scale to deploy case solutions.

This is some of what we've been telling our clients, but what follows on these pages is a deeper dive into the *Adaptive Case Management Revolution.* I was thrilled when Keith Swenson asked me to write this foreword to lend my voice to this powerful topic. I've known Keith for many years, and I have profound respect for his knowledge of the process marketplace and technical understanding of the software that underpins the discipline of BPM and workflow. Keith and the other industry experts that contributed to this book have done us all a great service by adding to our knowledgebase and providing clarity about this important subject. Right now, case management is the next new big thing in process technology and it's critically important that we take a deep, informed look to make sure that we understand how to apply it to our business-transformation efforts. Thank you, Keith, for providing that look.

—Connie Moore
Vice President and Research Director, Forrester Research
April 2010

INTRODUCTION

It is fitting, yet in fact coincidental, that the first formal work behind this text coincided with the centennial anniversary of Peter Drucker's birth. Just a few days before Drucker would have turned one hundred years old on November 19, 2009, a meeting of minds was held in Maidenhead England attended by each of the authors whose combined expertise and effort made this book possible. Although this book was never intended as an official tribute to Drucker, his influence on the ideas presented here is inescapable.

During the early twentieth century when the study of business was limited to either finance or operations research, in the spirit of Frederick Taylor and scientific management, Drucker invented the modern concept of management. Although the examination of strategies and management practices to optimize outcomes had existed for centuries—from the military strategies of Sun Tzu to Adam Smith's pin factory—these management theories focused on increasing certainty, while Drucker, in stark contrast, focused on the greater wisdom of embracing uncertainty.

Mastering the Unpredictable both embraces and extends Drucker's lessons for managers and their role in the organization. In "Planning for Uncertainty," Drucker (1992) explains that "matching a company's strengths to the changes that have already taken place produces, in effect, a plan of action. It enables a business to turn the unexpected into advantage. Uncertainty ceases to be a threat and becomes an opportunity." Competitive advantage comes not from steely corporate rigor, but from organizational agility and the adaptability of support systems. Those companies that transition from a command-and-control model (where certainty and repeatability is required) to a sense-and-respond model (where work is dynamic and rarely, if ever, repeated the same way) will be positioned to master the unpredictable by unleashing the creativity and productivity of their most strategic and valuable asset—their knowledge workers.

"The most valuable assets of a 20th-century company were its production equipment. The most valuable asset of a 21st-century institution, whether business or non-business, will be its knowledge workers and their productivity" (Drucker 1999). For most firms today, while the know-how of employees is considered to be the most valuable asset, the conversion of that acknowledgement into increased profit has not materialized. Achieving mastery of the unpredictable in a way that delivers sustainable business value requires more than a shift in policy or attitude: It requires fundamentally rethinking the tools required to support the transition from a command-and-control model into a sense-and-respond ecosystem with the understanding that the introduction of a software system to support organizational work changes the way that people work and the way that they are organized. In other words, it is not sufficient to think of your current organization and how it might use a software system to support organizational work; you must instead imagine how that organization will be transformed by the system, and how that transformed organization will use the system.

As is examined in Chapter 1: *The Nature of Knowledge Work*, supporting the knowledge worker requires a different set of tools than those that have largely defined the common IT environments and office automation investments over the last few decades. Drawing from Taylorist principles, systems such as enterprise resource planning (ERP) and even more contemporary approaches such as business process management (BPM) focus exclusively upon repeatable, predictable kinds of work. They are designed to enforce a command-and-control management model where the focus is the process route, where the item of work or case information follows a predefined path, and efficiency gains are sought through standardizing how work is performed. Yet scripting the work process in advance offers little benefit for increasing knowledge-worker productivity, much less the ability to adapt to changes in the business environment.

Supporting the dynamic nature of both constantly shifting business environments and the self-directed, nonrepeatable nature of knowledge-worker processes requires the ability to assemble structured and unstructured processes from basic predefined business entities, content, social interactions, and business rules. It requires capturing actionable information and supporting decisions based on patterns defined by business users without having to model or re-engineer processes in advance. *In this new process-management orientation that we introduce through this book as adaptive case management (ACM), the case itself is the focus.*

This is an orientation or management practice that Drucker has labeled "management by objectives" (MBO). With this approach, knowledge workers and management establish specific goals or objectives within the organization so that the outcome is mutually understood, but the specific course of actions and decision making is left to the knowledge worker. ACM provides for guidance and measurement of outcomes, as well as the long-term maintaining of data surrounding the process to demonstrate how objectives were realized and decisions were made.

The concept of supporting the knowledge worker through adaptive IT systems is not entirely new; indeed, it can be traced back for nearly three decades to the first emergence of a field called computer supported collaborative work (CSCW). CSCW is where the genesis of this book and some of the original research on computer-aided workflow management can be found. The idea of supporting knowledge workers without stifling the process of innovation and the social nature of collaboration—a challenge referred to as the socio-technical gap—was a key theme in those years. In fact, the very notion of innovation management appears to be an oxymoron in the context of traditional BPM; however, in CHAPTER 10: *Innovation Management* Henk de Man et al. offer a critical proof point for the inherent advantages of ACM.

Yet as it always seems to happen, the IT world swings back and forth in exaggerated swings to extremes. After 2000, we saw a swing in process technology away from flexible processes and strongly into the tightly programmed processes and elaborate modeling that define the majority of today's BPM sector. The limits of this approach have become increasingly apparent to those actually implementing the systems, and a loud chorus of opposition has emerged from practitioners and others who see the potential of process technology to increase knowledge-worker productivity while recognizing the inherent limitations of command-and-control environments.

One of those voices is that of John Matthias, the author of CHAPTER 4: *Technology for Case Management,* who joined this particular conversation in 2007 during a Workflow Management Coalition (WfMC) tutorial session. Having spent years working with the U.S. state courts, he realized that they required something different than what was in place, yet he also recognized that the current crop of BPM solutions could not support the kinds of interactions that court workers need. This ignited a background conversation within the WfMC on this topic and how to handle it, which reinforced the growing recognition for the need to support business processes that cannot be fully anticipated and/or modeled in advance. It was in this climate that the WfMC decided to hold a *Thought Leader's Summit* in Maidenhead England in November 2009.

Max Pucher, author of CHAPTER 5: *The Elements of Adaptive Case Management,* introduced "adaptive" into the group's vernacular at the summit by illustrating the need for knowledge-worker support systems that are not programmed by specialists, as they have been in the past, but instead can be dynamically modified by ordinary users in the course of their work. This is the orientation that frames our definition of ACM used throughout this book:

> Systems that are able to support decision making and data capture while providing the freedom for knowledge workers to apply their own understanding and subject matter expertise to respond to unique or changing circumstances within the business environment.

In many ways, this represents the shift from requiring business practices to contort themselves to fit the design of IT systems, to building IT systems that reflect how work is actually performed—one size does not fit all. The former statement spotlights the traditional gap between business and IT understanding, and the latter is the way all IT projects should be approached.

During the summit, there was a clear consensus about the importance of adding not only our voices to the chorus of opposition to command-and-control management models, but our pens as well, however, not to just decry the current situation, but to provide a framework and a detailed view of an approach to case management that views uncertainty as opportunity and discusses how to turn mastering the unpredictable into a competitive advantage.

This book is the result of that strong consensus that it is incredibly important to let people know that there is a way to avoid much of the waste in organizations today. As is often the case in a young, rapidly evolving discipline such as ACM, getting the experts to reach a consensus that something needed to be done is one thing, achieving a consensus on how to bring that about is impossible—just as in all areas of management strategy, there will be some points of disagreement. So instead of manufacturing an artificial consensus that would have made for a consistent, tidy book, we opted to allow the authors (who represent a broad spectrum of expertise) to each write from their unique viewpoint to produce a synergistic compilation about ACM: the ideas, concerns, methods, and technology at the forefront of case management.

The passion that each author has for adaptive case management is unmistakable and unedited. All of the authors' strong opinions remain intact so that readers may gain a visceral understanding of this exciting new discipline as they move through the chapters, rereading parts as necessary, incorporating bits of information along the way, assessing and adapting with each turn of the page.

CHAPTER 1

THE NATURE OF KNOWLEDGE WORK

KEITH D. SWENSON

This chapter introduces the concept of knowledge work and how it differs from routine work. Scientific management, from Frederick Winslow Taylor, has been at the heart of business process automation to date, but we see that it only works for predictable, repeatable processes. Knowledge work is not predictable in that way and requires a different approach. Several examples of knowledge work are presented to provide an understanding of the kind of work that is to be supported.

About 6:00 p.m. on June 25, 2008, Jeff Young, a fire captain for the California Department of Forestry and Fire Protection, received information about a hiker trapped by a falling boulder in the mountains east of Fresno. For the next ten hours, he was intensely engaged in a type of work that leveraged his knowledge and training to make decisions that drove the course of events and affected the success of the outcome (Galvan 2008).

Imagine the kinds of choices that he was faced with: how to free the boy, what equipment to bring, how to get there, how quickly can it be accomplished, and what contingencies are there. A team of rescue workers was assembled and prepared to go into the field.

The urgency of the situation led to the decision to bring in an Army National Guard Black Hawk helicopter with night vision technology. The helicopter arrived at about 11:00 p.m. with a surprise: the entire rescue team would not be able to go along. There was only one seat free for a rescue worker; a seat that Fire Captain Young volunteered to take. He had to carefully select from all the equipment available to rescue the hiker, taking only what was absolutely necessary to avoid exceeding the helicopter's weight limitations.

The closest, safe landing place was a treacherous forty-five minutes away from the hiker, and it was dark. It took three hours to free the boy's leg from the boulder. After Captain Young administered first aid and carried the boy out of the canyon, a task taking an hour, the helicopter was finally able to deliver the boy to the nearest trauma center.

Fire Captain Young received the California Medal of Valor for his extraordinary bravery and heroism in this particular case (Cal-Fire 2009), but it's decisions like this that make up this work and are far from unusual for emergency workers. As will be explained later, these kinds of decisions and this pattern of work are examples of *knowledge work*.

Lawrence McDonald was a bond trader for Lehman Brothers. On the morning of September 14, 2005, he went to work expecting a day like any other. At about 5:11 p.m., a news flash appeared on his screen: Delta Airlines files for bankruptcy protection. He, like many in Wall Street, knew that this news would lead to a flurry of bond selling by bondholders afraid that Delta bonds were about to become worthless. There was money to be made, if he could act quickly enough (McDonald 2009).

What happened in the next hour was a scene familiar only to Wall Street insiders. Colleagues quickly collected together and poised for the calls. As they did, Mr. McDonald had to bring all of his experience and knowledge about the market to bear in calling the price at which the bonds would be traded. There was no way for him to know exactly how many clients would want to sell at that time or what price they would find acceptable. One thing he did was to leverage a colleague who had made a study of the airline. Other colleagues played other roles without explicit instructions from anyone. By the end of the day, the Lehman Brothers traders had bought about $350 million in bonds that quadrupled in value a few months later. This style of work—knowledge work—might be thought of as less of a process and more of an informed "rolling with the punches."

THIS BOOK

This book is an exploration into new techniques that increase the efficiency of all workers engaged in knowledge work. The invited authors are all experts in the latest business process management (BPM) and other process technology techniques. While these experts have found BPM useful for many work patterns, for many others it is difficult and in some cases impossible to support them with existing process management techniques. It's not that BPM technology is buggy or incomplete; indeed, we will see that the entire approach of up-front modeling and execution is not appropriate for all forms of work—the issue is deep.

These experts have come together to express a common vision for the next step to use in the operational support of an organization. Like all progressions, this next step is both an extension of the previous approach and one distinctly different from it. This new approach aims to support a style of work known as knowledge work.

We must understand the nature of knowledge work before we can discuss in detail an approach that supports it. In particular, we need to understand how knowledge work is different from other forms of work. Then through this understanding, the reason for the failures of earlier process management techniques when applied to knowledge work will be apparent, as too will be the realization that success was never an option. We will also gain insight into the suitability of this proposed new approach.

What Is Knowledge Work?

Knowledge work does not look like a traditional business process (where work is performed according to a detailed plan prepared in advance) because as knowledge work proceeds, the sequence of actions depends so much upon the specifics of the situation (for example, who is available and what particular options exist at the time) necessitating that part of doing the work is to make the plan itself. An initial plan is drawn up with whatever information is available at the time. It may incorporate elements of prepared procedures. The plan may draw upon roles that individuals have been trained to play. The specifics of the situation will drive a unique plan with a unique collection of individuals to meet the needs of a particular case.

While it may be surprising to think of the Cal-Fire rescue workers as knowledge workers, clearly, rescue workers must be knowledgeable about many possible situations and many types of equipment that might be used. There are many aspects of Fire Captain Young's story that illustrate the planning and flexibility needed for the successful execution of a rescue. It is easy to recognize that knowledge is used for this work. When the initial report of trouble came in, facts about the case were collected quickly to assess the situation. There were many people involved who all needed to quickly put together a shared understanding of the situation, so as plans were made, information was shared by electronic means: email, shared documents, and online maps were used to support the rescue.

Additionally, Fire Captain Young's story illustrates another aspect of knowledge work. The initial plan involved rescue workers from American Ambulance, Cal-Fire, U.S. Forest Service, PGE, and the Huntington Lake Volunteer Fire Department (FCSO 2008). However, after only a few hours into the operation, that plan had to be discarded when it was learned that only one helicopter seat was available and the lifting capability of the helicopter was limited. A new plan had to be drawn up at that time. This is the nature of knowledge work: as the situational information changes, so too must the plan. It is not simply a matter of assess, plan, then execute—it is an ongoing activity of continuous assessment, continuous planning, and continuous execution. No plan is ever final until the goal is achieved.

Forest fires are increasingly battled with the aid of IT (Gogek 2007). Satellite pictures are requested and then analyzed with increasing sophistication to produce an accurate outline of the area on fire. Sophisticated models are used to project the position of the front of the fire. Databases of toxic hazards are accessed and symbols are overlaid onto maps warning workers of dangers. This knowledge helps fire fighters deploy resources as effectively and safely as possible. Detailed instructions flow to the people in the field and detailed status information, including GPS coordinates, comes back in near real time. Before Twitter use became widespread, one of the first notable examples of it was by the Los Angeles Fire Department when it used Twitter to communicate with people in a particular geographical region (Havenstein 2007).

What does this have to do with business? Consider how often businesspeople describe their day as having been spent "putting out fires." Workers who leverage knowledge and make decisions about the course of actions account for 25% to 50% of the workforce (Davenport 2005). A stock trader goes to work without a predefined script for the day, instead, news from many sources will guide the actions of that stock trader on that day. A medical doctor does not usually have a complete script for the treatment of all patients, but instead, he must follow the progression and make decisions about patient care at many points along the way. A social worker does not have a prescribed way to handle all cases, but he must make decisions along the way to decide what to do next. If you look past the special skills required for a particular line of work, many jobs consist of being prepared for and handling emergencies.

The case of Mr. McDonald on the bond trading floor may seem more relevant to office workers. Bond trading itself is normally fairly routine work, if you examine only the mechanics of taking and processing orders. But deciding the price of a bond in the midst of a rush of trading is far from routine. Doubtlessly, Mr. McDonald considers it lucky that he was at his desk at the time the news about Delta Airlines came in. All the people involved were those who happened to be there at the time, and the job of anyone that was absent had to be filled by someone who was present. There was no time to lay out a formal plan for this situation, but people coordinated their own actions based on their knowledge of the others to accomplish the goal. Again, the point is to reflect on how little it looks like a business process. Yet business is dependent on these kinds of unpredictable patterns of work. In this case, the benefit was to the tune of almost one billion dollars of profit.

The purpose of this book is to explore the extent to which such unpredictable work can be supported with technology. The purpose of this chapter is to clarify the nature of knowledge work and use that as a criterion for judging the fitness of process technologies—current and proposed—to support this kind of work.

KNOWLEDGE WORK REFERENCES

> "Knowledge workers have been around for thousands of years, and knowledge work (complete with its tools, such as brushes, tablets, books, pens, and other data handling items) for an even longer period of time. What is very new is the categorization of these people, activities, and tools into a discrete field— knowledge work—binding together practices and professions that were previously considered separately."
>
> —James W. Cortada
> *"Where Did Knowledge Workers Come From?"*
> *Rise of the Knowledge Worker (1998)*

Peter F. Drucker made the first reference to knowledge work in his 1959 book *Landmarks of Tomorrow*. He loosely defined a knowledge worker as "someone who knows more about his or her job than anyone else in the organization." What Drucker reflects here is the uniqueness of the job that a knowledge worker does. Drucker also reflects that knowledge, and by extension knowledge work, is constantly in flux. "Knowledge is different from all other resources. It makes itself constantly obsolete, so that today's advanced knowledge is tomorrow's ignorance. And the knowledge that matters is subject to rapid and abrupt shifts—from pharmacology to genetics—in the health-care industry, for example, or from PCs to the Internet in the computer industry." A job based on knowledge will change when the knowledge does. Processes that depend upon knowledge and at the same time produce knowledge have a compound dynamic that makes them especially difficult to predict.

Thomas Davenport (2005) in his book *Thinking for a Living* defines knowledge workers: "Knowledge workers have high degrees of expertise, education, or experience, and the primary purpose of their jobs involves the creation, distribution, or application of knowledge."

The opposite of knowledge work might be called "routine work." Routine work is well known and can be planned to some level of detail. If there are many instances of routine work, then we find that routine work is done in a very similar way every time. Routine work can be analyzed and a common pattern derived. This is not to say that routine work is done mechanically, exactly the same way every time, but rather that there is enough similarity in each instance of it that there is a benefit in identifying a specific, detailed pattern for the work. Because routine work is so repeatable, it can be automated by traditional process automation means.

Knowledge work is not routine—it does not have the level of repeatability found in routine work. The detailed differences from case to case overwhelm the similarity of different cases: it is not that similarities between cases do not exist, but rather that the differences are greater than the similarities. When it comes to work automation, any advantage gained from similarities is overwhelmed by the additional costs of having to accommodate the differences. Only routine work will benefit from the economy of scale and recover the large up-front expense of automation.

Davenport (2005) is interested in identifying a category of people—knowledge workers—for the purpose of identifying strategies to motivate and manage those workers. He acknowledges that workers are not purely one or the other: knowledge workers will sometimes engage in routine work, while manual workers will occasionally engage in knowledge work. There is a distinction between knowledge workers and knowledge work. A knowledge worker is someone who predominantly performs knowledge work, possibly spending 95% of the workday engaging in knowledge work. A manual worker is someone who might spend only 2% of the workday engaging in knowledge work. Still others may find their work more evenly split between knowledge work and routine work.

To motivate a person, you might need to tune your strategy if they fall into the category of a knowledge worker. But the technology used to support work need be concerned only about the quality of the work being performed, and not necessarily the category of worker doing the work. The purpose of this book is to discuss ways to support knowledge work regardless of the category of worker.

Davenport points out that "knowledge workers do not necessarily work in knowledge intensive industries." You should not think of knowledge work as necessarily being the work of librarians who collect and organize information. It is instead about work that is not routine work, for which knowledge of the specifics of the situation is required to determine the pattern of the work.

There is no doubt that knowledge work is very important. In 1969, Drucker wrote: "To make knowledge work productive will be the great management task of this century." In 1998, Drucker wrote: "The productivity of knowledge and knowledge workers…is likely to become the decisive [competitive factor in the world economy], at least for most industries in the developed countries."

Davenport (2005) further expresses the importance of knowledge-worker productivity: "Within organizations, knowledge workers tend to be closely aligned with the organization's growth prospects. Knowledge workers in management roles come up with new strategies. Knowledge workers in R&D and engineering create new products. Knowledge workers in marketing package products and services in ways that appeal to customers. Without knowledge workers there would be no new products and services and no growth."

QUALITIES OF KNOWLEDGE WORK

NON-REPEATED

Knowledge work is rarely, if ever, repeated the same way many times in a row. In some cases, it is not possible to do the same work in the same manner twice, such as the negotiation of a merger of two companies. In other cases, it is simply unnecessary, such as the discovery of a new product idea.

There are always elements of similarity. For example, all news reporters might submit articles by a particular time of the day to make it into that day's newspaper. But the journalists' work over the entire life of the article—what is done, who is contacted, and where information is gathered—will have elements that are unique for any given article. A merger of two companies may follow a very familiar pattern: initial contact, hypothetical probing conversations, a getting-to-know-each-other phase, a proposal, a due diligence phase, agreement, and follow-through. This high-level pattern does not say anything specific about what a given individual would be doing at a particular time. A stock trader goes to work every day and buys and sells stocks, but that does not mean that the same work is repeated every day; quite the contrary, the actual trading patterns are adjusted over the course of the day in response to many factors.

Routine work cases may be very similar, but the cases are not entirely identical. A bank may open fifty accounts today with each account for a different person with different personal data. One might argue that every new account opening is unique, since it is for a different customer. These differences, such as the name and background of the customer, do not materially affect the course of actions that the bank must go through. There may be variants of the process, such as loans for high-income applicants might follow a different path than loans for low-income applicants. A loan application process is often visualized as having branches for treating cases differently. But even with the branches, the process can still be thought of as highly repeatable.

The key is the degree of repeatability: routine work will be repeatable enough that it might benefit from a formal description of the process to take. Whereas, knowledge work is not repeatable enough, and a formal description of the process tends to cost more than it would benefit.

UNPREDICTABLE

Routine work is predictable; knowledge work is unpredictable. When talking about unpredictable, we need to be clear about the level of the unpredictability. A bank branch manager may not know who is going to walk into the branch in a given day to sign up for a new account, but the process of signing a given person up is predictable and repeatable. A checkout clerk will not know ahead of time what items will be scanned, but the task of scanning the barcodes of all of the goods being bought and totaling the amount is very predictable.

We need not be concerned about unpredictability at the micro scale. A checkout clerk will not know exactly which items, or even how many items will be scanned in a particular sale, but it is unimportant to know that level of detail in advance.

When we talk about the course of events being unpredictable, we mean that the sequence of significant human acts is not knowable in advance, and the course may vary greatly from case to case. The course will depend greatly on the details of the situation itself, and the details themselves may change before the work is finished. We will see examples below of a hospital which will start with the relatively routine task of admitting a patient, but what happens next is entirely unpredictable: the care may involve a single procedure taking one hour, or it may involve hundreds of procedures taking many months.

Prediction of the course of events must be based on actual information that the organization has at the time. Omniscience might make knowledge work predictable, but we cannot claim omniscience. For example, care must be provided for a patient that arrives unconscious, without identification, and without retrievable medical history.

EMERGENT

Stories told about knowledge work have the quality of "unfolding" as they go along. As a knowledge-work scenario unfolds, an early step may yield some knowledge, and that discovered knowledge determines the next step to be taken. The second step yields more knowledge, which in turn determines the third step to be taken, and so on. This iterative unfolding aspect is what makes knowledge work so unpredictable.

If I were to ask you to run to the store and bring back a box of mints, I could probably generate a plan of how to accomplish this to an annoying level of detail. I could predict fairly accurately the route to walk and the number of paces to the car, the route to drive, the approximate place to park, the number of paces to the store, the aisle to visit, the location of the product, the approximate location of the cash register, the amount to pay, and similar details for the return trip. This is because the entire task can be known as a whole and given sufficiently detailed information, the entire plan can be laid out. In execution, problems may arise—such as needing to detour because a particular road is blocked or having to park farther away because the parking lot is full—but these unpredictable changes cause very little structural change in the overall plan. They remain minor perturbations from the original plan.

Investigation of a crime, which is knowledge work, has a completely different nature. One clue leads to the questioning of one individual. This in turn yields a clue that leads to another investigation and more clues. This may lead to a laboratory test that yields more clues. The details of the case exert a strong influence on the course of events for that case. A good detective will apply heuristics persistently in the hope that, eventually, enough clues will be discovered to solve the case, but at no point can the detective confidently map more than a few steps into the future. Often, there is a breakthrough that allows the next few steps to become clear—this is also known as an "ah ha!" moment. This sudden realization may change the current course of subsequent action. In knowledge work, even the concept of a plan has a special meaning, since plans are always tentative, contingent upon the next piece of knowledge uncovered. The hallmark of knowledge work is the mention of "Plan B," as this implies the very unpredictability of the situation.

This sort of work is not exclusively the domain of Sherlock Holmes, but it appears in many lines of work: for example, working together with a customer to find a new product direction, coming up with a new advertisement campaign, increasing the quality of a production line, and finding a source of funding for a public works project.

ROBUSTNESS IN THE FACE OF VARIABLE CONDITIONS

One of the most nonintuitive aspects of knowledge work is reliability and robustness in the face of variable conditions. Organizations that need a very high level of reliability make use of knowledge work techniques to ensure that.

The U.S. Marines train their soldiers to know that decisions are made "on the front line." Marines are not sent into the field with immutable instructions detailed to the finest level, but instead, they have the flexibility to adapt the plan as the situation evolves. This is not meant to imply that they act "willy-nilly" in any regard, nor do they modify the goals of the mission. The original orders represent the strict goals to be achieved, and there exist well-defined regulations on how they can be carried out. But the generals know that they don't have perfect knowledge of the situation the soldiers will face, and they must count on the behavior of intelligent adaptation as necessary to the specific situation as it unfolds. From the general's position, the exact details are not entirely predictable, but the goals can be achieved reliably.

This is counterintuitive because we normally think of machines as precise and reliable, while humans are error prone. Some might think that jobs left to the knowledge of the worker would be erratically implemented and error ridden. That is possible, but not usually the case.

Consider instead the reliability of an extremely rigid automated process. By defining the exact process too thoroughly, you can end up with a fragile process that breaks upon encountering the first exceptional situation. Realize that in any formalized work process, there is an assumed amount of knowledge work going on around it, either to handle the exceptional cases or to analyze and improve the process plan itself. Knowledge work exists outside of and all around the more routine practices making sure that cases that fall out of the routine course are picked back up and put back on track.

There are also cases where very well-defined, high-risk tasks are made considerably more reliable by layering knowledge work on top of the routine work. The U.S. Navy nuclear program has an unblemished record because of a practice of engaging every participant in the constant practice of looking for unexpected situations and continually suggesting improvements to the process (Spear 2009). Similarly, Toyota practices the same strategy with their Lean TPS (Toyota production system) method of developing cars. The knowledge work of suggesting improvements is unpredictable, but it serves to make the routine work processes more reliable.

SCIENTIFIC MANAGEMENT

The Industrial Revolution, along with mass production, hit the world in the late nineteenth century, and the field of management was not spared its effects. The concept of mass production is that a large amount of time and money is spent to set up for an automated production run, but the cost of that setup is recouped through the large number of identical products that result. Fredrick Winslow Taylor employed concepts of mass production in development of scientific management, where he observed a worker's actions in detail and wrote a precise description of what needed to be done for a particular job. This description of work becomes a plan that can be used to automate the work: if the correct description can be documented in sufficient detail, then a precise script can be developed and every piece produced will be identical and of similar quality.

Mass production concepts underpin most BPM tools available today, which, like Taylor, involve a large up-front effort to identify a rigid process that is then executed many times to recoup the expense of the up-front process development. For routine work, such as clerical tasks, this approach works very well.

In recent years, the information revolution brought a completely different approach to manufacturing: mass customization and just-in-time (JIT) management. Toyota excelled in this with its TPS that introduced the radical idea of small production runs. TPS prohibits working ahead to produce things before they are needed. Although radical in the mid-twentieth century, these ideas are commonly understood in manufacturing today. Management now has a chance to learn from this as well. Knowledge work will benefit from a mass-customization approach to BPM.

March (1958) in his book *Organizations* points out that an organization is successful not because it does everything in exactly the same way every time, but because it is flexible enough to adapt and respond to the changes around it. A rigidly specified organization that has every procedure fully planned in detail will find itself unable to respond to change. This does not mean that planning is useless and that one should swing to the opposite extreme.

In 1953, Eisenhower said that plans are useless; planning is everything. He meant that the act of planning is critical to success, but you should not view the output of this activity—the plan—as being the produced value of the planning. A plan is produced, but it cannot possibly anticipate the details of the specific situation, and thus the plan itself cannot possibly be useful over a long period of time.

How Do We Separate Knowledge Work from Routine Work?

How do we separate knowledge work from routine work? This is a trick question. Almost all work that people do consists of routine, predictable phases mixed together with nonroutine, unpredictable knowledge work. Take any given predictable work process, such as that of a bank opening a new account for a customer, and we will find that there is an unpredictable aspect of it, such as how many applications one will get in a particular day. There are outlier ("exceptional") cases that deviate from the norm and cannot be handled by the normal process. There is never work that is 100% predictable, nor is there work that is 100% unpredictable.

The two categories of work exist simply as the result of the application of the principles of scientific management. Any attempt to carefully and precisely define work to be done, will focus exclusively on the repeatable, predictable aspects of a particular job. The work that is not predictable cannot be analyzed, and therefore, disappears from the story, almost as if it does not exist. Detailed analysis is only worthwhile on work that is repeatable. Detailed analysis of unpredictable or unrepeatable work provides no benefit toward the goal of improving work processes.

BPM technology is based upon the Taylorist principles of scientific management, and for this reason, it has focused exclusively upon repeatable, predictable kinds of work. A knowledgeable practitioner of BPM will understand that the technology is useful to automate routine processes, such as allocating a new account for a new customer. That practitioner knows equally well that BPM technology cannot be applied to work that is unpredictable, such as responding to an unexpected stock market crash.

When people talk about work, they usually are referring to routine, repeatable work. It is well understood that repeatable work will be possible to study and optimize, while nonroutine, nonrepeatable work is left to using a brute-force approach. There are aspects of knowledge work in all fields, and knowledge work itself is common enough to be called regular work. However, theory of work and theory of optimization of work have focused on repeatable, routine work and have largely ignored unpredictable knowledge work.

UNPREDICTABLE DOES NOT MEAN BLIND

Though the exact course of work is unpredictable, we do not mean that people doing the work are completely without guidance. Knowledge workers are not free to do any action at any time, nor are they left entirely on their own to figure out what to do.

Rules, regulations, and laws certainly still constrain the actions of knowledge workers. Furthermore, organizations will have customs and standard operating procedures that employees are expected to follow. There may be training on particular recommended approaches as well as procedures to which the worker has become accustomed. All of these constrain the range of actions, but they still do not fully define what will happen in a particular instance.

Knowledge workers will often perform extensive drills to learn the proper way to handle situations. Firemen will practice particular procedures, especially when teamwork is required, to make sure that each team member learns how to perform their particular part. These rehearsed procedures can be considered process fragments, but there is an important difference between these process fragments and a fully defined process.

An American football team will learn a set of plays. One talks about the team's playbook that describes all of the specific plays. Teams practice so that each player can learn their part in each play. Then, during the actual game, a specific play will be selected at a specific time. It would not be possible before the game to specify which plays would be called in which order. When we say that the process is unpredictable, we do not mean that there are no patterns of interaction, nor do we mean simply that we don't know what the final score will be, but that we cannot tell until you are in the game which plays will be called. Indeed, there is plenty of evidence that suggests that the tactics of selecting the right play in response to the specifics of the situation is instrumental in winning the game. And so it is with a knowledge worker who picks the right play at the right time.

In process parlance, we would call these plays process fragments or procedures. A hospital will have many such procedures: a routine test may involve several people following a prespecified procedure. In the courts, there are procedures that are dictated by law and failing to follow a procedure can cost you the case. In any office situation, there are procedures that people are trained to follow for many reasons, one of which is simply that it is easier to remember to do everything if it is done in a particular order. These procedures are an important part of knowledge work because they can be easily brought together in the context of a specific situation into a plan.

Another reason that these procedures cannot be considered fully predefined processes is that the procedures are adapted to their particular situations. A football team will select a play, but it will also adapt the play to the situation against a specific team. A fire fighting squad will take a trained maneuver and then modify it for the specific situation accounting for the specific terrain or available manpower. No doubt the Cal-Fire team had practiced how to rescue trapped hikers, but they had to adapt their practiced maneuvers to the specific situation. The choices that knowledge workers make are not simply branch points that exist in a predefined program—they are choices that affect and modify the actual course of action. The knowledge worker modifies the process itself, the very sequence and assignment of actions.

The goal of BPM is to define a complete process definition to the level that it can be executed like a program. One examines all the past cases and finds what is believed to the best way to run the process. The process is enacted or executed in exactly that way every time. With BPM, there is no concept of adapting the process fragment to a particular case. In most cases, the users of a business process management suite (BPMS) have no tools or training that allow modification of the process at runtime, and in some systems, it is technically impossible to make such modifications. Later chapters will explore reasons for this. When we say that the sequence of activities for knowledge work is unpredictable, we don't mean that no one has a clue as to what will be done, we simply mean that it is not possible to specify the process ahead of time to the level of detail that would be necessary to execute that process like a program. The knowledge worker is involved as part of the job in adapting the procedure to the situation.

THE LEARNING ORGANIZATIONS

Peter Senge (1990) in *The Fifth Discipline* put forth the idea that the single most important capability for a successful organization is that of being able to assess current performance and learn from it. A learning organization is one that is constantly improving. A learning organization does not lay out the business processes once and for all, but instead, it uses process analytics to measure performance and then continually changes processes to improve them.

Steve Spear (2009) in *Chasing the Rabbit* talks about the workings of high-velocity organizations. These companies move quickly to realize their customers' desires. They also respond quickly to emergencies and appropriately manage highly dangerous situations. The automobile assembly line is a highly rigorous, defined manufacturing process (routine work). A high-velocity organization employs every worker in the assembly line in a continual practice of knowledge work to identify waste and to find ways to improve the processes used in the routine work. High-velocity organizations are interesting because they wrap a learning organization around what would normally be highly routine manufacturing work.

A traditional business based on the ideas of scientific management would separate the brains from the brawn—the people who plan the work from the people who perform the work—effectively separating those in planning from those who really know what is going on in the factory. It will increasingly become the goal of businesses to leverage the intelligence of all their workers, and this book is an investigation into how that might be accomplished.

EXAMPLES OF UNPREDICTABLE WORK

MEDICAL CARE

A patient arrives in an emergency room in conditions that vary anywhere from a minor abrasion to seriously wounded, barely holding onto life. The patient is accepted for care without the emergency room doctors knowing what care will be required. The course of treatment is completely unpredictable at that point. Part of the receiving doctor's job is to determine what care is needed and assign specialists as necessary. The timeline for diagnosis is not even predictable. Some symptoms are readily apparent; others are deeply hidden. Detection of certain conditions require tests that may be dangerous for a patient already in critical condition, so there is quite a bit of judgment required in deciding what tests should be run.

That is not to say that there are no repeatable activities within a hospital. Lab tests are predictable procedures, and in many cases, are scheduled to happen at a specified time. The administrative bookkeeping of checking a patient in or out is routine. The complete course of treatment for a particular patient cannot be predicted based on the information that is known at the time the patient is admitted. The receiving doctor's job is a good example of knowledge work, not because the doctor has to know so much, but because the job is one of continual reassessment of the situation and modification of the treatment plan if necessary. Doctors determine the treatment plan as they go along informed by the patient's response to treatment. Many treatment plans are unique to the individual patient.

CHAPTER 8: *Healthcare* will delve into the specific problems of knowledge work in the healthcare field and outline how to best support this kind of work.

COMPLEX TRANSACTION

Many of the processes performed by a bank or insurance company are routine, predictable, and repeatable; however, there are exceptional cases that defy the normal rules. For instance, in the case of a divorce where various insurances and assets need to be divided and transferred between multiple parties, the work that must be done cannot be entirely predetermined. The person coordinating this task has no fully specified script but instead must draw upon knowledge of laws, customs, and the wishes of the parties involved to determine the proper course of action. This is a case where the specifics of the situation will strongly affect the course of events. A similar example is the death of a policyholder. Again, the exact course of events is determined by the details of the situation.

LAW ENFORCEMENT

Investigation of a crime is almost the prototypical example of knowledge work that unfolds in an unpredictable pattern. The job of investigating a crime is accepted without any knowledge of how the investigation will play out. The details of the particular case, together with the knowledge and experience of the coordinating investigator, will determine the course of events. There exist routine procedures, such as a lab analysis or deposition of a witness. The investigator will decide as part of the job which procedures need to be called in—it cannot be all predetermined.

Legal case proceedings are knowledge work. Indeed, one could completely eliminate the court system if it were possible to easily and reliably predict the outcomes of legal cases. The complexity of the law, the need to interpret according to a wide range of criteria, and subtle details of the specific situation all make the results unpredictable. The story of a legal case unfolds as new information is uncovered and as decisions are made along the way. CHAPTER 4: *Technology for Case Management* provides a detailed view of the needs of the courts, how courts currently manage use cases, and how this use case management might be improved.

FINANCIAL AUDIT

What can be more common than the annual audit of a company? Still, no two audits are the same. Initial investigation leads to findings, which in turn lead to recommendations for corrective and preventative actions, and the ultimate follow-up to see that everything was done. No two audits look the same, even in exactly the same domain, because the exact course of events depends strongly upon the details of the situation. No two companies will have the same findings. The auditors and the financial leaders of the company draw upon legal and customary practices to guide their behavior.

MEETING COORDINATION

Hosting or presenting a meeting or conference is a complex activity that, once again, defies the use of a fixed process. Arrangements must be made, and the details depend strongly on the details of meeting itself: who is attending, where is the meeting to be held, what facilities are needed, and what are the acceptable compromises. Anyone with this experience can tell stories about all of the unexpected occurrences immediately before the meeting and how they were creatively worked around.

EXCEPTION HANDLING

Exceptions are by definition nonroutine. An exception is identified as something that did not work in the normal process and so must be accommodated by a more flexible approach. Just as all nonroutine knowledge work is accompanied by routine procedures within it, so it is also the case that all routine work is accompanied by some capability for handling exceptions.

CUSTOMER SUPPORT

A help desk or service desk is the classic knowledge job. It is very difficult or impossible to predict which path a support ticket will take when it first arrives. Different groups of experts are involved at a customer site and on the service provider side. The details of the particular case strongly determine the course of events, but many of these details are not uncovered until late in the process.

There is normally a high-level status that is tracked on a particular request, such as unverified, verified, solution identified, solution delivered, fix validated, closed, etc. It may be that all trouble tickets go through these states, but these states do not specify in detail what specific tasks a particular person will do. The trouble ticket status is a high-level indicator of the progress that has been made, but the actual work activities that are done are determined as the work unfolds depending upon what is found along the way.

CHAPTER 9: *Improving Knowledge Work* will follow a particular help desk worker through the kinds of decisions that must be made during the unfolding of a typical case.

START-UP MANAGEMENT

Any organization that starts small and expects to grow will have a few people at its inception who will adopt many roles. This is true of a start-up company, but it is equally true of a new department in an existing company or the reorganization of departments in existing companies. As people are added to the organizational unit, the roles of its members will change, and the processes within that unit will change. It is a period of great change, and the effort to fix processes in place will not be justified.

Such an organization must treat all work, even work that in a normal situation would be quite routine, as knowledge work.

How Is Process Technology Affected?

Workflow technology and BPM are based on the principles of scientific management, and they are built with the idea that there exists an underlying fixed process that can be used to automate the work. The job is to identify the correct underlying process, often through something known as process discovery; formalize that in a process model; and automate that process so that it can be run many times repeatedly. There may be some variation in the handling of individual cases, so branches are put into the process. In some cases, the branch conditions can be very sophisticated, utilizing a large and complex set of rules weighing many factors in determining how to handle a case.

Common to all of this is the assumption that the effort spent up front to identify the process—which can be quite large—will be recouped through the efficiency gain of executing the process. The cost of discovering and automating the process can be many times larger than the cost of a single instance of the process. But if the modeling can result in 10% improvement in the process, and that process is run hundreds of times, it is easy to see how there is a net benefit in the long run.

Because the cost is repaid over many instances of the process, this approach will only work on routine work processes that are predictable and repeatable. Using this approach to discover, implement, and execute knowledge work will not be economically beneficial. One would never use a traditional workflow or BPM process for knowledge work that will be done only once because the cost of the overhead would outweigh the benefit of automation.

Consider the case of Fire Captain Jeff Young. One could observe this rescue operation and make a fixed process representing all of the things that he and the other workers did. This could be drawn up as a process diagram and automated in a workflow system. But there is almost no likelihood that a future rescue attempt will follow the same course.

Some companies have found that such automation has restricted their ability to perform work because the cases are not as similar as they thought, and the formalized work process prevents their ability to do what is actually required. If the Cal-Fire team implemented the workflow as it had been discovered in this case and used that process on the next emergency, what they might find is that when the new case required something different, their burden would be increased. On top of doing the work, they would also need to expend effort to change the formalized process. The overhead that is incurred depends on the number of changes made times the amount of effort needed to make a change. When work is not repeatable, the cost of making changes to the process definition can outweigh any possible benefit of automation. Clearly, a different approach is needed.

The economic consideration for automating knowledge work is further exacerbated by its emergent nature. If the entire process was visible from the outset, you might be able to modify the process once and let it run from there, but knowledge work unfolds and the course of events is modified by new knowledge obtained while the process is moving forward. This means that there is no point in the process where the plan is fixed. There is always the possibility that you have to go back to the drawing board and modify the plan.

Consider the case of the bond trading floor. One could study exactly what happened during the trading of the Delta bonds and draw a process diagram. However, it is unlikely that the next rush to sell bonds will be similar enough to use that exact same process diagram. The roles that people played were dictated by many factors: what exactly did they know about the company, what client did they have, and to a large extent the dependencies upon who happened to be in the room at the moment the news crossed the screen. One might be able to analyze the situation, possibly though investigations of dozens of such events, and determine the underlying rules that might be used to determine who would play what parts, and what to do in all possible eventualities. Such a powerful process diagram might be useful to guide the work of the trader, but it would be prohibitively expensive to create and to maintain.

A FUNDAMENTALLY DIFFERENT APPROACH IS NEEDED

The conclusion is that the concept of predefining the work process ahead of the particular case is not appropriate for and will not work for knowledge work. This is not because a particular BPMS is flawed or is lacking features, but instead because of a fundamental problem with the application of scientific management to knowledge work.

This does not mean that these workers must be left to do things manually. There are tools and techniques that can help to make knowledge workers more efficient and effective. Early work on collaborative planning, the idea that people will work together to create a plan for a specific case is presented in Swenson (1994) based on a graphical formalism from Swenson (1993a). We found that the graphical formalism proved to be a barrier to end users. Swenson (2001) presented an easier-to-use, list-like approach for direct manipulation by knowledge workers. While this work laid the early groundwork, in recent years, the BPM community has focused almost exclusively on predefined Taylorist style process models that cannot be modified easily by the user at runtime.

A completely different approach from BPM is needed that is developed within the following guidelines:

◆ It is not based on the principles of scientific management.

◆ It does not require that a process diagram be discovered and formalized beforehand.

◆ It does not expect a large up-front cost to be recouped through a large number of repeated processes.

The rest of this book is devoted to exploring approaches to supporting knowledge work and making knowledge workers more effective. At this time, there is no agreement on how this can best be accomplished. The invited experts have devoted years to understanding exactly under what conditions Taylorist process technology fits and under what conditions it fails. For those situations that traditional process technology does not fit, they have come up with alternate approaches that avoid the drawbacks.

You will see that common themes appear. For example, instead of needing a large up-front planning cost, most approaches will incorporate planning as a low-cost effort that is part of the work itself. Instead of integrating systems with highly structured information transfers and transforms, most approaches will leverage unstructured and semistructured information documents. The approaches will focus less on standardizing all cases and more toward facilitating the knowledge worker to take unique actions based on their knowledge and judgment. There is a general theme of organizing all information and informing people, as opposed to isolating the specific data needed for a particular task.

We call this new approach *adaptive case management*. Knowledge workers adapt the system to their needs as they work, instead of following preprogrammed processes.

Adaptive case management will not replace workflow or BPM, but it will augment the arsenal of tools available to help organizations work. Workflow and BPM will continue to be used for routine work. Companies are deploying BPM and will continue to do so, and the use of BPM will continue to grow for many years. Adaptive case management, however, will be used for knowledge work for which previous approaches have never really worked.

Adaptive case management simply represents the newest generation of technology for making organizations more effective and efficient.

CHAPTER 2

WHAT TO DO WHEN MODELING DOESN'T WORK

JACOB P. UKELSON

Business process management teaches that you should start with a model of the process, but it is difficult to model a process for work that does not have a predictable process in the first place. The limitation of needing to model up front is explored. An alternative is proposed for handling these emergent processes. The answer is not to attempt to make all the decisions ahead of time, but rather to put the right resources in the hands of the workers, so they can make the right decisions at the right time. The result is an approach that can still achieve the goals of understanding, visibility, and control of these emergent processes.

Business process management (BPM) has received a lot of attention over the last few years as a way to enhance operational excellence. There are any number of definitions of BPM—some more technical, some more business oriented—but one that I like is business process management (BPM) is the understanding, visibility and control of business processes, enabling them to be managed as strategic assets. I think it summarizes nicely the business goals of deploying a BPM suite (BPMS) and gives the context of how BPM can help achieve greater operational excellence. In this chapter, I'll discuss why standard BPMSs work for routine processes but aren't appropriate for managing emergent business processes—those ad hoc human expert processes that make up the bulk of processes in organizations—and how adaptive case management (ACM) can be used to achieve understanding, visibility, and control of expert processes.

Even though there is a wide variety of technologies and approaches to BPM, there is wide agreement around the need for modeling processes. Understanding the model of existing processes and creating a model of the "to-be" processes is one of the first steps of any BPM project. Creating a model makes a lot of sense when the process is routine and repeatable—in other words, processes that can be driven by a predefined workflow describing in detail the flow of work between both the automated and the human participants, and the work to be done by each participant (whether automated or human). The ability to model a process end-to-end (i.e., structuring the process) is the cornerstone of any BPM implementation, and the resulting model is the key enabler of the rest of the BPM methodologies and technologies.

Given that modeling business processes is so beneficial to the process, participants, and organization, why isn't every business process modeled? Should businesses attempt to model all of their business processes? Is this desirable or even possible?

When you get right down to it, most business processes have not actually been modeled. There are a number of reasons for that: business process modeling technologies are relatively new, so it takes time until processes are modeled; modeling is both expensive and hard, so businesses are focusing their initial modeling efforts on specific processes that will give them the most "bang for the buck." In the 2009 report on the state of BPM, process analysis emerged as the main area of both activity and expenditure in BPM projects (Palmer 2010). But there is more to it than that—the business process community is starting to realize that most business processes can't be modeled. Many analysts and practitioners agree that repeatable, routine processes (the ones that can be modeled) cover only about 20%–40% of processes in modern organizations. In Manyika (2006), the term "tacit interactions" is used to define the type of unstructured, collaborative processes undertaken by knowledge workers. "An analysis of US Bureau of Labor statistics shows that the overwhelming majority of new jobs created in recent years in the US have been in occupations in which tacit interactions are the main component. Workers engaged in tacit interactions—such as complex negotiations—now make up 41 per cent of the US labor force." In his book *Thinking for a Living,* Davenport (2005) investigated these knowledge-intensive processes and the knowledge workers that engage in these processes (see FIGURE 2-1).

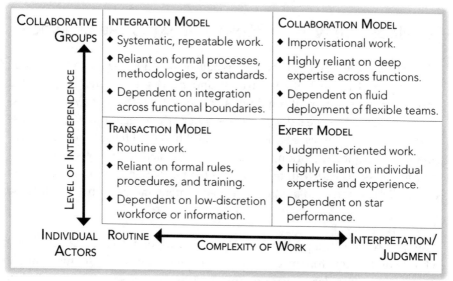

FIGURE 2-1: Classification Structure for Knowledge-Intensive Processes (Davenport 2005)

In Davenport's classification scheme, only the processes that belong to the transaction model and the integration model (i.e., routine work) lend themselves to process modeling. For those routine processes, it is possible to create a detailed model describing the work, but for the collaboration and expert models, it isn't desirable or possible to build a model. For lack of a better term, I'll use "expert processes" as a general name for the expert and collaboration processes shown in FIGURE 2-1.

One easy way to think about these processes is that they are the processes that knowledge workers do using the standard office tools of email, documents, and meetings. Some organizations are starting to use more modern office tools—

wikis instead of documents; email, instant messaging, and web conferencing instead of face-to-face meetings—but those don't really change the processes themselves: they remain unpredictable, barely repeatable human processes. People use these tools to combine process (a particular course of action intended to achieve a result) and collaboration (working together on a common enterprise) to do their work and reach their goals. Another way to think about the different process types is that routine processes have a prescribed workflow and structured\semi-structured data (i.e., databases and forms); while expert processes have an emergent flow and semi structured\unstructured data (i.e., forms and documents).

To Model or Not to Model—That Is the Question

Modeling a process and its flow has lots of benefits—it increases understanding, visibility, and control of the process and processes should be modeled whenever the creation of a model is cost effective. But not every process can be modeled—especially processes where the execution of the process changes on a case-by-case basis. Any attempt to model these types of process (the improvisational work in Figure 2-1) is doomed to failure since there is no routine associated with the process—the participants involved decide on the work to be done and modify its related content and flow on a case-by-case basis.

A simple example is a process initiated as a result of a decision taken during a board of directors (or any executive management) meeting. In this example, the meeting takes place, decisions are made, and processes are initiated—but the processes themselves are different every time, dependent on the context of the board meeting. For example, a bank's board is worried about the risk profile of the bank, especially their loans. So they initiate a process regarding the risk management of loans to European real estate and construction projects. In this case, the bank made large loans for the construction of commercial real estate projects in a number of European countries, and those projects have reached a point where they will be asking for additional funding to enable the project's completion. In the time since the original loans were granted, both the macroeconomic and microeconomic environments have changed, causing the bank to revisit the original assumptions underlying the loans. These loans now represent large, relatively risky loans and have the possibility of external scrutiny of the handling of those deals—so the board decided to take a closer look. The board requested that the international banking division and the real estate division jointly look into the viability and risk of the projects, taking into account various deal parameters such as the current legal situation of the country involved, the macroeconomic outlook, the expected amount of financing that will be requested, the financing sources for the projects, the capital structure of the projects, and the current viability of the developers. Of course such a deep dive process will generate a lot of activity involving numerous people throughout different divisions in the bank and experts from outside the bank—the specific participants and information assembled are dependent on the specifics of the loans being examined.

Even if such reevaluation becomes regular practice for all real estate loans over a certain value in specified geographies, each time it will be a case unto itself and will require different participants and different activities based on the specific circumstances of the loans. There is no way for someone trying to define a general model for the process to know which specific people need to be involved and the exact information needed for every instance (e.g., examining a real estate loan for a factory in Germany is very different from examining a real estate loan for a shopping mall in Russia). For such an expert process, the closest thing to a model would be a best-practice framework that describes the recommended work products needed by the board of directors described by a checklist of actions (e.g., the type of sign-off needed based on the type and value of the loans) and information (e.g., an external macroeconomic forecast for the country for the duration of the project). In some cases, the best-practice framework will also describe a recommended flow for the process, but it is not exhaustive and is mostly for illustration and training.

To execute a specific instance of an expert process that has a best-practice framework associated with it, the first step is to assign a process owner. The process owner would then tailor the general framework based on the specifics of the case being examined and initiate the first steps of the process. This tailored framework then becomes the template for the process instance. Even then, the participants will need to modify the specific process to take into account the unique attributes of the specific process instance as they are discovered.

Basic Attributes of Processes That Can't Be Modeled

In general, expert processes take many forms, but all have the same basic attributes as follows:

◆ The process consists mainly of interactions between human participants.
  ◇ Collaboration
  ◇ Negotiation

◆ Content is an integral part of the work; it is both consumed and produced as part of the process.

◆ The participants control the process and change it on a case-by-case basis.
  ◇ Flow changes
  ◇ Participant changes
  ◇ Activity changes

◆ Every process instance has an owner.

◆ Every process instance has a goal, deadline, and defined work product.

Interactions Between Human Participants

Expert processes are, for the most part, human processes taking place between human participants. These participants may be collaborating to complete the process (e.g., the creating of a joint document) or negotiating (discussing some topic trying to come to a consensus). Many expert processes consist of both collaboration and negotiation between the participants. Since these are human-based activities, documents play a large role in expert processes (and for many organizations, so do meetings).

Content Is an Integral Part of the Work

Since humans are the key participants, human-consumable information (content) is used heavily as part of an expert process. The content may be messages, documents, spreadsheets, and presentations, but it is central to the work being done, and the process provides the usage context for the content.

Participants Control the Process

The process is not dictated ahead of time but emerges as part of the collaboration and negotiation between the participants. The participants can decide to change the order of steps in the process, add new participants to process, change the type of information needed, and change their own activities related to the process—all dependent on the specific details of the process instance. Each participant controls their next step within the context of the process but has no control over the steps after that.

Every Process Instance Has an Owner

There is always someone responsible for the process results and who has a vested interest in the process completing in a timely manner with a useful result. They initiate the process and may tailor the best-practice framework if it exists. They play the role of taskmaster making sure that the process is on track and the work is being done. They don't always get any glory when the process completes successfully, but they always get grief when it doesn't.

Since the process is defined while it executes, the only way to determine that the process is stuck is that a deadline has been missed. The deadline may have been missed for a variety of reasons, but if there is no owner, there is a good chance that the process will remain in that state and will not advance. Expert processes are human processes that take place within a team and within an organizational hierarchy, and they rely on cultural, social, and managerial mechanisms to ensure that the work gets done. By providing a technical layer enabling greater visibility, ACM provides teams and process owners with a better way to leverage existing cultural and social norms to manage and control expert processes.

Every Process Instance Has a Goal, Deadline, and Defined Work Product

The process itself has a defined purpose and a required work product that allows the process to be declared complete. Since the work product cannot be completely defined in all cases, sometimes it is up to the process owner to decide when the process is complete. Also, processes cannot go on forever—they must be completed within a proscribed, but adjustable, time frame. The existence of defined goals, deadlines, and defined work product differentiates between expert processes and "regular" collaboration, which is outside the context of a process.

Goal, Guidelines, Monitoring, and Tracking

The main purpose of modeling in BPM (and one of the key business benefits) is to enable the understanding, visibility and control of business processes, so what is the equivalent for processes that can't be modeled? How does ACM enable understanding, visibility and control for expert processes?

First, every expert process must have a goal associated with it. The goal describes what must be done and it replaces the model that describes how the process must be done. In some cases, they may also have an associated guideline or best practice that gives a generic outline of the process, however, the details of which will change for every process instance. These guidelines fulfill the same role as examples in a textbook: they help participants understand some of the basics of getting to the goal and the participants involved, but they don't dictate the work or its flow.

Second, since these expert processes are emergent, visibility and control can only be achieved in the context of the execution of a process instance or after it is complete. For expert processes, visibility is achieved by monitoring the process as it is executing and enabling the process owner (or anyone else that is permitted) to view the current and past states of the process. The monitoring provides details on both the emerging flow of the process (the hand-offs between participants) and the work done by each participant (either in summary or detail form).

Third, since these processes are people processes, control is achieved by tracking, deadlines, and goals. It is up to the participants to decide how they will achieve those goals, but there is always a mechanism that allows the owner to track the current state process, especially if it goes awry. Participants have the freedom to decide how to do their own tasks, involve others, and continue the process as long as they meet the deadlines and achieve the goal. This lack of explicit control doesn't mean they are completely free to do as they please since the visibility brought by ACM (i.e., knowledge that their work is tracked) brings to bear the social and cultural responsibilities of being part of a team and within an organizational hierarchy.

This level of freedom allows the participants to handle the unforeseen events and information that is the mainstay of unstructured processes. They can modify the flow to bring in other participants as needed (e.g., experts in a particular area related to the process instance), do usual tasks in a different order to accommodate changes in the availability of information or participants, and change what they do as a result of the information related to a particular instance.

Let's take the previous example of real estate loans. Each loan has its own structure, even though it may have started out as a variation of a standardized loan. Not only that, but as more is found out about the state of the loan and its environment today, the list of things to be checked (how to check them, and who needs to be involved) will change. The only way to model the process would be to investigate the specific loan in light of the current environment and use that information to build the model—in other words, modeling the instance itself—which defeats the purpose of a model.

Another example of a widely used expert process is an internal audit or compliance. Audits are done on a regular basis (e.g., regular audits of plant operations), but once started they immediately change. The auditor, John, starts with a guideline of what is to be checked, but he uses his skill and experience to modify as needed to take into account changing conditions. For example, in the last few weeks in discussions with his colleagues, he has heard of issues with a certain brand of fire extinguisher, so he has added special checks regarding fire extinguishers to the plant audit. John initiates the initial set of inspections and meetings that lead to a set of audit findings, which are a result of negotiations between the auditor and auditees. Jane, the plant manager, also got involved in defining some of the issues that need to be addressed. Based on the findings, specific recommendations are made for corrective and preventative actions that include a wide set of people throughout the organization and then, of course, follow up on the implementation of those actions. For example, there could be specific recommendations about where fire extinguishers are located, how often they are inspected, and where they are acquired. Jane will need to get her plant foreman and the purchasing department involved to handle these actions.

For some companies, the recommendation report is the goal of an audit and for others it is the corrective and preventative action (CAPA) details. Some companies also use those reports as a way to kick off new processes focused on the follow-up to the CAPAs. An audit is an emergent process: each instance of an audit is changed by the participants as the process progresses. It would be impossible to define a detailed audit model, since it changes with every instance—the only thing that can be defined is a goal and guideline for each type of audit.

CONNECTING MODELED AND MODEL-LESS PROCESSES

Many important business processes are actually a mix of routine and expert processes—a portion of the process can be modeled but other parts of the process cannot. The easiest example is an exception to an existing routine process. For example, a large customer (XYZ Corp.) calls in with a request to change a product in a specific way (adding support for Italian) that would result in a very large order. Liz, the salesperson, has no idea whether this is a sensible (or even doable) request, but of course she is very interested in closing the deal. This can't be handled by the standard sales process and requires special handling. Liz is used to handling standard orders through the standard customer relationship management (CRM) tool and routine process, but this sale is anything but routine. Even the best order process couldn't foresee this specific scenario. That means that this process instance has moved from the realm of standardized order taking (a routine process) to the realm of complex sales (an expert process). Liz will need to take ownership of the process and pull in a team of experts throughout the company to try to meet the request. Her goal (hence the process goal) is to present a proposal to the customer that meets their needs and is profitable for the company. She'll need to bring experts from the product group (is this a sensible request?), development (can it be executed in the time frame requested?), and finance (does the income justify the expense?) to complete this process. Each one of those participants may need to bring even more people (e.g., an external translation company) into the process. There will be collaboration between the participants (toward the common goal of making the sale), but there will also be negotiation between the different groups involved. Liz can't dictate how the process gets done, but she can use the visibility and control to make sure things are on track and do not fall between the cracks.

The first bridge for this process is from routine to expert: from the regular CRM or sales order system to the realm of a complex sale. This needs to be initiated by the sales rep—moving the opportunity from the standardized sales system to an unstructured complex sale. However, there is also a need to link the complex sales process back to the standardized order system (and person) that initiated it, since in many cases that is what drives compensation and other organizational processes. Today, bridging routine processes to expert processes is mostly done through email, which practically ensures that the two processes lose their linkage. Organizations would greatly benefit from enabling routine processes to launch an expert process (by selecting an appropriate template for the process instance to be handled or defining a first step) and enabling notification of completion (or other expert-process status) back to the routine process. This would enable true end-to-end visibility and control for real-world business processes.

As the complex sales process progresses, some of the participants may also need to interact with other routine processes as part of their goal (e.g., an enterprise resource planning [ERP] system to make sure the product can be made and delivered on time). In most enterprise environments, this linkage is left to the participant who needs to manually bridge between the expert and routine processes by taking the results of the routine process and using them as part of the expert process. Here, too, the organization would benefit from the ability to have the expert process launch the routine process providing a programmatic link between the two.

SUMMARY

Expert processes make up the bulk of all processes in many organizations and are done by the most expensive employees. Until now, business and IT have focused their energy on managing their routine processes, but they are now starting to understand that the next evolution in process management will be the management of expert business processes. ACM is starting to define the requirements of systems needed to manage expert processes. The needs of expert processes, and their participants, are very different than the needs of routine processes, and they require a very different (though complementary) set of tools. Combining ACM systems with BPMSs will finally enable true end-to-end visibility and control of the real-world business processes—structured, unstructured, and everything in between.

CHAPTER 3

MOVING FROM ANTICIPATION TO ADAPTATION

TOM SHEPHERD

Using examples of work from an insurance company, the qualities of emergent processes are examined to find that they are constantly changing. To handle this, tasks should not be rigidly fixed in an immutable process definition, but instead should be planned as the work proceeds. The planned tasks act as a guardrail to keep you from going off the road accidentally but can be changed as necessary during the work itself. This is the essence of "adaptability," which guides work and allows the plan to be modified at any time, but it does not enforce a particular pattern.

In CHAPTER 1: *The Nature of Knowledge Work,* we heard a compelling story about Jeff Young, a fire captain for the California Department of Forestry and Fire Protection. Faced with a challenging rescue, Jeff used his extensive experience to put together a plan, only to have an unforeseen event (a helicopter without adequate space for the rescue team) force him to rethink his plan. In the end, Jeff was able to rescue the young hiker and was given a Medal of Valor for his bravery. Jeff's ability to "think on his feet" and "overcome adversity" provides the key to his success.

To some of you reading this book, this might seem to be an extreme example, one that you have a hard time relating to your own business, and hopefully, none of you have been that hiker stuck out in the wilderness. While you may not be engaged in the business of rescuing wayward hikers, I would argue that situations like this occur every day in your world, so let's look at another.

Take the customer service representative answering the phone at a large health insurance company in the Northeast U.S. At the beginning of the conversation, Jill Michaels might know the caller's name and a membership ID number. A minute or two into the call, she now knows a little about the reason for the call, in this case a question regarding a denied claim for services Scott Thompson received after a car accident. Jill has at her disposal several systems meant to help her answer questions: she has access to a number of documents that might contain valuable information, she has a set of scripts meant to guide her through interactions with customers, and she has ten years of experience as a senior member of the team that deals with priority customer relationships (Scott is a director-level employee for a large financial services firm that provides its employees with health coverage from Jill's employer).

Jill asks Scott to hold for a minute while she does some quick research on the claim submittal. There are a number of reasons this claim could have been denied: everything from an uncovered procedure, to a lapse in coverage, to another insurance company being responsible for payment. Jill's job, in as short a time as possible, is to find the information needed to answer the question and then determine what action to take (if any). It turns out that the claim was denied for much more complicated reasons, and Jill can't resolve the problem in this call. This requires Jill to refer Scott to an appeals process to try to resolve the differences of opinion related to the claim.

If you've ever had a problem with a healthcare claim, a disputed credit card charge, or even a simple misunderstanding over a phone bill, chances are you can appreciate the challenges both parties feel in this scenario. Scott and Jill may have a longer relationship than either would want, and there's no telling how the call will end or which party will be satisfied with the outcome.

You probably also know that no two calls, claims, disputes, or applications go the same way, regardless of our best attempts at planning.

Looking at virtually any industry, it is possible to find circumstances that dictate a less rigid approach to managing work and tracking performance. Case management provides the capabilities necessary to solve this problem. This chapter will show you how.

THE CHALLENGES OF ANTICIPATING HOW WORK WILL HAPPEN

In his book *The Black Swan,* author Nassim Nicholas Taleb introduces the concepts of narrativity and causality as related to the prediction of defining events in history (Taleb 2007). As humans describing our lives, we are innately drawn to storytelling (narrativity) and establishing a sense of linear cause and effect (causality). The gotcha here is that Taleb actually refers to this as the narrative fallacy, and he goes on to explain how this tendency is an artificial construct that allows humans to more easily digest and explain experiences. When we talk about our past accomplishments, our tendency is to describe a chain of events linked neatly through time. It's no wonder then that we try to describe our work using that same approach, especially when presented with process modeling tools like those offered in conventional business process management suites (BPMSs). When discussing a business process, most people try to distill it to a set of repeatable steps governed by if/then logic, even if this isn't actually how the work gets done.

Let's talk about how that relates to knowledge work for a few minutes.

GAINING CONSENSUS ON REQUIREMENTS—HOW WORK IS DONE

How many of you have participated in a requirements gathering effort for something like an enterprise resource planning (ERP) system, a custom underwriting solution, or another large software implementation? In the late 1990s and early 2000s, these were referred to as joint application development (JAD) sessions. JAD sessions are characterized by multiday meetings attended by many constituents from different areas of the company sponsoring the meetings, most often with the intent of defining the requirements for a large software solution. Whether you call it a JAD session, requirements gathering, or some other name, the goal of these kinds of meetings is to (1) understand how work should be done in the system being implemented and (2) eliminate misunderstanding between the people who will use the system (knowledge workers) and the people implementing the system (IT professionals).

I've spent my fair share of time in these kinds of meetings with customers of various software companies. In every one that I can remember, a significant amount of time was spent trying to get the many different parties to agree on how a proposal should flow, how to decide a risk rating, or what documents and information were required before issuing a policy. Inevitably, those discussions came down to differences of opinion between highly respected, highly qualified individual contributors in specific departments. What was easy to define were the entry and exits to a specific group or department. Less easy to get to was an agreement on the exact steps and approach to completing the work to be done.

Standing in front of a room of thirty people as a facilitator, it's hard to decide what to do in this sort of situation. The entire point of a JAD session is to eliminate confusion and discord around how an application should work when it is finally rolled out for use. In most cases, the parties disagreeing on the how and what of how they each do their work were selected for their expertise, making it challenging to pick the "right" answer. Complicating things further, it isn't always the most experienced, qualified, or successful person whose voice is heard, simply the most persistent or most vocal.

In the early 2000s, I participated in meetings to define a new rating, quoting, and enrollment system at a large insurance company in the Midwest. Quoting was particularly challenging because of the multiple distribution channels (direct, captive agent, independent broker) and different markets (individual, small group, large group) that the company served. Even within the same group (small group, captive agent) there was a disagreement over the information that was required prior to issuing a quote. Kelly Tavernier and Adam Benfield were two of the agent services reps that were particularly at odds with each other over the "right" way to proceed. Ultimately, Adam backed down, not necessarily because he agreed, but because he was tired and wanted to get past the issue.

The most common occurrence in situations where there is a difference of opinion is to compromise on a solution with the understanding that not everyone is completely in agreement. Editorializing a bit, this really means that someone gave up. All fine and good but for two potential issues: (1) the compromise isn't always the best answer, and (2) the compromise exists alongside a strong-willed, experienced knowledge worker.

By no means am I suggesting that every compromise was a shortcut or a mistake. In fact, many of the challenging discussions ended up driving very successful applications. But in some scenarios, specifically ones involving knowledge-intensive work, the compromise meant that the solution wasn't meeting someone's needs before the implementation was even finished. The next section deals with this implication.

FINDING THEIR WAY

Knowledge workers are, by nature, an inquisitive, intelligent, and sometimes challenging bunch. The characteristics that we look for in an underwriter, rescue worker, bond trader, salesperson, or product manager are the same personality traits that cause issues with conventional, rigid approaches to work.

We expect the actuary to be able to come up with refined approaches to setting rates for life insurance using complex mathematical theory. The salesperson is encouraged to find a way to "get high and wide" in an organization and never to take no as an answer. Our customer support representatives are expected to take minimal information and track down the answer to questions ranging from the mundane (can you change my address?) to the complex (is my college-aged daughter eligible for maternity benefits while she's covered on my policy?).

Should it then surprise us that Adam, the agent services rep from our JAD session, struggles with the quoting system put in place or that he bucks the system a bit in the interest of getting his job done? Given the dilemma we put him in by forcing him to compromise and sacrificing his autonomy, there are two potential outcomes we should discuss.

Process Flows and Work-Arounds

If you've ever spent time talking to a business analyst describing a business process, chances are that they showed you a very comprehensive, ordered, structured process diagram that describes in some detail how the work at their company gets done. Remember the narrative fallacy, the concept Taleb introduced us to? They've likely spent countless hours trying to make sense of a complex, unpredictable business problem with the goal of distilling it to this efficient, streamlined process model, even going so far as to include process narratives (see, there's that word again) that describe exactly how work gets done.

Walk down the hall and go meet with Adam for a bit. Ask him if you can simply watch him work while holding the process model for reference. In the best of circumstances, some of Adam's work will actually flow the way the diagram shows it. In the worst though, Adam will have to do work that isn't represented in the process model. He'll create work-arounds to deal with the things that aren't specifically defined or called out as procedures. And those activities will generally be outside the system, untracked, rarely auditable (unless you consider his notebook as a source of truth), and wildly different than the approach we all agreed on during the requirements-gathering process.

It's not that Adam doesn't want to do things like Kelly, it's that sometimes he's forced to think outside the box and deal with unforeseen circumstances. In other words, he's forced to think on his feet and deal with unpredictable events. It is simply a fact of his work world that the business analyst couldn't account for in his neatly organized process diagram.

In some of the enterprises we've interviewed, we've even found a sort of "shadow IT" organization that deals with these sorts of problems. Maybe someone creates a really advanced spreadsheet using Microsoft Excel that calculates filing fees, since the system doesn't do it automatically. Or they have a manual process for generating their TPS (testing procedure specification) reports because the data they needed wasn't accounted for. Most commonly, we see Post-it Notes covering the sides of a processor's monitor, reminding her of the right keystrokes or product codes to use.

The fact is, traditional applications, even BPMSs, don't deal well with variability, and it is the knowledge workers that often suffer as a result.

I Know a Better Way

I'd be remiss if I didn't talk about Adam's colleague Jackson. Jackson is an agent services rep who wasn't asked to participate in the JAD sessions. Turns out, Jackson is a bit of a rogue who likes to do things his own way. He means well, and he's quite a bright guy, but he suffers from a bit of arrogance. He feels that he's smarter than all of his co-workers and that he "knows a better way." Where Adam finds work-arounds because he has to, Jackson tends to find shortcuts to make his performance numbers look better. In a sense, he and Adam are doing the same thing, unfortunately, Jackson's actions can expose the company to risk and cost because of his reckless behavior.

I'm happy to say that I haven't met nearly as many Jacksons as I have Adams, but I've run across a few. Interestingly enough, we can use case management to provide Adam a solution to his problems as well as to correct Jackson's issues.

THE CHALLENGES OF THE LAST MILE

It goes without saying that companies implement software solutions to lower costs, improve worker productivity, enhance visibility into the state of the business, or some other worthwhile goal. If there were no tangible goal, it would be very difficult to generate executive interest in a given project and to obtain funding. But too often, the return on investment promised as a result of these goals doesn't materialize, at least not at the levels promised during the planning stages of the project.

Take what should be a fairly routine and therefore simple question: What forms are required to process an application for a life insurance policy? Well, the standard application form includes sections like personal information, lifestyle questionnaires, and benefit selections. But what if there are two people on the policy, for example, a husband and wife? Do we require two applications or do we offer a single application? We obviously need to know about each person individually to be able to accurately determine the risk they represent. So now we include additional sections for each applicant's personal health questions: Is there an existing policy that is being replaced? Is cash being received with the policy? In what circumstances do we allow that?

You're probably getting the sense that there's a lot that goes into the application for life insurance. If you've ever applied for whole life or variable universal life alongside term life to balance your investment, you might be wincing a little now—and we're just at the "application" stage—the complexity goes up exponentially when you move on to underwriting the policy, especially when you involve a reinsurer to cover a high-value policy.

In the course of implementing a solution for new business and underwriting, we can choose to try to capture every possible requirement and automate everything, which is the promise of conventional BPM solutions. We can try to plan every choice, task, and document that could possibly be required to get through the business process. After all, it is human nature to try to fully solve the problem.

One way to accomplish this is to eliminate all the variation associated with how the company does business, so we can fit the process on a diagram. This approach forces us to sacrifice the flexibility that often defines our competitive advantage. If your customers—be they consumers, businesses, or a distribution channel—ever say to you that they do business with you because of your "extraordinary service" or your "long-standing relationship," then you may automate them away by trying to find the "one true process" that fits on a process diagram.

The other option is to spend an extraordinary amount of time and money attempting to predefine all the possible "if-then-else" choices that make up the order in which work happens, in an attempt to deal with the unpredictable nature of knowledge work. The problem with this approach is that trying to go the "last mile" and structure the business process in this way would take an inordinate amount of time and money, and if it is even possible to do so, by the time you finish implementation, the business will have evolved, forcing you to start all over.

The better approach would be to capture whatever structure is possible in as short a cycle as possible, and find a solution that helps you handle the unpredictable work as part of the course of doing business.

THE NEW WAY: ADAPTING TO WORK IN REAL TIME

Okay, let's stop for a moment and take a breath. It's entirely possible that by now you're not feeling too good about the prospect of improving productivity through the implementation of new solutions. That certainly isn't the intent of this chapter. Instead, it's meant to point out that knowledge work isn't well suited to traditional approaches, especially more rigid solutions like conventional model-centric BPMSs.

The key here is that we've spent our time so far talking about trying to anticipate how work happens even though we know it isn't possible with knowledge work. We simply can't predict the future. That isn't to say that we can't embrace repeatable processes when we find them, but we'll get to that shortly.

Case management offers a chance to leverage a new paradigm: adaptation to work as it happens. The concept of just-in-time (JIT) production isn't new, but the ability to apply it to unpredictable work is. We need to move past assembly-line thinking, where we try to eliminate every variation, and focus on how to deal with the reality of work that changes from one situation to the next.

STEP ONE: ADMIT YOU HAVE A PROBLEM

Back to *The Black Swan*. Taleb produces multiple examples of events that had a major impact on the world that couldn't reasonably have been predicted— the terrorist attack on the World Trade Center in 2001 and the stock market crash of 1987 are two notable ones in this lifetime. While it is not my intent to link knowledge work with the tragedies of our lives, there are certain similarities between these extreme examples and much of the work we refer to as knowledge work. The most important similarity being that knowledge work is very often unpredictable in how it unfolds, and as a result, doesn't lend itself to automation through conventional BPM solutions.

It's tempting to shrug off unpredictable events as being impossible to plan for, or even worse, presenting acceptable risk because the odds of a significant yet unpredictable event occurring are so low. And in some situations, this would be completely valid. The issue is that with knowledge work, the odds of an unpredictable event aren't low at all. Customers call to cancel an order when it is in production or even shipped. People like Scott from our first example have their claims denied and ask you to take action to reconcile the situation. Contracts are broken and recourse needs to be taken. With knowledge work, unpredictable events aren't the exception, they are the norm and cannot be ignored or simply absorbed.

Can you predict when your customer will call to cancel a significant order? or when your client's demeanor will have an adverse effect on a judge during a court case requiring you to change strategies? and what about when your star salesperson will quit to work for a competitor, leaving the entire pipeline in that territory in limbo? If you can predict these events with certainty, I'd recommend a career change to professional lottery player. For the rest of us, there's case management.

Now that we all agree that we're not omniscient, let's see how this comes into play in your business.

SUPPORTING EMERGENT PROCESSES

Highly profitable, successful companies that last tend to be driven by outstanding, yet sometimes anonymous, leaders. A great CEO surrounds herself with a top-notch senior management team. And being a successful executive means having people in your employ that excel in their respective areas. Truly great companies breed a culture in which everyone is contributing at the highest level and driving the business forward. The author of *Good to Great*, Jim Collins, introduces the concept of "the right people on the bus in the right seats" as he discusses a number of industry-leading companies (Collins 2001). The book showcases eleven companies that have surpassed all others in their growth and sustainability, and the book discusses how they managed to accomplish remarkable gains over a long time period. While several of those companies have since ceased to exist, the lessons learned are still valuable.

One of the critical success factors identified in the great companies is a continuous evolution inside the company. Success isn't always about a dramatic change, but great companies need to evolve to survive. Take Amazon.com for example. Who would have thought that a company originally created as an online equivalent of a brick-and-mortar bookstore could have evolved into one of the most profitable and successful retailers, or that the same company would bring about the start of the cloud computing revolution? Clearly, great leadership and vision from Jeff Bezos had a huge impact on the direction of the company, but the ability to adapt was equally critical.

An important aspect of knowledge work becomes apparent when you constantly evolve: you need to support emergent processes, or processes that are different every time they run. And you need to roll out solutions to support knowledge work in a highly flexible way so that your trusted employees can deal with the dynamic nature of the processes they are engaged in. If you can find a way to get over the mental hurdle of accepting that the process isn't fully predefined, there is much to be gained in terms of speed and flexibility. As work flows through the system, more details of the process may become clear. We'll discuss analytics and the role this plays in a bit, but the concept is to go with the flow more often than traditional systems allow for. In many scenarios, you'll be able to bring more structure and repeatability as the business process matures. Of course the flip-side of this is that some process will never be able to be fully predefined as required by conventional BPM solutions. Case management allows you to deal with even the most amorphous processes. This brings us to our next section.

DEALING WITH THE REALITY OF CONSTANT CHANGE

One of the great challenges of automating knowledge work is in the translation of business requirements to an actionable system while allowing the level of flexibility required for most knowledge workers. As discussed regarding gaining consensus on requirements, the first hurdle is simply in getting knowledge workers to agree on how work should be done. Equally challenging is the fact that between the time requirements are gathered and the system is rolled out for usage, the requirements will have typically changed. This results in a never-ending cycle of "catch-up" and requires that the solutions need to constantly evolve. The typical software development lifecycle approach that is applied to implementing systems simply isn't suited to adapting to changing business climates. Put together, the problem presents a "nontrivial issue," as my college professor was fond of saying.

As a knowledge worker myself and having interviewed my fair share of other knowledge workers over the course of my professional life, I can say with some certainty that the primary reason this is so hard is we just don't know what's going to happen next. It's not a lack of interest in trying to determine the process or a desire to keep our "best practices" to ourselves. It is simply that knowledge work is not consistently predictable. I say consistently because there are aspects of knowledge work that are repetitive and routine, and in that right, easily automated. But that only accounts for a small percentage of what a knowledge worker does each day to get the job done.

One of the greatest benefits of case management solutions comes from the concept of a template. Think in terms of the corporate presentations you've given. Did you start every single one from a blank white slide? Chances are that unless you work in a startup, you started either from a predefined presentation template or from a prior presentation. Templates in case management are very similar. The initial version may be quite empty (like that first presentation), but as we know more about the business, we add standard tasks, placeholders for documents we might expect to see, and data we want to capture. As we learn more and more through our experience, we refine the pieces that make up the case, and we capture the experience of our workers in the template.

Rather than having to follow the typical development process where your IT organization codes, compiles, tests, deploys, and repeats, templates provide a configurable way to capture business logic and make it available to users. Certainly there are components that require IT intervention at times, but the goal is to put the knowledge workers in control by enabling them with the capabilities they need to capture their work.

When done correctly, a case management solution evolves constantly, allowing you to course-correct as your business changes or even as customers or external events behave in unexpected ways.

GET HELP FROM THE EXPERTS: YOUR KNOWLEDGE WORKERS

You already have access to the most valuable assets you could hope to acquire in order to improve your business: your knowledge workers. These are the people who really know how your business works because they live and breathe it every day. There is often room for improvement in how they approach a problem, and we want to maximize their potential, but your researchers, analysts, data entry operators, and customer service people have a wealth of knowledge waiting to be extracted.

I'm not suggesting that traditional development and process improvement approaches don't incorporate feedback from the end users, as that would clearly be inaccurate. The difference with case management is that the advice and guidance we seek isn't limited to during our requirements gathering sessions and the occasional focus group during testing, but part and parcel of the implementation and ongoing improvement. The ultimate goal is to put control of the templates in the hands of the people doing knowledge work so that they can contribute their experience to their colleagues.

Templates enable the end user to exercise judgment and control over their tools. If a second-level support person sees that he has to perform a specific task over and over again on every incident, he should be able to make that task part of the template so that the next time he's working on an incident, he can save a little bit more time.

One aspect of this that shouldn't be overlooked, as it can also drive significant value, is that "not all those who wander are lost." Just because a particular knowledge worker doesn't follow the same happy path as others doesn't mean that it's the wrong way to go. There are times when variation from the norm is positive. Some of the best insights into how to improve the flow of work can come from observing how someone does it differently.

Shifting from Rigid Flows to Planned Tasks

We've established that change is constant and that knowledge workers are hard pressed to predict in what order various events will occur in the course of business. So it's only natural that we need to find a way to deal with this unpredictability.

The first step is changing how we look at work. Rather than taking the BPM approach of predefining the exact flow, we should acknowledge that some of the work involved in knowledge work requires planning effort, and we need to incorporate it into how we support the work. Think back to Jill dealing with Scott's denied claim early in this chapter. At the end of the call, Jill was referring Scott to an appeals process where his claim was escalated and sent for further review. In some cases, this will involve far more than just a claims specialist, it may require pulling in doctors for medical review and lawyers on both sides if the claim is not resolved. To kick off the appeals process, Jill's job will probably include setting expectations for Scott so that he knows what will happen next and selecting a set of tasks that need to be done for a set of individuals yet to be determined. She's effectively planning the first part of the appeals process and either directly or indirectly assigning work for others to be involved in various capacities. Jill probably didn't know that this was going to happen at the beginning of her call with Scott, but her systems certainly need to support her in this business process.

This requires a fundamental shift in how we think about knowledge work to where we think in more granular terms as well as allowing for more flexible work patterns. Rather than a process with many subprocesses and hard-coded activities, we need to present work more fluidly through dynamic views of the work as it is being done. This change in mindset also provides us the opportunity to break work into two distinct parts: planning of work and completion of work.

If we think in terms of a project to build a new website, the first part of the project involves setting up the project plan. The project manager sets the goals, the deliverables, and the timeline associated with the work with the help of the project team and stakeholders. This is the planning part.

Each phase of the project has tasks for the various team members: the designer creates mockups of the site, a graphic artist creates images and buttons, a programmer might be enlisted to create some technical widgets, and the various departments involved create collateral and review the designs. The tasks are interdependent to some degree and, as such, can affect the delivery date and overall time to complete because within each task there is the potential for a lot of on-the-fly decisions, a hallmark of knowledge work. This represents the completion of the work.

Interestingly enough, even in situations where this type of project occurs repetitively, say in a web design firm, each project or implementation is different, requiring the team to adapt to the differences that the client brings to the table. So even if we could approach this with a milestone-based process, we're still going to need the flexibility to adapt on the fly. Many of your internal business processes will be similar in how you approach them, although some may not require as much planning for each incident.

Tasks as a Unit of Work

With this new mode of thinking, we need to redefine the work to be done. The most effective way to do this is to start to think of a task as a unit of work. In knowledge work in general, tasks will mostly be work that a human completes. Often, these will be steps like "verify form is signed" or "perform interview." The very nature of these tasks is such that they won't always be done within the case management system. The value that the solution brings is in presenting the user with the appropriate tasks for the current state of the case as well as providing a mechanism for tracking the progress of tasks.

An important consideration here is that while many tasks are very much dependant on a human worker, we should automate whatever is possible to automate. Tasks requiring human judgment really can't be automated, nor can nonrepeatable activities. However, we can begin to incorporate technology behind the tasks where it makes sense to do so, especially as we see patterns and repeatable behaviors occurring. The ability to link a structured process from a BPM solution, or some other technology, to a script can dramatically improve productivity. An example of this can be seen in a task like "calculate risk score." A smart loan officer can calculate a risk score given the rules, but if we integrate an automated calculator into the solution, the loan officer will have more time to focus on the softer qualifications.

SUPPORT FOR THE UNPREDICTABLE

One of the key attributes of tasks in a case management solution should be the ability to create and complete them on the fly as needed. Our case template might have a set of tasks that we expect to be completed in every new product introduction such as creation of product requirements, writing of data sheets, creation of training, and dozens of other standard tasks. But what if the product manager decides that for this product she wants to create a special focus group to provide consumer input, something the company has never done before. Should we exclude the focus group because we have never had one before? or have a predefined task for this on the chance that we might someday have one? or should we simply give this trusted employee the ability to handle this new requirement at the point she needs to do so?

The ability to dynamically add tasks is critical because it allows our experts to use their experience and judgment while still enabling a level of audit and accountability that isn't traditionally present in a BPM solution.

The tasks that a user adds on the fly can be analyzed over time, and they may provide the means to standardize and make the process more repeatable. For example, if we see that employees who were interviewed by five people rather than four have a lower attrition rate over the first six months of employment, we may choose to add a fifth interview to our standard talent acquisition process. Or perhaps the focus group our product manager introduced in the last product introduction gave us feedback that we chose to incorporate, and it made the product significantly more successful.

The key here is that we need to let users adapt to the changing conditions faced in a work environment through ad hoc capabilities.

STANDARDIZATION ON SETS OF TASKS

The logical extension to using preplanned tasks is that there may be scenarios where we can standardize on groups or sets of tasks. It stands to reason that if we have some level of repeatability, there may be logical groupings of tasks that we need to complete. For example, while underwriting a mortgage, there are several repeatable steps that most companies would follow that would be captured in a template. Examples include running a credit check on the applicant, performing a title search, putting money in escrow, etc. Those steps, or the sets of tasks, might vary based on the data captured about the applicant or based on the product applied for. An adjustable-rate mortgage and a fixed-rate mortgage would likely have different sets of qualifications. Mortgages in California would likely be subject to different rules and regulations than those in Florida, driving a different set of requirements for the underwriter. Task sets let you predefine chunks of reusable work so that the planning phase is that much quicker and more efficient. If the mortgage covers a property in Florida, we use the appropriate set of tasks to meet those requirements. Similarly, we might have a different set of standard tasks for properties in California.

FOLLOW-UP AND DEADLINES

A recurring theme in interviews with knowledge workers is that their workload is such that they struggle to keep track of everything they should be attending to. Not from a lack of desire to do so, but because in most companies, employees are working on many cases at the same time. If an underwriter could focus on a single policy from start to finish, follow-ups and deadlines would be less important. But since not every case can be worked from start to finish in a single sitting and not every case has all the required information when it shows up on someone's desk, we need to provide a mechanism to help keep on top of the state of each case. Complicating matters, a good portion of knowledge work is time sensitive in nature, either because of service-level agreements, regulations, or competitive pressures.

It stands to reason that deadlines, reminders, and calendaring are critical components of a case management solution. All work should be able to be given a deadline, and that deadline should support business time, not just elapsed time. Users also need reminders, either via email or front and center in the case management application. The intent should be to get ahead of the curve and be proactive rather than penalizing people for missing deadlines. A nice-to-have feature is a configurable list of work that is coming due in some period of time, a sort of "my expiring work" view. Effectively, the system needs to provide a series of soft, but insistent, reminders of work to be done to help move the knowledge worker along.

Think back to Jill dealing with Scott's newly started appeal. Jill might have asked Scott to provide additional information in support of the claim, for example, an additional bill for services rendered. As diligent as Jill might be, once she's off the phone with Scott and on another call, she might not remember to follow-up with Scott in three days (the company-mandated period) to ensure he followed through on her request. Wouldn't it be better if the system reminded her of what to do and when based on the tasks she determined were required?

Assignment, Routing, and Collaboration

When starting process improvement initiatives, there is a tendency on the part of the analysts to view workers as having very structured work environments where work is assigned to them on a "push" basis, mostly out of their control. While this is certainly characteristic of some heads-down types of processes, it is not an accurate view of how knowledge workers acquire their day-to-day work.

BPM enables the assembly-line approach of feeding a worker a steady stream of piecework. Case management, on the other hand, allows more flexibility in the obtaining of work. This is not to say that there is no higher-level control of work to be done, or prioritization of critical tasks, but rather a level of flexibility in how and when work is started and stopped. The primary reason for this is to enable the deadlines and follow-up work inherent in knowledge work. An assembly-line approach to specialization of work is effective where workers are expected to do a small part of an overall job, but what about the underwriter at the life insurance company? She doesn't get to do a single task and move the pile of paper down the line. She, instead, has responsibility for a number of tasks associated with underwriting the risk on the policy, and she needs the assistance of a number of her colleagues.

Earlier we discussed planning tasks rather than predefining the flow of work in a rigid process model. Instead of a fixed "route on" or "forward" button, the knowledge worker is given the power to exercise judgment on who is best suited to a particular task and how and when to complete the tasks required. This enables the person responsible for the case to manage the overall progress of the case toward resolution while involving multiple parties to do the work simultaneously. What we end up with is the visibility of a managed process with the flexibility and compressed duration of a collaborative working environment. Tasks are defined as dependent on data, documents, or other tasks so work proceeds in an orderly fashion and not in a random order. The challenge this presents is that we need to be sure the knowledge worker knows how to proceed appropriately, which leads us to our next section.

OF GUARDRAILS AND GUIDING PRINCIPLES

Much of what we expect our knowledge workers to know about how to do their job is determined by business rules, policies, and procedures. These manifest themselves throughout the organization in everything from benefits and human resources policies, to exact steps describing how to handle a call or address change. Some larger organizations have entire departments dedicated to keeping policies and procedures up to date, others rely on the line managers to define them. Whatever the case, rules are a fact of life and something we need to account for in knowledge work. In fact, the application of these rules to work is an effective means of driving the work forward with an empowered business user. For simplicity's sake, we'll refer to business rules, policies, and procedures as "rules" for the remainder of this section.

Rules can be categorized in two major buckets: hard-and-fast rules that cannot be broken and soft rules that are either optional or used as guidance.

ABSOLUTELY

In every business scenario, there are rules that simply can't be broken. Examples of these can be seen in HIPAA rules governing privacy, in licensing requirements for professionals like stock brokers, or in any number of other ways.

Clearly, we need a mechanism to enforce these rules and to be sure that the end user understands the how and why. In many cases, these type of rules are embedded into the templates in the form of required documents, calculations used in many different ways, or as gates between stages of a case.

Examples of absolute rules applied to various business problems are as follows:

◆ The task "verify form signature" must be performed before the life application can be underwritten.

◆ Stock certificates must be received within three days of trade confirmation.

◆ Applicants must be eighteen years or older.

Absolute rules can also be used to enforce work qualifications or skills. For example, a junior underwriter might be limited to loan values less than $250,000, so the system must not allow her to work on any cases with larger loan values. Or we might see that an agent is licensed in New Hampshire and Massachusetts but not in Vermont, so he should not be able to quote business in Vermont.

Shades of Gray

Where knowledge work and the application of rules get interesting is when we look at soft rules. By soft rules, I am referring to rules that are less rigid, often not required, and in many cases, are best practices or recommendations.

Examples of soft rules include the following:

◆ Allowing an underwriter to override a risk rating that was calculated based on his judgment.

◆ Softening the requirements for documented proof of income when the applicant's credit score is over 750.

◆ Deciding to have a different department head interview the product management candidate.

As you can see from the examples, we've established guidelines and procedures for the tasks to be done. However, we've allowed the knowledge worker to deviate from the norm either because of some unique scenario or because her experience dictates that the standard approach isn't effective.

These shades of gray are critical to the success of case management because of the nature of knowledge work. It is important to plan tasks as discussed earlier, but it is even more important to leave room for the unpredictable.

Rules as Guardrails

The challenging part of mastering knowledge work is that we need to be able to adapt to the way work needs to be done. Rules, both absolute and soft, are powerful tools to help guide and protect the knowledge worker while allowing them to adapt to the changing dynamics they face every day. It is sometimes helpful to think of the rules we apply as being like the guardrails and the painted edge lines on roads. The guardrails (the absolute rules) keep the driver on the road and safe from going too far off the edge. With a skilled driver, good weather, and a little luck, the guardrails are simply there as a precaution never to be used. The same could be said of rules as the knowledge worker becomes more skilled in the application of their expertise. The painted edge lines (soft rules) help guide the driver along their journey.

BUILDING YOUR GUARDRAILS

As we've discussed, rules are inherently part of knowledge work, whether they are codified into the system, part of an extensive policies and procedures manual, or simply ingrained in peoples' experience. Because of this, it's critical that case management solutions provide a way to capture those rules into the templates that define the solution. The rules can be implemented as scripts, process fragments, or simply logic tests associated with tasks.

In some cases, integration with an external business rules management solution might be advantageous, but a case management solution should provide a level of capability without having to integrate as well. Otherwise, building your guardrails becomes a job that necessitates traditional software implementation approaches, somewhat negating the benefits of a template-based approach with case management.

THE GUIDING PRINCIPLE

When we put all this into action, a final variable needs to be factored in: the skill and preferences of the underwriter, lawyer, customer service representative, or analyst. Not all users are created equal. You might have senior underwriters that mentor associate ones. Or, in the case of our customer service representative Jill, we have a senior member of the team who is quite familiar with what she's capable of and allowed to do. The tasks people do and the rules that are applied should allow for differences in skill. For example, providing more guidance to and potentially placing restrictions on those who are less experienced. While it is easy to understand how we need to guide a new employee, it is equally important to provide a level of autonomy to your top people. Having interviewed a sizeable number of people considered knowledge workers, it has become very apparent to me that they thrive when given autonomy and purpose, just as they become disillusioned when given overly restrictive systems. Trusting your more experienced people allows them to thrive, and in many cases, they will self regulate.

THE NEW THREE A'S: ANALYTICS, AUDIT, AND ACCOUNTABILITY

Elsewhere in this book, you'll read about the importance of data as it relates to case management. One of the reasons it is so critical is to enable analytics, audit, and, ultimately, accountability. As work flows through the case management system, it will be tracked, measured, and analyzed. The goal is to understand everything from the average time to complete a task, to the time that work sits in a backlog waiting to be done, to the frequency certain rules are used, to who has the highest average premium value. It is no small feat to be able to capture and report against tasks that might or might not happen, but the data gathered is extremely valuable.

Aside from a general picture of the state of the business, analytics can help find patterns in work that may enable repeatability. Over time, we may see a certain type of task being done in a large percentage of successful cases, and we may decide to implement it as a required task. Without data, none of this is possible.

One of the ultimate goals of a case management system is really accountability. Knowledge work has been regarded as a black box as far as process improvement is concerned. Case management solutions enable companies to see into that black box and look for ways to make it more effective.

CONCLUSION—SUPPORTING KNOWLEDGE WORK

Throughout this book, one common thread is evident: knowledge work is unique and necessitates solutions that can handle those differences. Further, knowledge work is more pervasive than most companies and managers realize. While there are clearly classes of workers who do knowledge work day in and day out, there are also quite a few who do knowledge work some of the time, and as a result, they need the same tools and capabilities.

Leverage templates rather than fully constrained applications so that your internal experts can evolve their capabilities without total reliance on traditional system implementation restrictions. Move from predefined processes to supporting planned tasks. Support ad hoc tasks and content to enable users to deal with the unknown. Implement rules that can guide users and keep them on track as needed without introducing too much rigidity. Leverage analytics to ensure that performance is appropriate and to find trends and repeatability.

People who do knowledge work are experienced, intelligent, and autonomous, and as a result, they need solutions that guide them without over-constraining them. Give them the tools to adapt to work as it happens instead of having to find a way around the systems they use.

The ultimate goal of case management is to better support knowledge work by allowing you to move from trying to anticipate what might happen to being able to adapt to what does happen. After all, we're not all-knowing, and business, like life, just happens.

CHAPTER 4

TECHNOLOGY FOR CASE MANAGEMENT

JOHN T. MATTHIAS

This chapter discusses how case management systems have been marginally successful for courts in the past, and it envisions a new approach for identifying requirements and implementing systems. It presents a detailed view of the need for technology support of case management, how such systems have been constructed in the past, what possible improvements can be expected in the near future, and what one might be able to achieve with the right improvements.

The need for adaptive case management (ACM) has emerged from the joint failure of the software industry and in-house people responsible for addressing the needs of knowledge workers in enterprises who handle cases—both in the private and public sectors. Knowledge work will be described in more detail, but briefly, it is work involving ad hoc, nonsequential, and nondeterministic processes driven primarily by external events and handled with human discretion and judgment in an environment requiring collaboration among case participants with rich information. Part of industry's failure to automate case management derives from a lack of understanding of what knowledge workers need to do their work and an inability to discover requirements.

An organization's ability to manage cases effectively is strategic. In both the private and public sectors, the ability to provide an enabling environment for knowledge work is strategic in capturing the best ideas of employees as they find better ways to perform their jobs in a changing external and internal environment. Although the goals of private and public organizations are different, they share a common need to allow their knowledge workers to handle cases efficiently and effectively.

Software technology, since its invention, has been searching for the "holy grail": methods to develop systems for knowledge workers that (1) fulfill the mission of knowledge workers and the enterprise and (2) evolve under the guidance of businesspeople (not IT professionals) as the business environment continuously changes. Case management is difficult to design and implement because of incomplete, contradictory, changing requirements (which are often difficult to discover from knowledge workers) and complex interdependencies of data and knowledge workers. Conventional approaches to software development do not capture the kinds of interaction needed between knowledge workers and IT professionals to achieve this goal. Hitting this target will make a strategic difference for an organization.

CASE MANAGEMENT ENCOMPASSES WORK BEYOND TRADITIONAL "CASES"

Work with cases is pervasive in the private and public sectors, and the term "case" includes more than one may initially assume. Work on a case involves a group of knowledge workers performing a series of activities in the course of multiple, interlinked processes to deliver a product or service. A case has a beginning and an end and is distinct from other cases, but the course of a case is unpredictable because of external events, the need for the knowledge worker to apply judgment during performance of activities, and the need to collaborate with the human subjects of the case, as well as with other knowledge workers, within and outside the organization by exchanging information.

Attempts to automate case management have met with only partial success. Though not for lack of trying over a period of decades, knowledge workers and software developers have produced systems that only partially automate or facilitate activities and processes. Typical systems developed in response to case management needs seriously compromise the promise of automation and are unable to evolve with the enterprise's business environment. In the American justice system, for example, courts typically keep a system for ten to twenty years—modifying it every few years (or upgrading with a vendor's new releases) at considerable expense—but they only migrate to a new system at the point that no one can stand it any longer. By then, much of the operational and decision-making information is in innumerable spreadsheets, Microsoft Word documents, and handwritten checklists or ledgers that workers rely on to perform their activities.

Both custom/bespoke software development and commercial off-the-shelf (COTS) software, whether developed in Windows or Java environments or using toolsets like business process management suites (BPMSs), historically have serious shortcomings because of their failures to address the dynamic nature of handling and managing cases, multiple interactions with internal and external stakeholders, and rapid change capabilities needed.

Analyst Sandy Kemsley's *A Short History of BPM* (2006) proposes that business process management (BPM) is not just workflow plus enterprise application integration (EAI) plus business activity monitoring (BAM) plus business rules, etc.: it's the near-seamless integration of all of these tools into a single suite that provides workers with the ability to do things that an organization could never do before. Proponents of BPM may insist that it is an effective toolset for developing case management systems, although others will disagree. BPM is an evolving technology, so reasonable people with different facts and ideas will disagree.

This chapter's purpose is to raise the bar for the following groups of people:

◆ Knowledge workers (and their supervisors) to conceptualize why their jobs are more difficult without proper system support (though they understand it anecdotally).

◆ Software developers and vendors to understand what capabilities are required for case work and provide better functionality for it.

◆ Executives who have a duty to provide resources to support their knowledge workers to fulfill the purpose of their organizations.

◆ Chief technology officers need to be aware of what technology is delivering—or failing to deliver—to their organizations.

While this chapter takes case management in courts as its reference point, it will evoke recognition of characteristics of case management in other fields.

BRIEF HISTORY OF CASE MANAGEMENT AND ATTEMPTS TO AUTOMATE IT

While not a comprehensive history of computing, this discussion provides some context for how case management has evolved to its current state.

PAPER FILES

As long as there have been courts operating under laws and rules, paper documentation has provided a public record of the activities of this arm of government. (The same applies to business organizations and their internal recordkeeping needs.) The form and method of creating and using paper records have evolved, but surprisingly, many kinds of recordkeeping are still recognizable in their nineteenth century form. FIGURE 4-1 depicts a common sight in many offices.

FIGURE 4-1: Paper-Based Records

When case records are in paper form, physical folders can be used by only one person at a time. Folders are often "lost" because someone else is using them in an unanticipated location. The need to record information in a paper folder involves labor in moving the folder to where it will be used, handwriting notes about the interaction, and then re-filing the folder into its usual location. There is delay in entering data into an automated system (assuming there is some computer support).

FIRST-GENERATION COMPUTER SUPPORT

Character-based systems (mainframes and minicomputers) automated manual processes without significantly retooling their paper-based approach, resulting in "paving the cow path." Summary and detailed information at least was available online. FIGURE 4-2 shows a typical screenshot of a "green screen" application (named for the green characters on a black background).

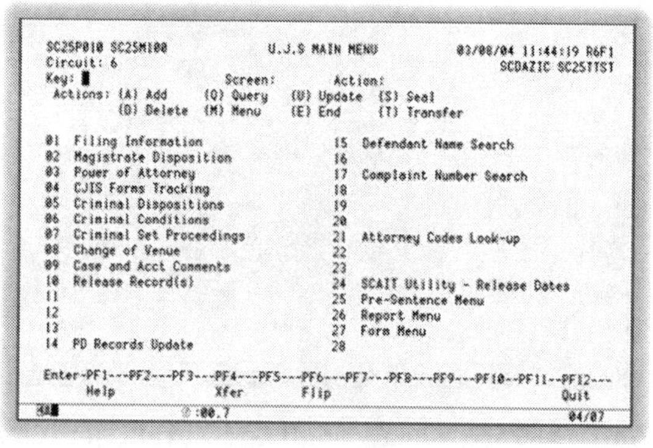

FIGURE 4-2: Character-Based "Green Screen"

System knowledge workers relied on function keys for navigation through multiple screens to perform a function, a very structured activity. There was a general lack of data input validation or enforcement of data entry/update rules, and significant amounts of data were entered into nonsearchable text fields. Systems were rigid, although workers created work-arounds to use available capabilities in unexpected ways, and stored information in information sources external to the system. This generation of technology saw the migration from hierarchical to relational database technology, and there was little or no ad hoc reporting. Software development tools were predominantly COBOL and RPG custom coding, although COTS packages often formed a basis for customizing applications.

FIRST-GENERATION GRAPHICAL USER INTERFACE SYSTEMS

The advent of PCs brought the advent of client/server computing and its relatively lower cost. The trend continued of automating manual processes without retooling work approaches, although the GUI opened windows on rethinking how applications could support knowledge workers. Workers were able to use a mouse to navigate, although usually it required many screens to perform a function. Software development toolsets made it easier to validate data being entered, and knowledge workers could select an item from a pick list with a mouse rather than a function key. FIGURE 4-3 shows a typical case management GUI.

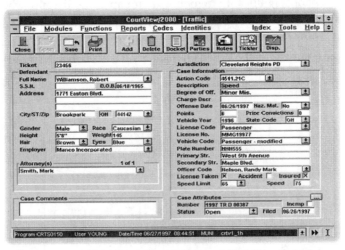

FIGURE 4-3: Case Management Graphical User Interface

Despite the advances in usability, these systems were still quite rigid, requiring workers to create work-arounds and find recourse in storing essential information in external sources outside the system. These systems were developed predominantly in C++ and fourth-generation languages for custom coding, and the COTS business model moved from forming a basis for customizing applications to offering new releases/upgrades of the package. For management information, there was still fairly limited ad hoc reporting.

BROWSER-BASED, HIGHLY-CONFIGURABLE CASE MANAGEMENT SYSTEMS

A new generation of event-driven case management systems has emerged as COTS products. These products are realizing the potential to retool the approach to case management work. Configuration of the system, now a framework rather than a customized code base, provides flexibility in setting the system up to match the needs of the environment rather than forcing the organization to meet the computational needs of the system. In addition to responding to external events by entering data, the system performs more functions automatically in a workflow, presenting workers with activities to perform in a work queue (analogous to an email inbox, a widely known metaphor).

FIGURE 4-4 shows a case management GUI using event-driven architecture (Caseflow). Caseflow adapts to events as they actually occur and serves as an automatic tickler mechanism. Exceptions to normal caseflow are handled "in-flight" by adding activities and continue to be tracked within the system. The system facilitates central monitoring of work in process and reallocation of activities to other workers, reflecting priorities and balancing of knowledge-worker workloads. Caseflow's functions, screens, forms, and reports are configurable for each court, judge, and case type.

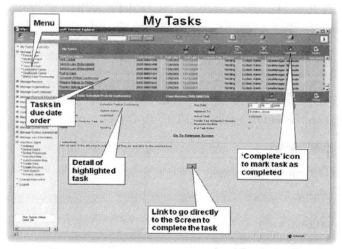

FIGURE 4-4: Event-Driven Case Management

Management of operations is becoming easier through business activity monitoring of worker work queues, relatively easier ad hoc reporting, and allowing knowledge workers to maintain the business rules and workflow.

These systems are typically developed as proprietary products in Windows or Java environments (though a trend may emerge involving open source code) increasingly using web-based service-oriented architecture (SOA). Whether

BPMSs can be used as a platform to meet the needs of case management has yet to be demonstrated in court case management.

THREE MISCONCEPTIONS ABOUT CASE MANAGEMENT AND WHY IT MATTERS

All areas of private and public sector activity conduct case management, whether they know it or not. Knowledge workers who manage cases are not well served either by the COTS software industry or the in-house development capabilities of the workers' organizations. This section describes the characteristics of cases and presents the challenge of automating case management.

MISCONCEPTION 1: Case management involves only traditional cases in the sense of professional services (e.g., legal, medical, and psychological).

Case management is, in fact, more pervasive in the private and public sectors than one may initially assume. Much of how government touches our lives at the local, state, and national levels involves case management, including the following:

◆ Social welfare benefits

◆ Child support enforcement and Title IV-D recovery

◆ Immigration status

◆ Unemployment insurance

◆ Public utilities rates

◆ Occupational safety

◆ Equal employment opportunity

◆ Driver licensing

◆ Professional licensing

◆ Government permits

◆ Freedom of Information Act requests

Types of cases discussed in this chapter focus on public sector areas, primarily court-related (e.g., prosecution, court case adjudication, and execution of judicial judgments such as probation, fine collection, and forced sale of property). The court system provides a procedural framework within which all of the cases that come through it are handled individually according to rules, each according to a case's characteristics.

Case management is similar to other business activities that are supported by computer applications, but case management requires a different mix of technology support capabilities.

MISCONCEPTION 2: If we can get a man to the moon, software projects shouldn't be so hard.

The failure rate of case management software projects is high, in part because case management system requirements are difficult to specify and to implement, whether custom software development or COTS products. Although software engineering techniques are intended to deliver good systems, there are many reasons for the failure rate, and it is beyond the scope of this chapter to enumerate them. One reason, addressed later, is the translation from business requirement to system function required in many implementations because business users do not have the tools to adapt the system to their needs.

The Standish Group (2009) has followed project resolution since at least 1998. Its "Chaos Summary 2009" reports the highest failure rate in over a decade with 32% of all projects succeeding (delivered on time, on budget, with required features and functions), 44% challenged (late, over budget, and/or with less than the required features and functions), and 24% failing (cancelled prior to completion or delivered and never used).

MISCONCEPTION 3: Systems to manage cases aren't much different from other applications of computer technology, like manufacturing goods or running a business.

Managing cases is, in fact, very different from other uses of computer technology because of the inherent difference of cases compared to business activities like tracking inventory or performing transactions. Cases are more difficult to manage, and current case management technology falls short because of the following characteristics of cases.

◆ **A case unfolds over potentially a relatively long duration and culminates with one or more decisions by one or more authoritative decision makers.**

Cases conclude after decisions are made and may persist over significant periods of time.

◇ **Decision Making**—A case worker who is authoritative within a certain sphere of case activity will make one or more decisions with respect to the case. Case workers make procedural decisions and substantive decisions within the scope of their authority both before and after the primary authoritative decision.

◇ **Duration**—A case may span days, weeks, months, or years. Recordkeeping is critical to maintaining a knowledgebase for case workers to refer to later, since a person may or may not have worked on the case previously.

◆ **Database organization for cases requires both person-centric and case-centric views of data.**

Cases have both a person orientation and a case orientation, so the database of a case management system must encompass both.

◇ **Person-Centric Views**—Person-centric views of the database show person-related data across all cases and courts (e.g., financial obligations, multiple demographic data like aliases and addresses, and scheduled events for a person).

◆ Able to model complex relationships among customers and case participants. For example, the state of Texas' data dictionary diagram for juvenile cases identifies twenty-one different potential roles in a juvenile case and seventeen potential relationships among participants in a case (TX-OCA 2008).

◆ Able to identify possible duplicate identities among customers.

◇ **Case-Centric Views**—Case-centric views show case-related data essential for case workers and decision makers to understand a current event or state in the context of their experience with similar cases (e.g., case participants, event log, performance measures like number of continuances, time standards like age of case and milestones, and links to other cases that will be considered at the same time).

◆ **A case is event driven by human participants reacting to a changing context and external events.**

External events and a case's own internal dynamics create an unfolding case.

◇ **State of the Case**—Case workers must be aware of the status of the case and the parties when they are ready to add value to the process. Participants make choices expressed through external events like filing a document in a case or attending an event, or failing to do so. The process itself has certain imperatives that a knowledge worker must attend to such as time standards set by policy or practice.

◇ **Impact of Stakeholders on Internal Case State**—Other stakeholders are often involved in a case and communication of the status of the case in the stakeholder environment may have far-reaching consequences on internal handling of the case. When a judge is making a bail decision, being informed by the pretrial services unit about the defendant's adult criminal history and whether the defendant is likely to return for the next hearing will have a bearing on how high to set bail or whether to allow release for any amount of security.

◆ **Case handling involves recording complex customer and service interactions.**

A potentially complex and drawn-out case with multiple interactions with a customer needs a methodology for tracking steps taken in the case in a system of record.

◇ **Variability of Path Through Processes**—A case worker must be able to react to ad hoc changes and exceptions through addition of new activities in handling the unpredictability of intermediate and final outcomes.

◇ **Need Visibility of Case Progress**—Customers are justifiably dissatisfied when their cases appear to "fall through the cracks" of a long process. If customers are unable to track the process themselves (analogous to tracking a shipped package), a case worker should be able to look it up easily to answer a question.

◇ **Need Variety of Information to Make the Best Decisions**—A case worker (a judge, especially) needs an accessible and concise case history of actions and decisions in a case to be ready to take further action. Workers need to be able to make ongoing log entries about correspondence and personal interactions.

◇ **Cases Can Be Interrelated in Processing or Outcome**—Cases involving the same person or incident may be handled at the same time to achieve economy.

◆ **Capture results of knowledge-worker decisions and stakeholder inputs in real time, updating the state of the case.**

The concept "information delayed is information denied" applies to the availability of information to make decisions: information must be available in a timely manner to be useful. If data entry of decisions does not keep up with events, the participants and stakeholders will not have the information they need.

◇ **Configuration of Data Capture and Validation for Each Activity**—The knowledge worker interface for capturing data in real time is critical to making information available when it is needed. This includes configuration of data validation during keyboard entry and stakeholder data import to avoid the "garbage in, garbage out" problem.

◇ **Configuration of Screen Navigation**—Real-time data capture requires well-designed screen navigation to keep up with events as they transpire. There are enough subtle differences between organizations and decision makers within those organizations—in processes, work styles, and input documents (even among organizations and persons that perform ostensibly the same functions)—that navigation must be flexible to accommodate those differences without significant underlying code differences.

◆ **Secure access to information and the application based on case type and role of the knowledge worker and the groups of which a worker is a part.**

Role-based access to information is a widely accepted concept in contemporary systems. Data that is required by law or regulation to be confidential has to be assuredly made secure.

◇ **Protection of Confidential Information**—Certain case-related information must be excluded from public access according to federal or state law, administrative rule, court rule, court order, or case law. Court-related examples of confidential information include adoptions, juvenile abuse and neglect cases, and mental health cases.

◇ **Redaction of Personal Information**—Information on publicly available scanned documents must be redacted to prevent its appropriation by unauthorized persons, to protect individual knowledge workers, and the public interest.

◆ **Application of individual judgment by knowledge worker following business rules and through collaboration with colleagues.**

A range of staff roles is required to complete a case, usually through collaboration.

◇ **Hand-Offs**—Review or authorization by other knowledge workers may be required to meet business accountability requirements.

◇ **Configuration of Business Rules That Guide, Track, and Constrain the Process**—Case management systems either rely heavily on a knowledge worker knowing how to handle a particular event (which produces training issues), or are highly structured in guiding the worker to the next step (which removes discretion in handling exceptions and tends to force the worker to follow the built-in processes in the system). An event driven/business rules approach steers the middle course between these two problems.

◆ **Information is available for management of the process to spot bottlenecks and reallocate work dynamically.**

Elimination of paper files calls for replacement of visual cues of workers and supervisors to manage which workers are performing activities and who is doing the work.

◇ **Work Queues**—Information must be presented to a case worker based on role and appropriate to the activity needing completion.

Developmental Deficiencies of Current Case Management Applications

Since the 1980s, court case management systems (both statewide and local jurisdictions) have trended from custom-developed to COTS packages. *Automating Court Systems* (Webster 1996) notes this trend and urged courts to participate in system design. The advice is dated but sound considering that systems had to be hard-code modified to have any hope that they would fit a court's needs—more often, the court has had to bend its practices to the system. System modifications also have had to be hard coded, requiring significant time and expense to modify a system.

One of the primary realities of private and public sector business is constant change in the external environment and internal business objectives and policies. A solution must be able to keep up with changes or knowledge workers will be forced to cope any way they can—they develop system work-arounds and a variety of subsidiary manual and computer-supported mechanisms, including Microsoft Access databases, spreadsheets, checklists, and other aids to help them automate their work or perform it more efficiently.

The time and expense to modify a system, and the constant change in external and internal imperatives, make system development deficient in meeting the automation needs of an organization.

Functional Requirements Are Not Enough

The perennial challenge of software engineering (and software development in general) is the development, operation, and maintenance of software for users that is adaptive, resilient, and "good enough" for its intended purpose. In the court case management area, the court community—both court people and court case management system vendors—responded to a call for guidance for case management system requirements through a standards process.

Beginning in 2001, the National Consortium on State Court Automation Standards issued the first so-called Case Management System Functional Standards for case types of civil, domestic, criminal, juvenile, and traffic (NCSC 2001). Followed in 2005 by the "Consolidated Case Management System Functional Standards" (NCSC 2005). The premise of functional standards is that they identify what the case management system should perform, leaving the question of how the system should accomplish those functions to the designer because such questions are design issues.

Court customers continue to use some variant of these requirements in their requests for proposals in acquiring new case management systems. Functional requirements (even including "nonfunctional" system requirements involving security and performance issues), although serving some useful purpose, are not enough to adequately specify a court case management system, although no generally accepted alternative approach has been developed.

Case management system vendors respond to these functional requirements during procurement saying that their systems purportedly meet most of them, at least partially. Despite best efforts at clarity, requirements are worded ambiguously and are capable of being interpreted in subjective ways.

Examination of one functional requirement will illustrate the difficulty in specifying a requirement that is meaningful, complete, easily understood, implemented, and tested. For instance, 1.5.5 "Assign Person Identifiers," in "Consolidated Case Management System Functional Standards" (NCSC 2006), provides the following requirement:

> "Generate (or retrieve and assign existing) separate person identifier for each plaintiff, defendant, appellant, and/or other party and enter the corresponding contact information."

This requirement says, simply, that each person should have separate and unique person identifiers in the case management system—this is obvious. It envisions associating an entity, such as a party in a case, with data elements identifying that person by finding existing persons in the database or by entering the data. This requirement also implies a user search process with business rules resulting in a display for the user to make a decision. The sample requirement does not address, however, the issue of criteria to use to determine whether the identity of a person already in the database is the same as the person at hand, which is implicit in giving a party a separate identifier. There is great variation in approaching this issue, both in what court people want and what vendors provide. Multiplying this process for hundreds or thousands of requirements multiplies the problem nearly beyond manageability.

Translation is required from functional requirements to the configuration setup, and this creates room for misunderstanding. Functional requirements were a first attempt to impose some order on a chaotic marketplace, and while functional requirements are necessary in some form, use of them by themselves is not sufficient to facilitate success in automating case management tasks.

Failure to Adapt to External and Internal Change in Business Practices

The main deficiency of most case management systems has been a failure to provide a flexible framework for configuring processes in a way that they can be modified as business practices change. In court case management, beginning in 2007, a majority of case management system vendors announced and marketed a new generation of highly configurable systems, frameworks. (For one of the earliest descriptions of frameworks in the case management system context, see "Moving Courts into the Future: The Organizational Agility Imperative," Kasten 2006.) Case management's characteristics require architectural foresight in a system to enable it to fit local business practices and avoid hard-coded changes to match changes in legislation or business rules, for example.

To the extent that system managers can avoid the delay and expense of software developer involvement in changing system settings, a case management system will evolve more easily to meet the changing needs of knowledge workers. Highly configurable systems may meet these needs.

Assumption That All Paths Through a Process Can Be Identified at Design Time

Most customized/bespoke and packaged software is developed through a waterfall process where the requirements are identified and the software is developed to meet those requirements. Requirements tend to change during development, and the relatively high rate of project failures is attributable in part to human nature which, in matters of software, is unable to know what one wants until one sees it. Other approaches such as rapid application development have been developed to be more agile in responding to what knowledge workers think they need. This is a persistent problem, and there are still as many techniques as there are software development managers and knowledge-worker organizations.

Even if an organization developed or acquired a case management application that met its needs, before many months will have passed, it is likely that external or internal imperatives would require adding one or more steps to processes. Unless a case management application continues to evolve, it will force knowledge workers to employ other means to cope.

Unpredictable, Unfolding Cases

The course of the case is unpredictable because of (1) external events, (2) the need for the knowledge worker to apply judgment during performance of activities, and (3) the need to collaborate with the human subjects of the case, as well as with other knowledge workers, within and outside the organization by exchanging information.

The relatively simple case of a motorist receiving a traffic citation for an illegal left turn illustrates a case from a customer's point of view (see FIGURE 4-5). A defendant has a number of choices ranging from simply paying the ticket before the due date ("Forfeit") to ignoring it entirely and eventually being arrested on a warrant.

From the court's design point of view, there is a routine procedure for handling and recording any choice that a defendant makes and to that extent is routine. If the case goes to court ("Be arraigned"), the outcome is pushed in one direction or another by the human element, and the outcome will be routine. Cases have routine elements that are predictable and to this extent can be automated with a solution/application using any software development toolset. The unpredictability is not at this lower level but in a larger context. Even with this relatively simple case example, other external forces are at work.

The citation in this example may have been issued in connection with a more serious offense and was merely the probable cause that drew law enforcement attention to the driver—who was driving while intoxicated, or who attempted to elude police when the lights started flashing because he had drugs in his car. Where a more serious offense is an external factor in the citation for illegal left turn, the citation may be linked to the other offense, and its disposition will be similarly linked. It is common in a plea agreement to drop lesser charges in exchange for a plea to another offense. Those choices do not appear in Figure 4-5, and a case management system cannot be designed to anticipate such an eventuality: where this little gear is turned by a bigger gear.

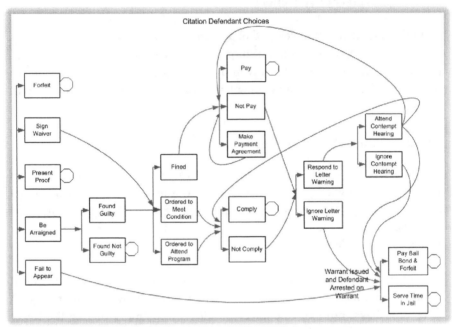

Figure 4-5: Defendant's Unfolding Citation Choices

Knowledge worker jobs have both routine and nonroutine (or problem-solving) aspects. Figure 4-6 depicts the distribution of routine and problem-solving work by two main participants in court cases.

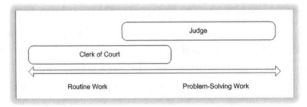

Figure 4-6: Proportions of Routine Work and Problem-Solving Work

While clerical functions related to the citation are routine, the judicial functions range from routine (especially in citation cases) to problem solving (in most other kinds of cases), where the judge applies discretion in light of individual circumstances. In terms of legal rules and precedent, a given judicial decision may be considered predictable, but judicial decisions often make news because they appear to be arbitrary. Judicial decision making is an emergent process where a plan is evolved as the work evolves.

LACK OF INTEGRATION BETWEEN PROCESS AND KNOWLEDGE

Most case management systems do not provide knowledge workers with the information needed at the moment it is needed. Knowledge workers must use other information sources, and this adds delay to completing activities and making decisions. A case worker must stop to look up information outside the system, typically spreadsheets and other nonintegrated data sources.

Most case management systems do not provide the means for nonroutine, high-level collaboration or organization learning, they only provide isolated, topical email messages and notifications. Most systems lack process configurability or a means to build progressive improvement into processes or other methods to move knowledge into the system for the benefit of other workers.

Only limited worker performance measurement is available in most case management systems: limited to counting activities or other activities at a coarse level. This limits the ability to gather management knowledge about how processes are performed for analysis and ongoing improvement. Workload measurement is widespread in American court systems at a macro level to develop information to establish the number of judges and court staff needed to handle and resolve all cases coming before the court effectively without delay while also delivering quality service to the public. This approach, while state-of-the-art for determining manpower levels, is not process oriented and is not capable of determining resources at a finer granular level.

LACK OF MODULE, DATA, AND DEVICE/SERVICE INTEGRATION

Part of case management complexity is workers' need for access to a variety of ancillary capabilities including functional modules, data integration, hardware devices, and online services.

Custom developed systems and COTS packages require integration with multiple applications to provide needed information and functionality for communication, collaboration, and decision making. TABLE 4-1 identifies court examples of functional module integration.

TABLE 4-1: Functional Module Integration

Type of Module	Integration Capability
Email system	Send emails to external case participants (receiving emails is problematic because of spam).
Document management system	Attach and retrieve document images related to an event.
E-filing system	Receive documents filed electronically by attorneys and self-represented litigants and acknowledge receipt and acceptance via email.
Double-entry accounting system	Collect fee revenue and pass-through money and account for its distribution.
Scheduling module to handle scheduling conflict resolution	Find schedule openings in calendars of participants.
Generation of documents	Merge data fields from the database with word-processing templates.
Ad hoc reporting module	Generate reports using nonstandard criteria.

Case management workers usually require information from external stakeholder systems. State and local court systems typically do not receive or send dynamically updated data from or to their stakeholders without a concerted development effort to exchange this data. Where this integration has been achieved, point-to-point interfaces predominate and standards-based information exchange is proceeding between government jurisdictions using the National Information Exchange Model (NIEM). A robust case management system will interface with a data integration hub with import and export capability. TABLE 4-2 identifies case participants in a court/justice environment who need each others' data.

TABLE 4-2: Data Integration

Stakeholder	Information Exchanged
Prosecutor	Complaints and affidavits for initiating cases.

STAKEHOLDER	INFORMATION EXCHANGED
Sheriff (jail, service of civil process, service of warrants, execution sale)	Bail information, custody status, transport, and court orders.
Pretrial Services	Bail recommendations.
Probation	Person information and court orders.
Division of Motor Vehicles (driver's licenses, vehicle registration)	Report convictions and driver's license suspension/reinstatement, look up information.
Criminal History Repository	Report convictions, look up information.
Child Support Enforcement (filing of IV-D cases)	Report payments or lack thereof.
Child Protective Services	Evaluations and status reports.
Collection Services Contractor	Receive accounts to collect, report payments made on account.
Vital Statistics	Report divorces, access death information.

A highly functional case management system may integrate with a number of hardware devices and online services. TABLE 4-3 identifies hardware devices and online services that make court knowledge workers more productive.

TABLE 4-3: Hardware Device and Service Integration

HARDWARE DEVICE/SERVICE	FUNCTION
Document scanner	Scan paper documents filed by case participants.
IVR (telephone interactive voice response)	Provide access to case information, payment of fines by credit card.
Web payment	Payment of fines by credit card, deposit funds in bank account.
Cash drawer/cash register	Track receipt of payments.
Digital audio system	Record court proceedings, play back on demand.

HARDWARE DEVICE/SERVICE	FUNCTION
Fingerprint reader	Capture fingerprint minutiae, verify identity when presented again.
Bar code reader	Manage document scanning process.
Signature pad	Capture signature and apply electronically to a document.
Address verification service	Verify that an address is valid and that a person has a particular address.

Case management requires high degrees of interaction with customers, colleagues, and stakeholders. Other processing models and applications have elements beneficial for case management but usually do not provide the broad range of functional, data, and hardware device/service integration described above. These applications include the following:

◆ Customer relationship management: short-lived, high-volume, single-customer interactions.

◆ Content management systems with predefined, limited workflow.

◆ Online transaction processing (OLTP) with limited follow-up (e.g., retail, job sites, and credit card transaction processing).

Hypothetically, these applications could be extended to provide additional integration capabilities, but the question remains whether their architectures would be sufficiently extensible.

How to Get Good Case Management System Requirements

There are still as many techniques for requirement gathering and software development as there are software development managers and knowledge-worker organizations (or industry pundits). No one disputes the importance of good requirements, but an organization may be conflicted about what constitutes good requirements.

The effects of not-so-good case management system requirements are continued high rates of failure or dissatisfaction with software development and COTS implementation projects. When requirements are not clearly defined and traceable, the crucial question is: How does the provider or the customer know when the project is completed? This section provides advice on why and how to develop good case management system requirements.

REASONS TO DEVELOP CASE MANAGEMENT SYSTEM REQUIREMENTS

An organization that manages cases will develop requirements for a number of purposes, as depicted in FIGURE 4-7.

◆   Developing a custom case management system.

◆   Selecting a COTS package case management system.

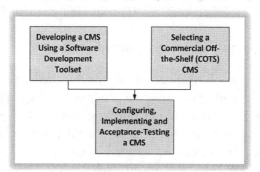

FIGURE 4-7: Reasons to Develop Case Management System Requirements

Once a system is developed or selected, requirements will be used for configuring, implementing, and acceptance testing a case management system to ensure that its function and performance meet specific knowledge-worker needs and the higher-level goals originally set.

IDENTIFY USER SCENARIOS

Knowledge workers know what work they need to perform and can provide lists of features/capabilities. The list may include dozens or hundreds of items. It is difficult to prioritize such a list, but it will provide the basis for the system provider and customer to determine: When are we done? A few examples of court user case management system scenarios are set forth in TABLE 4-4.

TABLE 4-4: Court User Case Management System Scenarios

Clerk generate warrant, send to a judge for review and electronic signature, return to clerk for sending to law enforcement, and automatically docket issuance of the warrant.
When scheduling a case for a given case type, see next available date, displaying time slot/session limits on the online calendar view for greater detail about the scheduled events for that session.
Configure an alert for fine payment past-due, driven by a flag automatically set based on time a payment was due.
Receipt a payment on a case including type of payment, payee, cashier identifier, amount tendered, payment amount, change given, time of payment, and location (e.g., mail, counter, Internet).
Reassign several cases with the same court event setting from one judicial officer to another and generate a notice for each judicial officer.

PICK A TOOLSET OR FRAMEWORK WITH FLEXIBILITY

Elsewhere in this book, you've read about the challenges of automating knowledge work. While it is beyond the scope of this chapter to describe what flexibility means in terms a software developer could use, in general, it seems clear that case management requirements should adopt multiple approaches for case management system requirements. TABLE 4-5 sets forth types of case management system requirements on a relative scale of abstraction, where data is the foundation.

TABLE 4-5: Types of Case Management System Requirements

LEVEL	TYPE OF CMS REQUIREMENT
6	Information Exchange/Devices/Services
5	Reports/Generated Documents
4	User Interface: Navigation, Search, Entry
3	Process Definitions: Business Logic, Rules
2	Linking of Persons/Cases
1	Data Objects/Data Model

A software development toolset or framework that is capable of providing structure and function seamlessly at all levels of abstraction, may be a platform for constructing a good case management system. Theoretically, such a system could be successfully written in COBOL or Fortran, but the issue is how flexible the toolset or framework will be to implement the requirement cited herein for person identifiers, when, for example, another person identifier is mandated by law or regulation, or when the business unit decides to change a processing flow.

Robust organizations are capable of tapping the energy and creativity of knowledge workers on the front lines. If a system is not capable of changing relatively easily and quickly to meet their needs, they will look elsewhere and develop subsidiary systems or other work-arounds to enable them to perform their jobs. This disintegrates the integrity of the system, however, and ultimately, leads down the path to loss of productivity because data and process are not managed from a single platform.

The goal of supporting case management automation is providing a system to knowledge workers that fits their business data and process needs and does not require them to bend their processes to fit the system. To the extent that businesspeople can modify workflow and business rules without the assistance of IT professionals (subject to a governance process, of course), the more flexible and successful the system will be.

INSIST ON AN AGILE REQUIREMENT DISCOVERY/CONFIGURATION/ DEPLOYMENT PROCESS

Case management system requirements will be most useful and result in a successful system through an agile requirement discovery/configuration/ deployment process. Knowledge workers must be involved in discovering requirements and in deciding that the requirements are met during configuration and deployment.

The Paradox of What Users Want

Although you must rely on your knowledge workers to know what they want, the paradox is that there are limits to what they know. It's commonly said that court people are anecdotal, not conceptual, and this plays out in the following ways:

◆ People don't analyze what they do and can't tell you how they do it.

◆ People base what they want on what's wrong with what they have.

◆ People know what they don't want when they see it in prototype form.

◆ People don't know what they want until they see it in prototype form, and then it takes awhile to sink in before they can think critically about it—and they may agree to every step of the process but refuse to accept the final product.

One solution is to use a third party that is knowledgeable in case management systems to facilitate the discovery/configuration/deployment process. Requiring users to identify work scenarios and requiring the case management system provider to enact them in the system will ensure that the system has functions that knowledge workers need.

The Question of When Are We Done?

Implementation of any system—whether custom developed or a configurable framework—can be abandoned or fail to meet objectives if the system provider and customer cannot agree on when a requirement is met. The customer cannot endlessly change their mind about what they want, and the system provider must make a good faith effort to meet requirements. Good contract sanctions and project management are necessary to reach a point that was mutually agreed to at the beginning.

The best way to get a good case management system is to understand the principles of ACM, use an agile process, and use a toolset or package with flexibility to enable making ongoing adjustments after deployment is "complete" because internal and external environments will continue to change and evolve. That's the blessing and the curse of case management.

CHAPTER 5

THE ELEMENTS OF ADAPTIVE CASE MANAGEMENT

MAX J. PUCHER

Many current implementations of process and case management solutions are at odds with modern management concepts. While that applies to all workers, it is especially relevant for highly skilled knowledge workers. Motivation is achieved by empowering people to be valuable team members rather than through command-and-control-oriented process implementations. Adaptive case management sits at the center of gravity for process, content, and customer relationship management and therefore plays a key role for effective execution toward business goals. This chapter examines the requirements for the necessary technology components.

> "There is no such thing as a logical method of having new ideas, or a logical reconstruction of this process. My view may be expressed by saying that every discovery contains 'an irrational element', or 'a creative intuition'."
>
> —Karl Popper
> *The Logic of Scientific Discovery (2002)*

Despite being around for twenty-five years, the terminology and acronyms of process management remain ambiguous. BPM means different things to different people. I will use the following terminology and acronyms:

◆ BPO for the management paradigm business process orientation.

◆ BPM for the methodology of analyzing and managing business processes.

◆ BPMS for business process management software products.

I consider understanding a business in terms of its processes—which I translate to mean customer outcomes—an important element of good management. As long as processes remain an abstraction—used to provide a better understanding of which organization structure will achieve certain outcomes and goals—then process orientation can reduce costs and increase quality for some processes but most likely not both at the same time. The cost of managing a business by means of BPM as a methodology, getting processes analyzed and implemented in software, and the resulting bureaucratic delays are, in my experience, never properly considered in return on investment (ROI) considerations.

BPO is not a magic bullet that solves all business problems or improves any business activity. Only some business activities can be well enough analyzed, defined, and automated by means of BPM. How many processes of a business can be optimized is a matter of perspective and opinion: between 20% and 80% is suggested by various experts—I lean more toward 20%. The general benefits of automation and industrialization achieved for manufacturing cannot simply be copied for service-oriented businesses. Nonmanufacturing work can be split into simple, repeatable administrative tasks and knowledge-oriented tasks. Knowledge work will suffer from too much automation as it reduces the ability of the knowledge worker to apply his skill. The necessity of detailed flowchart analysis and the complexity of BPMS implementation amplify the already long change cycle and push project leaders toward lesser quality quick fixes with some financial bonus. Various improvements toward even stricter BPM methodology and more analysis and monitoring software have tried to solve that. I still feel that the benefits are overestimated.

Custom case management solutions fill some of the gap for knowledge workers. It seems that there are opportunities to improve case management collaboration by replacing the hard-coded logic or complex rule engine integration with a more-user-friendly infrastructure and more adaptability, rather than just flexibility. The case functionality could improve over time from business user input rather than through programmed add-on functions or being completely ad hoc. If knowledge workers could be supported by *sharing and learning from each other's experience*, then the benefits for the business would be substantial. It would also be a first step toward a more adaptive process management infrastructure that could reduce process analysis effort substantially.

Let me propose that existing BPMS implementations probably reduce the resilience of a business in terms of its ability to deal with outside change. Controlling workers with encoded business processes does not improve the way a business operates in the long term. There are, in fact, no vendor-independent, long-term studies that compare businesses with and without BPM that would prove that all-out BPM is beneficial beyond reducing cost and wait time for some processes (quick fixes).

Over the years, the management of business processes has used and been given different names, and it has also been enhanced with various adjectives. I propose that all of these variants of BPMS were created because the principal concept of automating human business interactions based on process analysis is not as effective as theory assumes. There is an ongoing discussion as to which kind of BPMS is best for which type of work. Consultants and vendors use the terms quite differently, so for our purposes, these variants of BPMS are defined as follows:

◆ **Ad Hoc Process**—Instantly created activities by the business user.

◆ **Agile Process**—Processes can be changed by business analysts.

◆ **Case Management**—No fixed process; goal oriented and collaborative.

◆ **Dynamic Process**—Activity sequence can be changed during runtime.

◆ **Flexible Process**—Activities in processes can be modified by an actor.

◆ **Human Process**—Enables business users to define and execute their processes.

◆ **Orchestrated Process**—Linking various business services into a sequence.

◆ **Straight-Through Process**—Lights-out execution without human interaction.

◆ **Structured Process**—Fully automated execution without actor decisions.

◆ **Workflow**—Routing each type of scanned content through a fixed sequence.

While some software systems enable more than one of the above variants, most are hard coded to a particular kind. The problem is that a single-process-owning team may need more than one variant, possibly most of them. Many human activities and business interactions when seen as processes—and I propose that all processes are human until they are dehumanized into step-by-step flows—defy analysis and automation.

The focus of *Mastering the Unpredictable* are the needs of business users who perform emergent or unstructured knowledge work as opposed to repeatable production work. The needs of these knowledge workers requires a technological empowerment rather than a new management methodology. While the business strategy is a top-down definition targeting cost, process innovation targeting quality is most likely more effective bottom up. Technology has to support both targets—costs and quality—to be acceptable and beneficial to management, employees, and customers.

Most case management solutions (as well as BPM solutions) need a substantial amount of software implementation for data interfaces, user front ends, rule engine integration, and back-end orchestration. But they don't do much for the business user or customer at all. They just enforce a process landscape regardless. You might disagree with that, but the focus defines what the business is about: if you focus on processes, then that's what you'll produce—not happy employees and satisfied customers. Process is a means, not a target or asset. In difference to conventional IT wisdom, the use of out of principle well-defined and thus rigid process methodology to make better use of technology becomes a hindrance to innovation. Modularization and standardization create fragmentation and the additional complexity of integration.

To improve the IT support for at least the knowledge worker, I have proposed moving the knowledge gathering process in the lifecycle from the template analysis phase into process execution. We refer to this as adaptive case management (ACM). The ACM system collects "actionable knowledge" based on process patterns created by business users. Actionable knowledge is not just data, information, and descriptive text, but it is also knowing which action will lead from the current situation to the desired situation. The ACM solution has to provide the transparency to document what the desired outcome for the customer is from the top-down strategy. Transparency is also needed up the hierarchy to report process outcomes. Bidirectional transparency includes partners and customers in the virtual process organization for managed collaboration. Regardless of how processes are implemented and ultimately executed, the team owning the process must be in charge of additions, improvements, and corrections. Business users are enabled by the technology to implement many small, low-cost improvements that follow the business architecture and can be verified for benefits within days.

ACM technology has to provide the following:

◆ Master data models mapped to back-end interfaces.

◆ Process manageability and adaptability.

◆ Embedded business rules mapped to master data and processes.

◆ Inbound content to be classified, data extracted, and validated.

◆ Outbound business content maintained by business users.

◆ Embedded security on the object and function level.

◆ Actor role/policy has to be authenticated (ideally biometric authentication).

◆ All changes to templates and definitions must be audited.

I briefly introduce the concept of "adaptive process" that when combined with an empowerment management paradigm turns more production workers into knowledge workers. In reality, it is quite difficult to use BPM for top-down analysis and simulation of business processes and linking key performance indicators (KPIs) to achieve a continuous improvement cycle. Measure-to-manage optimization is counterproductive to improvement and innovation. Only empowered actors can use their intuition and experience for sensible action. The dynamics of economy require a self-organizing structure that is resilient to fast changes through its ability to adapt.

ADAPTIVE CASE MANAGEMENT

"When it comes to individuals, companies, cities, or economies…
the system, to a large extent, causes its own behavior…
A diverse system with multiple pathways and redundancies
is more stable and less vulnerable to external shock than a
uniform system with little diversity…It may exhibit adaptive,
dynamic, goal seeking, self-preserving, and sometimes
evolutionary behavior."

—Donella H. Meadows
Thinking in Systems (2008)

Business processes in all kinds of organizations continuously adapt one way
or the other: people use the communication means at their disposal—paper
and pencil have worked fine for centuries. If management isn't attentive,
organizations may adapt in an undesired direction. Forms can create very
rigid paper-based processes. Structured/designed and unstructured/emergent
processes are equally adaptable given the chance because the individual
human agents make a business a complex adaptive system and not a simplified
complicated one.

The introduction of BPM, enterprise content management (ECM), or any
kind of hard-coded process technology will initially kill an organization's
ability to adapt because of process definition, mandatory simplification, and
process methodology bureaucracy. Formal innovation processes will have
to be artificially instigated, but innovation can't be enforced. A business that
runs like clockwork has lost its ability to respond to external change with
innovation. Ideally, we could bring in a software system that will not take away
the organization's natural adaptive capability but will enhance it and make the
outcomes and individual perception patterns transparent for improvement.

IS CASE MANAGEMENT THE MAGIC BULLET?...

"Case management departs from the traditional view of structured and sequential predefined processes. Instead, workflows are nondeterministic, meaning they have one or more points where different continuations are possible. They are driven more by human decision making and content status than other factors."

— Marc Kerremans
Case Management Is a Challenging Use Case for BPM (Gartner 2008)

This definition does sound encouraging and will provide more flexibility than your typical BPMS, but it clearly provides less guidance. For most content management vendors, however, providing case management is mostly about creating a case folder and presenting all the documents in it for collaboration. The case itself is driven by the business user. The metadata on the case and the documents are used mostly for searching. For a rule or a user to advance the case from state to state, code has to be written to link the case state to the content, to external events, and to inform back-end systems of the process progress. (See FIGURE 5-1.)

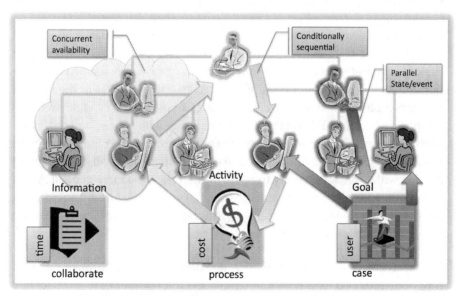

FIGURE 5-1: Collaboration vs. Process vs. Case

In 2006, Andrew McAfee proposed that it might be beneficial to bring the social networking capabilities of Web 2.0 into businesses to enhance their collaborative creativity and named that Enterprise 2.0. Many vendors have since added collaboration features with wikis and chat to the analysis and documentation phase of BPMS. While that is beneficial, I propose that social interaction is needed in the execution phase of a process. Many case management solutions offer such collaboration, but it is quite restrictive due to the nature of work. There should not be a technological border between collaboration, process management, and case management.

The most common properties of a typical case are as follows:

◆   A case has an execution state, not a lifecycle.

◆   Users define the states that a case can have.

◆   Several subprocesses might be available at each state.

◆   A case has to be uniquely owned overall.

◆   A case can belong to an individual at any given state.

◆   Appropriate actions are available on the task form.

◆   Business rules control mandatory items.

Case management does not tightly control the case from initiation to its final resolution. Arbitrary document content, collaborative decision making, and customer interactions are important elements of case management. A large portion of case-related information is received and managed in the form of business content rather than structured data. Complex cases can take weeks to complete. It becomes difficult to enforce compliance with policies and regulation due to a lack of transparency into desired outcomes. Complex integration with rule engines and back-end systems make case management very requirement specific with little opportunity to adapt to changes. Case management brings no benefit to knowledge workers who need to make decisions by automating them. Human judgment is more powerful than Boolean logic even for using long-gone experience (Hertwig 2009).

In case management, human judgment, external events, and business rules cannot be modeled as a path following a two-dimensional diagram. Reality is four-dimensional and the necessary abstraction causes inaccuracies in the model. Some tasks to complete the case may be defined in advance through case templates, but ad hoc tasks are a critical distinguishing element of case management. These tasks are often related to creating, obtaining, reviewing, and approving documents and some represent conventional subprocesses involving multiple participants.

Most case management products are specialist solutions for a particular service business, such as medical case management or legal work. For most other needs, case management is created by means of custom, conglomerate functionality of several complex products that are hardwired together by a systems integrator.

Custom case management solutions (as well as most BPM solutions) need a substantial amount of software implementation for data interfaces, user front ends, rule engine integration, content creation, and back-end orchestration. These software products include:

◆ A content management product.

◆ A customer communications product.

◆ A database product.

◆ A transaction application server (Java).

◆ A process management product.

◆ A rule engine.

◆ A portal or rich Internet application (RIA) functionality.

◆ A change management or system management product.

◆ A fault tolerant application environment.

◆ Lots of custom Java coding…

…No; HENCE *ADAPTIVE* CASE MANAGEMENT

I am presenting the shortest possible definition of ACM. I propose that it involves three distinct paradigm shifts.

1. ACM is a productive system that deploys the organization and process structure from defined architecture that through back-end interfaces becomes the system of record for the business data entities and content involved. All processes are completely transparent, as per access authorization, and fully auditable.

2. ACM enables nontechnical business users in virtual organizations to seamlessly create/consolidate structured and unstructured processes from basic predefined business entities, GUI components, content, social interactions, and business rules.

3. ACM moves the knowledge-gathering process in the lifecycle from the template analysis phase to the process execution phase. The ACM system collects actionable knowledge—without an intermediate analysis phase—based on process patterns created by business users.

Traditional BPMS and case management implementations require a huge project management infrastructure to handle the complexity of analysis, modeling, simulation, and implementation, which is so risky that it needs rollback and contingency plans. To make a BPMS project feasible requires even more reductions in personnel through automation who could have been turned into knowledge workers. For case management, the complexity means that only a small number of unstructured processes can be handled, while truly unpredictable business activities fall by the wayside and remain unsupported.

I propose that all work-activity classes map along a scale of designed to emergent processes (see FIGURE 5-2). All processes emerge in principle, but there are those that are more cost relevant and others that are more quality oriented. Efficiency is a measurable, manageable aspect, while effectiveness is in the end customer perception only. They cannot be targeted simultaneously and not by the same means.

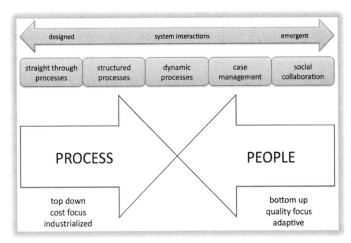

FIGURE 5-2: Mapping Process and People into Designed vs. Emergent

Schadler (2009) of Forrester Research writes in "Harness the Power of Workforce Personas" that there are four general types of workers: mobile professionals, deskbound contributors, offline practitioners, and accidental workers.

◆ **Mobile professionals** (28%) in management, marketing, or sales who use several knowledge tools.

◆ **Deskbound contributors** (24%) often in finance or HR who use collaboration tools.

◆ **Offline practitioners** (13%) who feel that work IT is lacking compared to home PCs.

◆ **Accidental workers** (35%) who use computers because they have to.

I suggest that knowledge workers are predominantly found in mobile professionals and deskbound contributors. That would mean that 52% of the business workforce cannot be supported well by predefined processes implemented in a BPMS.

For ACM, neither the use of a methodology nor BPM-like flowcharting of process components with dynamic execution will be sufficient. For such a system to be flexible enough, it must not require programming or substantial analysis to implement the case functionality. BPM methodology is unable to predefine all of the necessary processes with all variants and exceptions that stretch across the process landscape from purely expert designed to purely emergent from human interaction.

ADAPTIVE, DYNAMIC, FLEXIBLE, AND AGILE

Over the years, the industry has used several adjectives—dynamic, flexible, and agile—to distinguish their approach or software from others. From my perspective, businesses have to be managed with a complex-adaptive (social) system mindset, and therefore, I started to use the term "adaptive" for their process requirements a few years ago. It is turning into another buzzword as we write this book. The adjectives/properties are defined as follows:

◆ **Adaptive**—Internal changes to an entity caused by outside conditions that become permanent and make the entity more fitting to those new conditions. It does imply that those changes are performed by means of the entity itself and not by some external force.

◆ **Dynamic**—A real-time change of conditions or parameters.

◆ **Flexible**—Something that is not rigid and that can be varied (bent) while being used; however, it returns to its original shape.

◆ **Agile**—The ability to move quickly and without much preparation or support.

Traditional BPMS-style process flowcharting cannot be referred to as adaptive because it requires a person to make changes outside the environment that executes the process. Some BPM concepts are dynamic and allow subprocess selection, while others are flexible and allow user-defined process parameters. Given the substantial BPM bureaucracy, I question how agile most BPMSs truly are. If ACM is implemented properly, it should offer all four properties at the same time.

Adaptive knowledge work is distinguished from flowcharted processes by the following characteristics:

◆ Unpredictable in execution and decisions, not predefined.

◆ Defined by goal rules rather than steps and gateways.

◆ Planning is part of execution, not a design activity.

◆ Subgoals are rules, not simple sign-off check marks.

◆ Participants are added as necessary, not fixed.

◆ Inbound and outbound content is added as necessary, not by default.

◆ Secure Web 2.0-like collaboration, not simple form filling.

◆ Transparency and auditability, not just user authentication.

Business Architecture for ACM

How can the long and complex analysis to monitoring and improvement loop be shortened for ACM? The most important element is transparent communication between management, process owners, process teams, and customers. Communication is always built on a well-defined, common language.

The descriptive elements of such a communication scheme is referred to as "business architecture." A business architecture is not about controlling execution—it's about understanding. It should be communicated to the process owners in simple terms and enable them to execute as needed.

A short list of the important elements of business architecture for ACM is as follows:

◆ A business model presents the market segments, distribution channels, and partner networks and the company's value proposition.

◆ The organizational model defines the structure of the business in terms of hierarchies and overall responsibilities, not necessarily identical to capabilities.

◆ A capability model (often called a map) places the necessary business abilities (end-to-end process) as a logical view in the organizational structure.

◆ A process model describes process owner responsibility and people skills within the organization and clearly defines their goals and outcomes.

◆ The IT model (infrastructure) must enable the support processes for the process owner's goal fulfillment.

However, if business architecture has to be—as it is today—modeled, encoded, and assembled by using a large number of tools and software components, it will be difficult and expensive to provide the benefits. Today's heavily fragmented and hard-coded integrated IT systems (including service-oriented architecture [SOA]) are too rigid to enable rapidly changing business environments. Most IT departments do not focus on adaptability and innovation because they have been instructed to focus on lowering costs and ensuring system stability. Therefore, six-month rollout cycles are the norm, with three months being the exception. Because of the substantial complexity, most IT projects take twelve to twenty-four months for implementation and over half fail to meet their goals.

Executive demands for lower costs and business user expectations of stability are incompatible with the need for an IT infrastructure that is competitive. The perfect and error-free application that has been designed, developed, tested, and delivered—and will be used the same way for ten years—is, for me at least, an artifact of the past. The business perspective of IT has to change in the following ways:

◆ Adaptive technology has to empower the business to create business services on demand without requiring complex IT implementation projects.

◆ Adaptive technology must enable simple interfacing to back-end application systems without demanding a switch to SOA first.

◆ Adaptive technology must shorten the change management cycle and allow changes and improvements within a week.

◆ Adaptive technology must empower the business user to perform all activities according to customer needs with full auditing.

The Five A's of Smart Computing

Bartels (2009) at Forrester Research sees "smart computing" that is: "A new generation of integrated hardware, software, and network technologies that provide IT systems with real-time awareness of the real world and advanced analytics to help people make more intelligent decisions about alternatives and actions that will optimize business processes and business balance sheet results." (See Figure 5-3.)

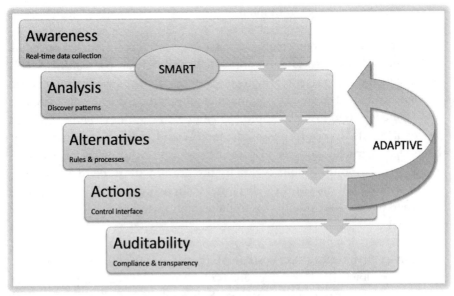

Figure 5-3: The Five A's of Smart Computing (Bartels 2009)

He sees the "Brave New World of 1984" descending upon us. Real-world sensors, interfaces using radio frequency identification (RFID), and GPS will capture data on the identity, status, condition, and location of people and physical assets. Using 3G (third generation) wireless networks, this data can be routed to central servers for predictive analytics where artificial intelligence agents will determine whether businesses or governments should act on a pattern. Rule engines and workflows will adapt on the fly. Human or rule engine decisions will immediately trigger actions to change quotes, place orders, change heater settings in thousands of households, and reroute cars around traffic jams. Bartels also sees smartness in monitoring and learning to improve decision making. He predicts that in 2017, 10% of all IT expenditure will be for smart applications. (Bartels 2009)

Bartels (2009) sees smart computing link up with Forrester's definition of dynamic business applications and digital business architecture to automate contract management, marketing, sales proposal generation, strategic planning, fulfillment of complex services, and to link demand chains with supply chains. Therefore, he proposes that this smartness will be purchased because of its direct impact on the balance sheet by providing a more current and accurate status of assets.

From my perspective, Bartels buys into the ideas and technology behind ACM. I am further in full agreement on the need for a core metadata base without which the consolidation of technology, and moreover, a common ontology of business terminology for aligning business and IT is impossible. *Rules engines, business services, and event handling need a common metadata base.*

I am less convinced about the proposed ability of predictive analytics in relationship to corrective and controlling actions. Control would require accurate and tested causal models of the real world, where causality could be verified and linked to leverage points. However, economy and business are social systems and not deterministic systems; therefore, control accuracy is not improved by more data because the high data rate will cause control oscillations. Real-time data gathering can substantially improve human awareness and understanding, as can be seen from navigation systems with embedded traffic monitoring. ACM can thus be seen as a smart navigation system for knowledge workers.

Bartels (2009) sees the need for an infrastructure to make it all work. Forrester's digital business architecture not only has the functional elements, but it includes configuration and change management as well as unified communications (see FIGURE 5-4). Yes, change management must be implemented in the technology infrastructure for all elements to make ACM feasible at all. If only a methodology is used to manage change, it creates expensive and slow bureaucracy. Ongoing change must be an inherent property of the infrastructure. If the business design ontology can be communicated by the infrastructure, it becomes irrelevant where and what process improvements are started. If technology enables up-the-line transparency, it allows immediate verification.

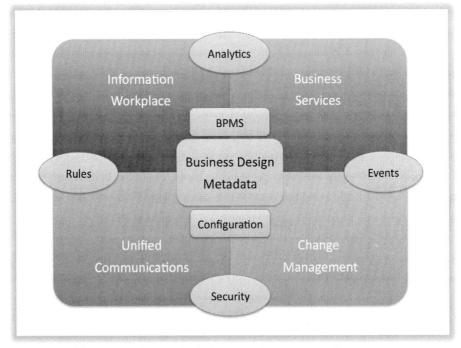

FIGURE 5-4: Digital Business Architecture (Heffner 2005)

THE ROLE OF TECHNOLOGY IN DELIVERING ACM

Smart systems are based on technology, Bartels (2009) suggests that until standards develop, solutions will have to be delivered by single vendors who consolidate all necessary functionality. I propose that the same consequence applies to ACM functionality. Adaptability requires simplicity; therefore, it is unlikely that a case management solution handcrafted by a systems integrator from many different products can ever be adaptive. It will not even be flexible or agile, but what programmers in the 1990s called a "big ball of mud."

Out of the box, an ACM system has to provide a central change management repository, a distributed execution environment, database and application interfaces, inbound and outbound content management, case management, (sub-)process management, business rules, a powerful but user configurable thick and thin client user front end, and let's not forget, deeply embedded security and records management. (See Figure 5-5.)

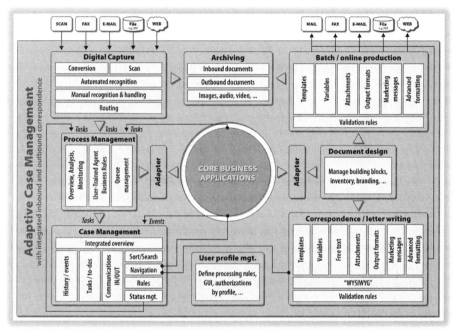

Figure 5-5: Adaptive Case Management Blueprint

ACM requires a comprehensive facility for creating, capturing, indexing, storing, finding, viewing, sharing, editing, versioning, and retaining a wide variety of content types. To ensure compliance and enable adaptability, both process managers and business users can apply rules to document events for automation and case status tracking at any point in the process, including required predefined tasks and documents via the case template and also allowing the addition of ad hoc activity and content at runtime.

A wizards facility that enables users to interactively create simple procedures is beneficial, as is some ability to train repeated information patterns as rule recommendations to other users. Such learning is not achieved through data mining and analytic prediction, but by observing in real time which data patterns cause users to take certain actions. Those tasks and activities define the case context and are visible, along with case documents, in the case environment, where the state of the case as a whole is determined by the combined state of all tasks and documents.

With ACM, a case is not a folder containing activities, processes, and documents; it is a consolidated, connected, and evolving entity progressing toward completion. The case is easily understood through the unified and customized view that summarizes the status and provides access to key content and details.

Rather than sequentially routing the case to the next task, department, or user role by user action or conditionally, ACM advances through both external and internal events. For external events—such as receipt of a phone call, letter, fax, or email related to the case—the message content is added to the case folder and new tasks or processes may be created. Such events can also be created by back-end application systems. This enables asynchronous processing, whereby the ACM system sends out a request and does not have to enter a wait loop for the result. Once the return message arrives, the event triggers the appropriate action, which can happen in parallel to other activities in most cases, substantially reducing the need for complex orchestration. For internal events created by business rules, for example, case workers assign tasks and initiate processes as needed to work on the case. Business rules can fire events, and they may automatically create and assign tasks or trigger fully automated actions based on either external events, completion of other case tasks, or expiration of task deadlines.

I propose that it will have to be consolidated technology to deliver that ACM capability because there are no standards that would support loose integration of different products. Technology that embeds a certain methodology, or worse, certain (case management) processes, is the reason why Carr (2004) wrote *Does IT Matter?* and questioned the competitive value of IT investments. When businesses buy IT because it has the business (process) knowledge embedded in the software, it becomes the great equalizer and is effectively irrelevant or even a detriment in terms of competitiveness.

Technology is changing the world, not management methodology or best practices. Technology will be the key competitive advantage. If technology is seen and managed as a commodity, as Carr (2004) suggests, then that ability is lost. If, for example, just one business had access to mobile phones for its salesforce and others did not, that would represent a substantial competitive advantage. It is the business strategy that defines the role of technology in providing competitive advantages. Technology can further be a powerful tool to enable the innovative and creative ability in a workforce.

While that is not for everyone, ACM technology can provide a mobile, collaborative IT environment that at least allows social network interaction on business activities and entities, and it opens up the creative opportunity to everyone (who is authorized, of course). It has to enable process owners to collaborate about real-world deliverables as their inputs and outputs and empower the process teams to execute as they see fit to achieve their well-defined outcomes. The ACM platform enables business actors to not only execute, but to actually add knowledge to the case template themselves. In some areas, software might be able to make suggestions on improvements but processes will not automate improvement or innovation. Relevant is the access of the actor to the template. Executives and managers have at all times complete transparency, and they can offer process coaching and guidance to process owners. Internal and external customers can enjoy full transparency into the processes (limited by security scope) within the organization and fully participate. Customers can see their own relevant detail but not business internal documents or data. Such choices are clearly made by the business, but the technology must not be a hindrance in principle.

KEY TECHNOLOGY FUNCTIONS OF ACM

Infrastructure Functionality

◆ Distributed (similar to grid computing) networking enablement of process systems.

◆ Consolidated central metadata repository (not archive) for change management.

◆ Simple mapping of back-end business systems to data entities (SOA or not).

◆ Simple linkage to external event-creating systems.

◆ Strong, distributed security with embedded access control on method and attribute levels.

◆ Seamless integration with all inbound and outbound content (back-end archives).

◆ Enable offline and mobile participation as authorized.

Top-Down Business Architecture Design

◆ Object model with state/event modeling without coding.

◆ Create a business architecture model of data entities in repository.

◆ Use organization charts to show authorized roles and departments or virtual organizations.

◆ User authorization (role/policy) and workgroup/queue assignment are independent.

◆ Consolidating process, business, and satisfaction data for the process owner.

◆ Enable a 100% change round trip for *all* elements of a process.

Bottom-Up Business User Empowerment

◆ Business users can access, create, and use data entities in repository.

◆ Users can write boundary rules in natural language (NL) accessing the object data.

◆ Enable authenticated users to create virtual organizations of case collaborators.

◆ Business users can create all the necessary business content with real-time data.

◆ Enable business users to define role-specific user interfaces as needed.

Adaptive Case Management Optimization

◆ Use timeline graphs to show past activities for documentation.

◆ Real-time business data are mapped into the process to measure business results.

◆ Customer-focused processes are set up to survey customer satisfaction.

◆ Business results are accumulated and dashboards and reports create transparency.

◆ Business trained document classification and routing.

◆ Business trained content capture and data extraction.

◆ Machine learning agents discover user-activity patterns in case.

Note that it is not simple at all to utilize neural networks or pattern matching on top of an existing BPM or case management engine because it cannot expose the state space for time-stamped user activities. It is also difficult to empower business users to define GUIs and write rules without a deeply embedded security layer as otherwise they can define themselves unauthorized data or content access. To auto-discover knowledge from user activity, one has to first give the users the opportunity and the environment (i.e., knowledge and functionality) in which they can freely act.

CREATING, DEPLOYING, AND MAINTAINING ACM TEMPLATES

The core issue for ACM is how the actual case/process templates are being created. Jeston (2008) says that a substantial bureaucracy is needed on top of locally defined processes to avoid high risk in the enterprise-wide implementation. It means that an ACM product or technology must focus on the problem points: communication and transparency, change management, enable variations, avoid bureaucracy, and support inline adaptation of processes during execution across all elements of a process.

The only way that such a change management function can be implemented is through a central, virtual "metadata repository." Virtual means that the entities managed in the repository are freely definable. Would the term "repository" not be so widely misused by the industry and analysts that is the only name we would need; a similar problem exists for the term "metadata."

repository

1. <database> See data dictionary.

2. <programming> The core of a computer aided software engineering tool, typically a DBMS where all development documents are stored. (CDO 2010)

meta

1. <philosophy> /me't*/ or /may't*/ or (Commonwealth) /mee't*/ A prefix meaning one level of description higher. If X is some concept, then meta-X is data about, or processes operating on, X.

   For example, a meta-syntax is syntax for specifying syntax, meta language is a language used to discuss language, meta-data is data about data, and meta-reasoning is reasoning about reasoning. (CDO 2010)

The common usage is that a digital item is archived in a repository using its metadata. However, a repository is clearly a development tool and not an archive (see Figure 5-6). Metadata should describe data properties and not search criteria, which are data elements of the document content. Other interpretations are that a repository is a place for safekeeping, but I would call that a vault, or as in the real world, an archive. Templates describing business entity metadata are managed in and deployed from the repository, while instances created from those templates are stored—ideally digitally signed—in the archive using search indexes from their attribute values.

The ACM platform uses the repository to store a business-architecture-based concept that supports discovery and documentation of user interactions performed on the entity models.

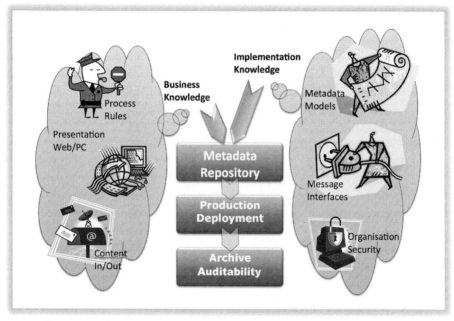

Figure 5-6: Repositories Store and Deploy Metadata Information

ACM enables an executive to define the goals and outcomes for each process owner. High-level flowcharts can be used for end-to-end process dependencies instead of step-by-step activities. The ACM repository enables the modeling of data and content entities that can be used by business users to assemble processes from application-specific framework libraries.

Business users must be able to define and refine activities independent of but linked to back-end application systems. The ACM platform should not restrict business users in execution but guide them by means of case definitions, monitored by business rules, and measured by goal fulfillment. Seamless consolidation of user-definable activities, rules, GUI, forms, and inbound and outbound content objects is required.

ACM consolidates the functions of process, content, and customer communications management without internal SOA functionality, but provides SOA and other interfaces to integrate with enterprise resource planning (ERP) and other internal systems. SOA is only practical for simple system functionality, such as storing and retrieving content from an archive by, for example, OASIS CMIS (Content Management Interoperability Services). ACM must support central project management and deployment for all definitions assets, including version control, a back-end service registry, and a user/role directory (linked via LDAP).

Management can continuously measure the quality parameters for process execution and business goal achievement. Auditing can be performed in real time using boundary rules or by postverification of archived process tasks. Processes in the ACM platform are collaborative activities performed on architecture data models and content. State/event chains of execution are used rather than rigid flowcharts.

ACM is uniquely consolidated with its ability to capture *all* incoming content, perform machine learning classification, extract and validate business data, execute automated business responses, and initiate straight-through or user-interactive processes. ACM should provide natural language rule (NLR) definition for business users that can be executed in the process environment directly and reused as templates in any process.

ACM should also enable rich Internet applications (RIAs), chat, wikis, blogging, user-configurable GUI presentation, and social interaction with co-workers all under control of the role/policy authorization and in context with the process. Most process management products are content blind, and most content products have limited or no process capability. While ACM uniquely consolidates both, it also provides consolidated content delivery through all outbound channels: print/mail, fax, email, web, and mobile.

A simple implementation plan for creating an ACM environment is as follows:

◆ **Derive/Define All Business Entities**—If available, derive all the business entities necessary from an existing enterprise and/or business architecture. If not available, define them together with the process owners.

◆ **Create a Role/Policy Hierarchy**—Create a role/policy hierarchy of the organization and high-level role-activity diagrams.

◆ **Define Real-World Entities**—Mostly content and products—to be delivered by service activities to customers according to cost and quality goals. Define the components that describe all standard content and building blocks, as well as the elements of information presentation in the GUI.

◆ **Define the Process Owners**—Utilize role-activity diagrams to model the hierarchy only of process owners for all processes that you need to improve. Map out through which real-world deliverables they serve each other.

◆ **Customer Service Outcomes (=processes)**—The goal achievement (customer satisfaction) optimization loop must be the responsibility of a process owner. The goal rules must link the case content together to create plausible process states. It can be easily improved by adding new entities, new rules, and new actors without redesign from scratch.

◆ **Real-Time Business Data**—The process owner needs real-time business data to measure goal achievement and have the authority to execute toward those goals. IT is the only option for transparency for the process owner and the executive.

◆ **Define All Business Rules**—Define all business rules in line with the relevant processes so that they can be managed and deployed in sync.

DECISION MAKING AND BUSINESS RULES

Because of our human ability to memorize data in sequential chains that we infer to be causal, we fail to see the complexity that appears when we fragment information into data, processes, and rules. That is, however, the state-of-the-art in IT. I use here the terms "process" and "case" interchangeably—the following statements apply to both terms.

The quantum physicist David Bohm (2002) wrote that fragmentation stops us from understanding and solving the most simple problems. I believe the same is true for IT.

People who see the world through a data analytics lens only, without processes and rules, overvalue the relevance and validity of statistical data generated from these models. Viewing business data makes no sense without understanding the process context. Looking at risk data is irrelevant if the causal links that generated these data and the causal actions that will influence them are not understood. These causal links can be approximately but only inaccurately modeled as a mix of processes and rules.

People who see the world through a process lens overvalue the significance of predefined action sequences. They fail to make room for the dynamics of daily life, business, and nature. Encoding processes and rules would require a solid data entity model that links all these together. Once there is an acceptable model, it has to be filled with data. Orchestration links processes to a business service back-end and passes and receives data through those. The data have to be filtered, weighted, and checked for relevancy. While using a canonical data model simplifies the project management, it creates substantial fragmentation and additional coordination complexity in each component that is being orchestrated. Additionally, the data being passed and used have to be reinterpreted and a local meaning assigned. If data values are passed for remote rule execution, they should really be write-locked until processed.

Rules make absolutely no sense without a context (i.e., state space) to execute in. It's a lot like university education without experience. Knowledge is not helpful without knowing when to apply it. This is what I refer to as actionable knowledge. Rules are not actionable knowledge without looking at real-world data and content in their process context. The more rules are connected, the more complex the data context has to be. The more data are synchronized or dependent/related to each other, the more complex a single rule set becomes. This is why local rules are a lot easier to manage than global ones. (See FIGURE 5-7.)

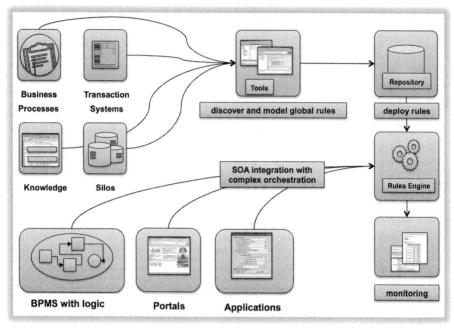

FIGURE 5-7: The Complexity of Stand-Alone Business Rules Engines

A business rules engine (BRE) generates complex results required for decisions based on a larger data set and a set of related rules. Business rules are business policies, goals, strategies, and guidelines that include declarative statements, constraints, or predicated actions. I question, however, the validity of the claim of BRE vendors that stand-alone declarative rules can capture management intent without being linked to the relevant processes. The linkage is as important as the data and the rules. Certain rules are only valid in certain situations. To identify the validity of *one* rule, many additional rules may have to be fired as prerequisites.

Business rules exist on all hierarchical levels, and it is advisable that they are also created and maintained at that level by the people responsible. Business users will typically not be able to enter business rules in the format necessary for a BRE. They usually cannot verify their global impact or correctly map them to the data model. A central BRE requires that all rules are abstracted, entered, and maintained by BRE experts. Not many people are aware that business process goals are not attribute values but rules. The same is true for process controlling parameters. Adjusting the value of a process parameter does not change the outcome of a process or optimize many processes for joint outcomes. Rules do! Business rules are a necessity to bypass many of the problems faced by BPM solutions based on a flowchart paradigm. Also, the more flexible state/event driven processes benefit from rules. One can only sensibly execute business rules in conjunction with process logic through asynchronous events.

Vendors of BREs, however, recommend that business logic and process logic should not be mixed. Because the implementation of any business process project is so complex, project managers often refuse to mix business logic and process logic. This is a good decision when the implementation would be done in some programming language; however, processes that do not contain business rules are no longer business processes. They only perform data conversion and mapping, service orchestration, organizational assignment, and process state changes. Business users are unable to implement such processes— they are unable to map such rules to a process engine and judge how they will execute. Consequently, an independent BRE eliminates adaptability, because the complete business process has to be analyzed so that it can be implemented by engineers.

Another often-cited reason for using an independent BRE is the ability to perform forward and/or backward chaining of rules. Forward chaining means that all the available data are passed to the BRE to execute all the rules of a particular rule set that can be mapped to the data fields. Forward chaining is often done in iterations because if a rule changes some data in the data set, those changes might trigger additional rules on the next pass of the rule set. Backward chaining means to fire a rule set to identify if some particular conditions are met. The data are selected by the rules and usually some control variable is set depending of the outcome of the rule set, for example: does this person qualify for a social security payment? The backward chaining rule set usually contains all the rules for all possible situations that would apply to the situation in question, causing substantial maintenance issues as this rule set maps to a large number of processes or applications and has to be verified and tested extensively.

That rules are stored and maintained in one place in the BRE seems to simplify maintenance, but it also means that all applications that want to use rules have to be redeveloped, or at least changed, dramatically. Just imagine that only the car manufacturer in Japan can maintain a car (and not a local workshop). Ideally, a car should be so simple that it could be maintained by the driver.

The claim that separating processes and rules makes their maintenance simpler is thus unproven. When rules are executed within the process engine, they can be executed as needed while still being globally defined and usable from a central repository. Many different, independent rules defined by business users can set the relevant control values for processes. This simplifies maintenance when the rules are embedded in the actual process. They can still be reused, but their relationship to the process is always visible. When a BPMS and a BRE communicate via a service interface (e.g., SOA), then the rule set does not know in what condition the process is except if the status is explicitly passed. As soon as process states are passed, the rule sets cease to be generally usable. To keep them generally usable, rule sets have to be large and have to process completely the same data set as the BPMS. (See FIGURE 5-8.)

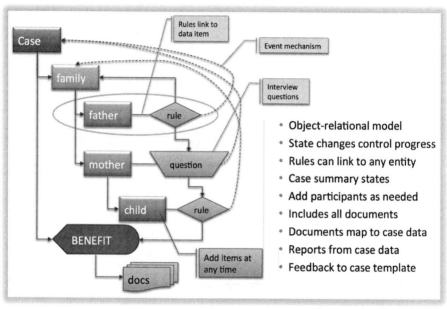

FIGURE 5-8: Business Rules Represent Control and Boundaries

During rule development for a BRE, IT requires that the business provide full test data sets and manpower for testing, as IT people neither have all the knowledge nor the necessary data. Business analysts and IT will always need last-minute fixes to the business rules and the processes, requiring changes on both sides, which in principle require a complete retesting of all rule sets that use the changed rules or are called by the changed processes. Validation testing of rule sets is not a simple task.

IT architects like BREs because they prefer to place system components onto one of the infrastructure layers where they would have their independent existence. At a lower layer, they would communicate with general functions and at a higher layer, they would aggregate functionality from different components into common ones. Given that the interfaces to those layers were standardized by, for example, SOA, the various components would theoretically be interchangeable. In reality, neither a process fragment nor a rule is freely reusable, no matter how standardized it seems. Particularly in ACM, it is common that a case activity drives the rules and equally often the rules drive a process.

Forrester's Karel (2009) writes, "Don't assume your business processes use master data!" The same point can be made for ECM, BRE, BPM, and customer relationship management (CRM). Don't assume that they use the same master-data model as your ERP. When different components of a system architecture use canonical data models, as in SOA, they do not use the same master data.

For users to understand the rules, the attribute names have to be unique across all applications. Technically, they have to be abstracted and mapped correctly from all applications into the rules engine. That alone is a humongous task that most businesses have failed to complete. As a consequence, in most BRE implementations, data are passed to the rule execution with the request. The performance and maintenance consequences of that I do not need to elaborate.

The issue of mapping business data that must be identical for two engines is not to be ignored. Most BREs still map business data by Java programming alone. Some use XML/XSD with similar disastrous results in scaling performance up when not used stand-alone. Keeping the data in sync between engines is an additional problem that is very difficult to solve. Additional technology such as NoSQL data stores, complex caching, and distributed database functionality has to be implemented.

Rule engine vendors tend to claim substantial performance advantages over the competition for very specific uses and in complex rule-optimization scenarios. Most rule systems create a few large rule sets that then are optimized by algorithms such as Rete, which deals with rule priority and conflict resolution. In a BPM or ACM environment, rules are not triggered as large sets but specifically those few that apply to the current business situation. If you use

SOA to call a large rule set in a BRE, you won't have that benefit, and you will fire thousands of rules when a few would have sufficed.

Because the technologies of ACM and BRE are so different, system integrators will argue that processes and rules ought to be defined and modeled separately by different teams. That is a disastrous decision in my mind. There is only one business process owner who tries to achieve a positive outcome for his customer and he defines both: the process and the related rules. When those rules are now defined in a different place than the processes, it is also not easy to change them. It will be difficult to test if their execution is perfect in all possible contexts. The frequent claim of "change once, use everywhere" is neither practical nor realistic. Business rules are part of business process architecture and change mostly in sync with the processes. (See FIGURE 5-9.)

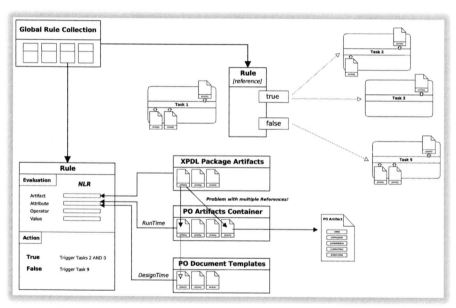

FIGURE 5-9: Rules Defined in ACM Access Real Business Data

One key element of defining rules is not just the logical syntax, but also, more importantly, the correct use of data entities. The rule entry should, therefore, be a NL capability without complex syntax that guides the user through rule entry and verifies that the rule can be executed for attributes and objects defined in the repository. NL rules have to be usable in the GUI as normal business user entry for queries also. That means that it must be multilingual in presentation and editing from a single rule definition. NL rules have to be able to access any data model stored in the central metadata repository. When a business user fires a rule he has just created, the execution of that rule has to be verified against and secured with the user role/policy setting. When the rules are executed in a different engine, the security aspects become very difficult to manage.

Buying best of breed BPM and BRE products and linking them by loose SOA coupling is identical to letting independent specialists develop the optimal parts for an airplane without a common design. BPM and BRE may be great individually, but together they won't fly without a common design and maintenance concept. Let's not forget that these two engines will be from two different vendors and keeping their product cycles in sync is a maintenance nightmare. Therefore, a stand-alone BRE just adds technical complexity without providing real benefits.

Rules should be defined in the process engine because they need to be signed-off on, deployed, and change managed just like the business processes, and that must happen synchronously. The rule also has to be tested and signed off by some authority. That change management has to be integrated with the normal process management. Let's not forget that deploying processes and rules out of sync would cause disaster! It would be nice if business rules could be so stable and independent that they could be completely decoupled from the processes and applications that they are used in. In my experience, that is never the case.

All of the above is relevant for an ACM environment. I believe that the full potential of business process orientation can most probably not be achieved without process embedded business rules. Especially, when a business does not have globally defined metadata models and the business user can add actors, data, content, and process elements at any time, there is absolutely no chance that independent BREs will be able to fulfill the needs.

I propose that ACM is not possible without a fully integrated embedded or consolidated rule engine with an NL editor that has access to real-time data modeled in a central repository with the rules being fired either by links in the process or by outside events to trigger actions in the process.

THE ROLE OF CONTENT FOR ACM

For ten years now, my motto has been: there is no process without content and content without process you don't need.

In 2001, I toured the U.S. to meet analysts and media representatives to announce an inbound/outbound content and process solutions scenario. The typical reaction was, "Has anyone asked for this?" Clearly, at the time neither business management nor analysts could imagine what capture, process, and printing technology could do together for a business. The link between inbound *and* outbound content and process was somehow not seen at all, despite the existence of capture workflows. Fortunately, that has changed.

Because content is the driver of processes, content state is an essential element for the state of the adaptive case/process too. ACM must be tightly integrated with content management to achieve the goal of a fully adaptive environment. Content is not just paper that has been scanned and digitized, but it is also all business documents that have to be created from business data. Content always must have a solid context to the case.

The official definition of ECM was created by AIIM (Association for Information and Image Management) in 2000 as "technologies used to Capture, Manage, Store, Preserve, and Deliver content and documents related to organizational processes." In 2008, AIIM changed the definition to: "Enterprise Content Management (ECM) is the strategies, methods and tools used to capture, manage, store, preserve, and deliver content and documents related to organizational processes. ECM tools and strategies allow the management of an organization's unstructured information, wherever that information exists" (AIIM 2009).

The key differences are that AIIM now sees the strategies and methods as part of ECM and not just the technology. AIIM also sees BPM as part of the overall strategy behind ECM. I see content as the carrier of the business process.

THE ROLE OF INBOUND BUSINESS CONTENT

Obviously, capturing and archiving inbound documents is an essential element of a full case management solution (see FIGURE 5-10). A huge number of documents of all types may reach the business from consumers or partners.

Typically, these contain known forms, semistructured accounting documents, and totally unstructured letters.

A primary challenge of ACM is the automated capture processing of these documents as they are received in an efficient way that will quickly start activities triggered by their content. One way to start the proper processing of inbound documents is the use of classification taxonomy. Documents are handled based on the way they look before any OCR reading has taken place. That can be combined with barcode reading to identify relevant detail information such as case or customer numbers.

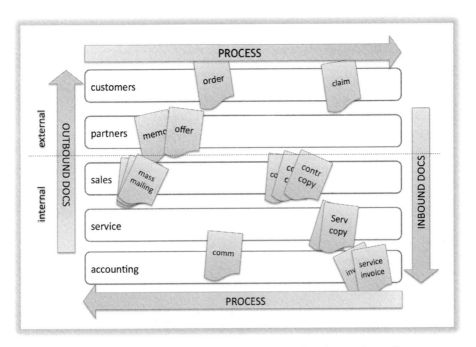

FIGURE 5-10: Inbound/Outbound Content Carries the Business Process

Goals for efficiency may include short scan-to-process rates for incoming documents, handling daily or monthly peaks without excess additional personnel, and easy distribution of various data completion work throughout an organization. Various products achieve automation rates of 60% to 90%. Modern solutions employ machine-learning algorithms that optimize automatic classification to nearly 100% for commonly received invoices, bills, delivery notes, work confirmations, orders, credit notes, and insurance claim documents.

Other needs are recognition for barcodes, printed and handwritten documents, support for multilingual documents, and GUI support for manual correction masks with rule-based data verification. Those rules must be editable with NL and cannot be outsourced to a BRE for performance reasons. Multiple methods of page classification enable document sorting for packs, high-speed extraction of geometrically structured documents, and unstructured documents, in formats such as MS Office, SMS, HTML, XML, PDF, audio, video, CAD/CAM, X-rays, photos, and more. It is obvious that the rules and processes for capture should be defined in the ACM environment, including execution for exceptions, corrections, and approvals and not in a separate capture product. Also inbound capture needs full security with a common definition as defined later.

THE MISUNDERSTOOD ROLE OF OUTBOUND CONTENT

Many document management products offer lifecycle functionality. For ACM, these have to be integrated transparently for the business user as he generates content interactively. It means to use defined processes for the creation, review, and sign off of customer- or partner-bound documents. What is mostly ignored in these products is the need for mapping variable business data into the document components that make up the business documents. (See Figure 5-11.)

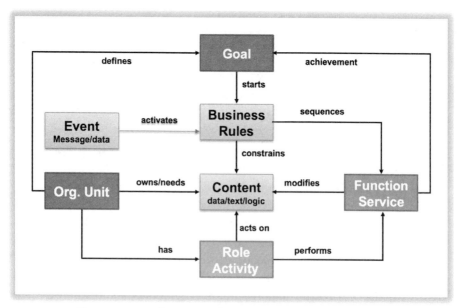

Figure 5-11: Content Relationships in Adaptive Cases

In ACM, the following functionality is needed for outbound content:

◆ Developers encapsulate interfaces into data sources or business services.

◆ Business users in various departments read documents and issue change requests.

◆ Administrators create and edit templates and map data into templates.

◆ Business, legal, and marketing verify templates for quality of wording, corporate identity, as well as regulatory compliance.

◆ Users assemble documents from templates and route them for review and sign off.

◆ Authorization controls who may view, print, or change documents.

◆ Define document properties, access permissions, and change management.

◆ Hierarchy for auditing and electronic sign off, optionally with electronic signatures.

◆ Automatically generate audit trails for events such as the creation, modification, and sign off of controlled documents.

◆ Custom headers, footers, and watermarks for documents for viewing and printing.

◆ Restrict printing, track printed copies, and provide secure central printing services.

Most of the following business needs cannot be addressed by using any PC-based office products. Because of the necessary programming, the current version of a PC-based office product is frozen into the ACM environment and restricts software change management. It is impossible to deploy the solution to other platforms and often other versions of Microsoft Windows. Managing document components in versions and variants can only be achieved by coding into the text-product binaries and thus becoming utterly dependent on those. Printing and archiving of content is impeded by the limitations of the printer driver architecture. Deployment to web user interfaces is complex to impossible. If a user opens any letter within PC-text, regardless of how well prepopulated, the result is uncertain and uncontrollable, requiring additional manual verification steps to ensure compliancy.

Businesses need to support and possibly enhance communications to their customers, clients, stakeholders, agents, and vendors. These documents can be any kind of letter, statement, request for information, rulings, contracts, claims payments or denials, status reports, account notices, serial letters, welcome letters/kits, new offers, and even litigation paperwork. Often, these have to be migrated from legacy correspondence systems, enable business users to maintain content, and support online/batch, interactive/ad hoc and web communications. Key needs are security, rapid development for new documents/applications, change management, compliance requirements, and standardization of corporate branding consistency and personalization. ACM needs to provide WYSIWYG design by business departments and IT; batch and client/server letter creation; generate/assemble letters from templates and building blocks with rules and processes for high-volume batch, online, ad hoc, browser, desktop, and offline PC laptop.

Data-driven specific business documents must be generalized or personalized. While the core structure is once defined by IT experts including the possibility to freely map business data, the final content must be under full control of the business users. Enablement of business users to maintain text/messages including multilanguage, resource management (fonts, forms, logos), change management supporting batch, online, interactive (thin and thick client), and web form/document solutions is essential for ACM.

To populate the business documents with data, the ACM platform has to access on the fly a variety of interfaces such as SOAP, MQ, XML, Java, LDAP, ERP interfaces, File, IMS, or transaction systems. In most BPM solutions, these interfaces are not platform- and compiler-independent and do need Java or .Net programming. Even when SOA interfaces are used, the mapping of data fields into the documents often requires such programming. Even if data mapping with XML/XSD definitions is used, it does require a lot of technical skill to deploy. The maintenance of these Java or XSD definitions is not linked to the change management of the documents, creating grave maintenance issues. This is against the requirements of the ACM concept. Data coming through an interface must be usable in a case business document without requiring a programmer or XML expert.

If one thousand users create ten documents of three pages each per day, the printing, enveloping, and mailing of thirty thousand pages correctly becomes a substantial cost and quality issue. Some businesses do over a million documents a day and some produce over a billion pages per year. Let's not forget the compliance problem of ensuring that the legal content of those documents is correct. ACM has to handle its outbound content through a user-managed correspondence facility that is tightly linked to output management with central bundling of different letters into one envelope, multichannel delivery (i.e., print, email, Web) and postal optimization, and obviously archiving. The actual status of the outbound document is a key element of the overall case progress. (See FIGURE 5-12.)

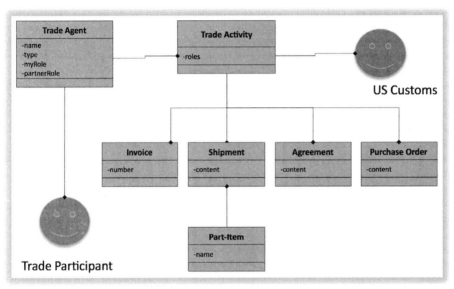

FIGURE 5-12: An Ontology Model of Actors and Content for a Trade Activity

The output management must create and deliver mission-critical business documents (high-volume, online, and ad hoc) across platforms and output channels. The ACM must link to the automation of print and mailroom production processes to ensure that documents that are sent can be traced and verified. That further requires complete centralized lifecycle management—across all platforms—of all document resources, such as fonts, images, forms, and text building blocks in all possible versions and variants (e.g., language and state). Documents must be tracked seamlessly from creation over centralized or decentralized printing to final enveloping in the mailroom. Document templates and resources are versioned including a full audit trail with who accessed what document applying which changes.

In relationship to inbound and outbound content, an ACM solution must offer the following:

◆ Consolidated facility for outbound and inbound communication with a single, consolidated view of all content processes across platforms.

◆ Central planning, control, and view of overall lights-out production with integration of existing hardware and software for optimized planning and utilization of resources and material.

◆ Real-time central resource management and versioning.

◆ Closed-loop print and postproduction, with print job and insert management for all applications, platforms, and hardware.

◆ Postal optimization and management with post office manifests.

◆ Document tracking and document-based reprinting.

In a recent *Financial Times* article, Galliers (2009) of Bentley University stated that it is utterly important that executives gain an understanding of what technology can and cannot do. Most executives are utterly unaware of the complexity they will encounter when they try to improve the work environment of knowledge workers, especially in relationship to content management. "We just want to send a letter, what could be so hard about that?" is the most common misunderstanding.

Technology is not just a means of cost reduction or automated execution, and the Internet is not just an additional marketing and sales channel and therefore influences business strategy. That understanding is even more relevant in the area of knowledge work.

The Role of Records Management for ACM

Because case management (adaptive or not) is a means of organizing business activities that are nonstandard and require a knowledge worker, it may be paramount that some or all content received, used, or created in the course of activity be treated as "evidence of an event" or as more commonly used a "record." ISO 15489 1:2001 defines records as "information created, received, and maintained as evidence and information by an organization or person, in pursuance of legal obligations or in the transaction of business."

The following records management functions are often needed for ACM:

◆ Creating, approving, and enforcing policies and practices regarding records, including their organization and disposal related to knowledge work.

◆ Linking the processes to a records storage plan, which includes the short- and long-term housing of physical records and digital information.

◆ Identifying, classifying, and storing records physically and electronically.

◆ Mapping the records management principles to the security requirements and also reflect them in the business rules.

◆ Digitally signing records to ensure authenticity.

◆ Link existing record archives (e.g., via OASIS CMIS).

THE SIGNIFICANT ROLE OF SECURITY FOR ACM

The need for transparency and the inclusion of outsiders, such as business partners and customers, into the virtual process organization and collaboration mandates the implementation of embedded security on the object and function level. Each access and function of any item has to be authorized. All objects, data, and content have to be authenticated. All actors have to be authenticated (ideally biometric authentication), and authorized in role/policy models. All changes to templates and definitions must be audited.

The key functions of ACM security are as follows:

◆ **Authentication**—Ensure that a user is identified with certainty.

◆ **Confidentiality**—Encrypt the document and data transmissions.

◆ **Authorization**—Control what someone can do with a document or workflow.

◆ **Accountability**—Track what someone did with a document.

◆ **Authenticity**—Verify the originality and source of a document.

◆ **Auditing**—Be able to create a full compliance record.

◆ **Digital Signatures**—Enable legally accepted digital signatures.

AUTHENTICATION

Authentication means verifying the identity of a user logging on to a network. Passwords, digital certificates, smart cards, and biometrics can be used to prove the identity of the user to the network. To log on to the ACM platform, the card itself (authentication by possession) as well as a PIN (authentication by knowledge) or an optional biometric fingerprint identification (authentication by identity) provides user authentication. Using a smart card with a fingerprint reader ensures a user's identity and enforces compliance without the possibility for human error. Once the smart card is pulled from the reader, all ACM platform applications (and optionally the workstation) are locked out. The user certificate and fingerprint are securely stored on the smart card, thus, authentication does not require network access. The authenticated user name is used as the key to obtain other security information, such as group membership and details about the person, to record a user as the owner of an object. The authentication service itself does not provide any details about a user other than whether authentication is successful or not.

An ACM platform should have an embedded authentication service to perform the following:

◆ Authenticate using a user name and password using a ticket.

◆ Create, update, and delete authentication information.

◆ Clear the current authentication and invalidate a ticket.

◆ Get the user name for an authenticated user.

◆ Provide a ticket for subsequent re-authentication.

CONFIDENTIALITY

Confidentiality must be ensured by encrypting the data transmissions and all data objects stored. There are many existing and widely used standards and means of encryption with public key infrastructure (PKI) being the most common one. I will therefore not discuss the complex technology issues related here.

AUTHORIZATION

Authorization defines what a person, once identified, is permitted to do with an application or system resource. This is usually determined by having a certain role and being a member of a particular group. When you go the cinema, you take the role of viewer, while the usher role works there. Your ticket is your policy giving you access to one theatre for a particular movie showtime. You have access to the theatre and a view privilege for the movie but not a record privilege. The usher has a default policy to access all theatres at all times. He also does not have a record privilege.

Each user receives at least one role. This role is authorized to perform either actions of a use-case or defined methods of an object. To define which resource instances a user is allowed to access, a policy authorization is also needed, which has to match the policy defined for the object. The user may be allowed to perform a method for a particular type of letter but is only allowed to access this type of letter of a specific department. The ACM platform should allow the use of existing user roles available in LDAP directories. (See FIGURE 5-13.)

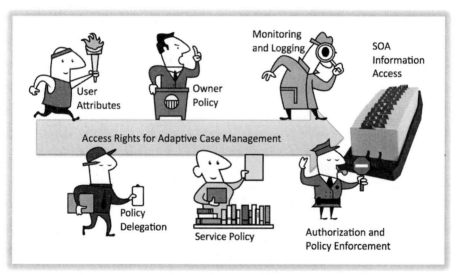

FIGURE 5-13: User Authorization for ACM

Authorities are objects defining a user name, group name, or role name. Global authorities are administrator, everyone, owner, and guest. Privileges are identified by objects granted or denied for an authority. A global privilege is assigned to an authority regardless of the resource type. A global privilege takes precedence over node-specific authority collections.

ACCOUNTABILITY

Accountability is achieved by a combination of user authentication and setting up the auditing functions for a workflow and its related documents. As you have identified the user by his smart card and fingerprint, his role and policy ensure what he can access, and all activities of the user can also be written into an audit log. Thus, at all times, the user can be held accountable for his actions. This is mostly important for system or security administrators, change management administrators, production managers, or users who sign off on application or document changes.

AUTHENTICITY

Authenticity of content has to be ensured and protected against tampering. Once a document becomes a corporate record or achieves a legal status as part of a contract, the document must be encrypted and digitally signed. The document can now only be opened by authorized parties, and as long as the signature is intact, the authenticity of the original can be verified without the need for storing the document to write-only media. Only users who have the authority to access the private key of the document can actually read it.

AUDITING

Auditing is the tracking of user activity as per the system's definition. This stored information allows authorized users to conduct audits. Typical audits are related to changes in security definitions or which way a document was routed and who accessed it. This is accomplished by using security functions such as authentication and data logging. Standard ACM platform document design, scheduling, and distribution features control when and which reports are formatted, how they are routed, and to whom they are distributed.

DIGITAL SIGNATURES

Many countries have legally validated the use of electronic signatures, as has the U.S. since October 1, 2000, but it does not specify a digital signature technology (ABA 2010). ACM may include dealings with clients or partners that require agreement or sign off, such as sales transactions, account openings, agreement to medical procedures, signing off on claims procedures, and many more. Signatures—digital or not—are not a part of such a transaction but rather of its formalized definition. Signing authenticates a form by linking the signer with it. A signature expresses the signer's approval or authorization. The signer's mark has to be distinctive and not easy to falsify.

A transaction is not invalid because it is not signed properly, but it may be unenforceable. While the act or intent is usually more important than form, formalized transactions are the norm. Formalization requires documenting the transaction and signing it, not necessarily with paper and ink. Today, the information exchanged for Internet transactions mostly never take paper form.

Signer and document authentication are a so-called nonrepudiation service or function. It assures the origin or delivery of information to protect the sender against false denial of receipt and to protect the recipient against false denial of sending. Also, a digital signature should represent an affirmative act as a ceremonial and approval function and establish the sense of having executed a transaction.

REAL-WORLD SECURITY ISSUES—HIPAA EXAMPLE

To make use of the full range of opportunities for effective quality improvements and enabling more efficient handling of complex knowledge work requires the consideration of security issues. In most situations, complex knowledge work takes place in cooperation with people from outside the organization with very different authority, such as partners or customers. Legal requirements such as U.S. HIPAA (Health Insurance Portability and Accountability Act of 1996, P.L. 104 191) regulation demands that personal information is handled securely and that fraudulent activities can be prevented. Similar regulation exists in Europe. The HIPAA Privacy Rule regulates the use and disclosure of patient information held by healthcare clearinghouses, employer sponsored health plans, health insurers, and medical service providers. Safeguards have to control physical access to equipment containing health information. Access to hardware and software must be limited to properly authorized individuals. That means that simple login procedures to the terminal or PC are not satisfactory—each action of a knowledge worker has to be properly authorized and must be auditable. These security requirements are continuously expanded evidenced by a new HIPAA subtitle enacted November 30, 2009, that extends the complete privacy and security provisions including civil and criminal penalties to business associates of covered entities. Due to these legal demands, only deeply embedded security can offer sufficient control.

Adaptive Process

> "Like resilience, self-organization is often sacrificed for purposes of short-term productivity and stability, which are the usual excuses for turning creative human beings into mechanical adjuncts to production processes."
>
> —Donella H. Meadows
> *Thinking in Systems (2008)*

While ACM is about bringing the benefits of adaptability to existing knowledge workers, I propose to expand that into "adaptive process" that combined with an empowerment management paradigm *turns more production workers into knowledge workers rather than just automating the production workers' work.*

There is an obvious need for dynamic processes that BPMS vendors are already addressing. The reality of BPM shows that it is very difficult to top-down analyze and simulate business processes and link them to KPIs in a continuous improvement cycle. Measure-to-manage optimization is counterproductive to improvement and innovation. Only empowered actors can use their intuition and experience for sensible action. The dynamics of economy require a self-organizing structure that is resilient to fast changes through its ability to adapt. Jeston (2008) writes about the complexities of getting orthodox BPM to fly:

♦ "Even if organizations were the same, the approach to the implementation of BPM varies enormously both from organization to organization and within an organization."

♦ "Continuous improvement, even if appropriate, is an extremely difficult program to implement 'continuously', year after year."

Process consultants tend to overestimate their understanding of the complete business problem, despite claiming an end-to-end business perspective. BPM believers are separated from the rest of the scientific world by their conviction that it is all about optimization of cost and quality, and as they know all about that, there is nothing new to be considered. This is why an evolutionary approach based on a complex-adaptive (social) system (Ackoff 1999) does not enter the BPM methodology and models.

From the perspective of complex systems and workplace psychology, we need to ask ourselves, what organizational strategy could be applied to combine the benefits of top-down business analysis with the needs of people management and still create a self-organizing structure that is resilient in a dynamic business environment? Must an organization choose between an autocratic, top-down, results-oriented leadership model and an empowering, bottom-up, people-oriented leadership model? In my experience, a well-balanced organization actually needs both. *Strategy, structure, and goals have to come from the top. Process knowledge, motivation, and execution have to come from the bottom.*

> "The process of institutional development is an evolutionary process, both linked and akin to the evolution of firms and industries. It is a groping, incremental process, in which the conditions of each day arise from the actual circumstances of the preceding day and in which uncertainty abounds."
>
> — Richard Nelson
> *An Evolutionary Theory of Economic Change (1982)*

Consider that a business is a social system of the complex-adaptive kind (Anderson 1988) with individually acting agents, and it is neither a deterministic manufacturing nor an animated one with a brain and a dumb body. Process modeling and simulation cannot ensure that the BPM model conforms to the real world or that any changes improve from before to after or achieve certain outcomes. BPM does not implicitly save costs and ensure proper resource usage. It certainly does not motivate people or answer what-if questions related to business goals.

I propose that modern businesses need process management systems that are like car navigation and information systems with arrival times, traffic warnings, weather reports, and fuel level, and consumption. It keeps me informed, but I turn the wheel and decide which route to drive. I, as the driver, need to make up my mind about where to go and how to drive the car and therefore know traffic regulation. I interpret signs and make decisions. I need to be considerate of other drivers and pedestrians. I decide if and when to go where, not the navigation system. Technology can improve my cognitive ability with lights, night vision, and distance sensors. In that simile, business activity monitoring (BAM) is like a radar speed camera: how would the average speed of cars at one point provide input into a model about how all people would get there faster and safer? Such models all fail miserably.

I concur with Blanchard (2001) in *The 3 Keys to Empowerment* that information transparency up and down the line, enabling autonomy through clear boundaries, and empowering teams in the hierarchy are the core elements of successful business leadership. People are at their best when they feel that their contribution is valued as an individual. Businesses will benefit from empowering employees and turning as many production workers as possible into knowledge workers—not the other way around.

Process management is not micromanaging everyday business processes from the board room. Empowerment is certainly not decision-making authority for everyone about everything. Empowerment truly means to give business users the power to create exactly what they need to achieve the best possible process outcome for the customer: this is effectiveness because it is measured at the customer. Empowerment is enabled by transparency (Pucher 2007). Transparency down the line helps knowledge workers to understand the business goals. Transparency up the line enables monitoring to verify the efficiency of that activity. If the customer can participate in that up-the-line transparency, then it will be substantially easier to judge his perception of quality. Amazon partners with their customers in product reviews and service ratings, and it encourages customers to cooperate. For a service business, transparency can best be achieved by a collaborative process support infrastructure that also supports the necessary improvement feedback loops. Transparency allows verification if goals are set sensibly and well understood, and it enables monitoring of business goal achievements of each team. In contrast to popular theory in MBA education, changing and therefore improving a business is *not* only a top-down management activity. Change happens slowly, as a social resonance of employees to motivating activities of the management! Meadows (2008) states that hierarchies are always built and always changed from the bottom up, while the highest hierarchy level has to provide the motivation and resources.

Agility cannot be enforced by methodology, and it is not a product feature. It can only be achieved through the agile mindset of management who will put the right technology in place that empowers agile employees. *Process maturity is not about how well processes control employees, but how much process control is given to employees to achieve goals and outcomes.*

Adaptive process technology exposes structured (business data) and unstructured (content) information to the members of structured (business) and unstructured (social) organizations to securely execute—and continuously *adapt* with knowledge interactively gathered during execution—structured (process) and unstructured (case) work in a transparent and auditable manner (Pucher 2009).

CHAPTER 6

DATA ORIENTATION

DANA KHOYI

Business process management technology considers the process to be the focal point around which business information is organized. Knowledge work does not have a predefined process. Adaptive case management (ACM) therefore uses case data as the focal point around which processes are arranged. Using the example of an employee onboarding situation, the effects of data orientation are explored. The conclusion is that an ACM system must provide rich data representation and relationships, and in the end, the ACM system becomes a system of record for the case.

Elsewhere in this book, you've read about how adaptive case management (ACM) provides a better approach to managing knowledge work. One of the reasons that an ACM solution is able to do this is because ACM systems allow you to describe your business in terms you already know rather than artificially fitting your business into a process diagram. The key here is that ACM allows you to capture the relationships of your business entities to the data that describe them. For the purposes of our discussion, a business entity is anything or anyone that is part of the knowledge work being done. ACM's data-driven approach is best understood through an example.

BUILDING THE SOLUTION WITH ACM

To illustrate the data-driven approach, let's walk through the steps involved in creating an employee onboarding solution.

Every corporation has a need to bring new employees into the enterprise, an activity called employee onboarding. This is generally a subset of what is commonly referred to as employee lifecycle management. This example illustrates the capabilities of case management well, as it often involves quite a bit of individual decision making and a lot of individual variability in how cases are handled. Some of you will have existing HR systems and may be thinking that you wouldn't need ACM as a result. While this may indeed be true, an ACM solution can augment HR systems where they are lacking or function as a stand-alone solution. We've simply chosen this as an example as it should be something most readers can relate to in concept.

DESCRIBE THE BUSINESS ENTITIES

The first step in setting up a solution with an ACM system is to list the business entities that are involved in the work. This should start as a brainstorming exercise—not all of these business entities will be needed for the system, but it is valuable to go through them and decide if you need them or not.

For the employee onboarding process, our brainstorming session resulted in the following list of business entities:

◆ **Candidates**—These cases represent the people who are under consideration for positions.

◆ **Managers**—These cases represent the people who are empowered to make hiring decisions.

◆ **Positions**—These cases represent the positions to be filled.

◆ **References**—These cases represent the references supplied by candidates.

◆ **Interviews**—These cases represent interviews that have occurred.

◆ **Recruiters**—These cases represent the recruiters that supplied candidates.

These business entities will be represented as cases in the ACM system. Dividing the problem into a well structured set of business entities enables the solution designer to minimize the amount of information in each entity, keeping each small and easy to understand. This is analogous to doing object-oriented design, and there are a number of design principles that have come out of that world (e.g., SIMPLE, DRY, etc.) that can be applied to this process.

DESCRIBE THE RELATIONSHIPS BETWEEN THE BUSINESS ENTITIES

The next step is to describe the relationships between the business entities. The business entities may have one-to-one, one-to-many, or many-to-many relationships. The most common relationship type is one-to-many, and in fact, all of the business entities in our example have one-to-many relationships.

FIGURE 6-1 illustrates these relationships with the arrows indicating which business entity is the one and which business entity is the many. For example, for each manager, there may be many positions and many interviews. For each recruiter, there may be many candidates. For each position, there may be many candidates.

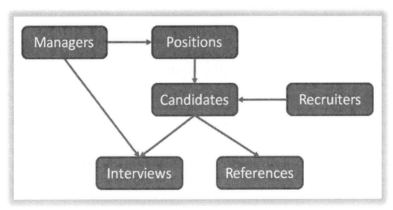

FIGURE 6-1: Relationships Between Business Entities

Add Detail to Each Business Entity

The next step is to start describing the business entities to the ACM system, creating templates in the ACM system to represent each business entity. Some ACM systems offer more than one type of object. Examples of object types that may be provided by an ACM system include documents, folders, forms, cases, and processes.

If your ACM system has more than one type of object, you'll need to decide which object type to use to represent each of the business entities. This decision will be made based on an understanding of the capabilities of these object types, which will vary between ACM systems. For the rest of this chapter, we will refer to the ACM objects representing the business entities as "cases."

The next step is to tell the ACM system something about each of the cases. You'll need to specify the information you want to associate with each case. This includes its relationships with other business entities. Some representative information for the business entities in our example is as follows:

◆ **Candidates**—Name, contact information, recruiter, make offer, offered position, and offered salary.

◆ **Managers**—Name, department, and open positions.

◆ **Positions**—Title and manager.

◆ **References**—Name, contact information, and comments.

◆ **Interviews**—Interviewer name, notes, and recommendation.

◆ **Recruiters**—Name, contact information, and placement fee.

Business entities in an ACM system usually have a concept of completion—what must be done to complete the case. In our example, a candidate is complete after all interviews have been completed, all references have been checked, and all associated managers have made a hire/no-hire decision. These decisions are captured as information associated with the business entities. For example, a candidate may include information about the decision to offer or not to offer a position to the candidate. An interview could include notes by the interviewer and a recommendation.

SPECIFY ASSOCIATED DOCUMENTS

A case may have associated documents. For example, a candidate will often have an associated resume. Ideally, the ACM system allows the solution designer to specify an expected set of documents to be associated with a case, so the people accessing the system can see what documents are expected and what documents are actually available.

SPECIFY THE TASKS

An important concept in most ACM systems is a task. A task represents some work to be done on the case. A case may have any number of associated tasks for the people that interact with the case to do. The users of a case are trusted to make good decisions about the tasks they do. Examples of tasks associated with the cases in our example are as follows:

◆ Candidate
  ◇ Get references
  ◇ Complete application form

◆ Manager
  ◇ Not applicable

◆ Position
  ◇ Approved for hiring
  ◇ Contact recruiters
  ◇ Post advertisement

◆ Reference
  ◇ Contact reference: confirm previous position, tenure, and salary

◆ Interview
  ◇ Conduct interview

◆ Recruiter
  ◇ Not applicable

Remember that the solution designer is specifying the initial set of tasks for each type of case. If a user decides that additional tasks are needed for a specific case, they can add them as needed. For example, if a recruiter sends in a notice that they are raising their placement rate, a user can add a task to that recruiter case to renegotiate the rate, with a note indicating that if the recruiter doesn't bring their rate down to a specified threshold, they will no longer be used.

CREATE A TEMPLATE LIBRARY

Some ACM systems enable the solution designer to define a library of template fragments that users can easily add to specific cases as needed. These can be used to create predefined sets of information, documents, and tasks that can be added to a case when a user decides it is appropriate. This is a fairly abstract concept and some examples will help.

In our example, there may be a library of predefined template fragments for a candidate case to add specific documents and tasks for various types of positions. For example, if the candidate is applying for a position as a programmer, we may want to ask them to complete a programming skills test. If the candidate is applying for a position as a graphic designer, we may want them to submit samples of their work. These two template fragments would be defined as follows:

◆ Programmer
  ◇ Documents: Test results
  ◇ Fields: Grade
  ◇ Tasks: Conduct test

◆ Graphic Designer
  ◇ Documents: Sample work
  ◇ Fields: Evaluation of sample work
  ◇ Tasks: Request samples

If your ACM system provides the capability, you can choose to empower your knowledge workers to add their own template fragments to their own personal libraries. These personal template fragments can be promoted to the case library—making them available to everyone.

Add Processes

Once cases have been defined to represent each business entity and the case definitions have been fleshed out, you can add the processes/tasks needed to transform the data toward the goal. There may or may not be one overarching process—there isn't one in this example.

However, an ACM system that includes BPM functionality results in a system that can be used to create inexpensive and manageable solutions for real-world business problems. Cases may trigger processes to perform well-structured sequences of activities and change the state of the case. In our example, a manager case may provide a button for a manager to create a new position. This can be done rather nicely using a structured process that gathers the necessary approvals and once complete creates a position case and links it to the manager case.

Specify the User Presentation

The last (and optional) step in defining an ACM solution is to tell the system how the information in each type of case should be presented to users. The productivity of your knowledge workers can be significantly improved by customizing the way the case is presented: making sure that the most commonly needed information is displayed when a case is accessed and the less frequently needed information is presented on tabs, for example. The presentation provides your users with tools to navigate through the data forest.

Foundation for Future Growth

Because the cases in your ACM system represent real business entities in your enterprise, the cases created for one solution will often be useful when creating additional solutions. One of the benefits of an ACM system is enabling incremental growth over time. The reuse of cases as you create new solutions is one of the ways this is accomplished.

In our employee onboarding example, the manager case may be reused and extended when adding a performance review management system. The candidate case may be changed into an employee case once a candidate has been hired.

ACM AS THE SYSTEM OF RECORD

While the cases in an ACM system can be used to update a separate system of record, often the cases are retained and the ACM system itself becomes the system of record. This implies a number of features that a good ACM must provide.

DATA MANAGEMENT

In BPM systems, since the information they manage is usually transient, enterprise architects do not worry very much about how they store the data they manage. With ACM systems, since they can become a system of record, enterprise architects care very much how the data is managed.

The preferred approach is to store all of the information in a database (avoiding "flat files"), ensuring that the database is well structured and ensuring that the database schema uses table and column names that are meaningful—preferably that can be specified by the solution designer as they create ACM solutions.

While it is reasonable for an ACM system to prohibit direct modification of the database—requiring that you use its application programming interfaces (APIs) to make changes—an ACM system should document the database structures so that you can do data mining and reporting.

RETENTION MANAGEMENT

As with any system of record, an ACM system must provide records management functionality. At the very least, it must offer retention management features: it should not be possible to delete content before it has expired, content should automatically be deleted after it has expired, and the automatic deletion mechanism should provide the ability to set a legal hold on content to prevent premature deletion. Ideally, an ACM system will be certified as compliant with appropriate records management standards (such as DoD 5015).

COMPARISON WITH BPM

It may be illustrative to contrast the ACM approach with how you might go about doing the same thing using a business process management system (BPMS). ACM and BPMSs differ in the way they approach business problems.

BPMSs start by describing the business process. The process instances in a BPMS are usually transient; when a process is done the process instance is deleted. ACM systems start by describing the business entities. Instances of these business entities interact with each other and users to reach their defined goal.

ISSUES WITH BPM

Trying to use BPM to create a solution for a problem that is not well structured is hard, and while it can be done, the resulting solution is usually unsatisfying. Some of the reasons for this are listed below.

Defining a structured process definition is hard for most processes. The process designer must negotiate with the process stakeholders to define a process that satisfies everyone. This is often the most time-consuming part of creating a BPM solution. In contrast, an ACM system allows the users to adapt cases to deal with the variations in the process.

A process has only one data object which must hold all the information involved in the process. Cramming all of the information associated with the problem into a single object (the process instance) makes that object complex and difficult to use. This can lead the designer into an incorrect conceptualization of the business problem—they treat every problem as if it were a single process (if all you have is a hammer, everything looks like a nail).

The process instance is transient: the process instance is deleted when the process completes. This means that all significant business information must be persisted in external systems. These systems must be accessed with integration tools (Web Services, MQ, Database Access, custom code, etc.) that require a developer's skill set to use. A custom user interface may have to be developed to provide users with access to this external information. This makes solutions more complex and expensive to build. Worse, moving information to a separate system of record and deleting the cases or process instances inevitably results in a loss of fidelity—you lose much of the history of how the work was done. This information can be very useful in finding ways to improve the business process.

ACM Needs BPM

While the majority of business problems do not have an overarching, easily definable structured process, most solutions do have areas that should be rigidly structured. These are portions of the solution that must adhere to regulatory requirements or where the enterprise has procedures that must be followed.

The best ACM solutions include BPM components to address these well-structured areas. Without a BPM tool, you end up implementing these areas with scripts or custom code. This makes the creation of the solution more expensive than it should be.

Conclusion

The reason that ACM is successful where other technologies are not is because ACM starts by describing your business. It allows you to think in terms of your existing business entities. You don't have to change how you think about your business in order to fit the needs of the tool—the tool adapts to fit what you do.

The problems that are best solved using ACM systems are those that are the competitive differentiators for enterprises. Why do we try to hire the best salesperson? the best underwriter? Why do we value experience? Why do we pay knowledge workers? (If all knowledge workers do is click buttons, couldn't we automate their work? The key is to know which buttons to click.) When people interact with a case they make decisions that are important to their enterprise.

Chapter 7

TEMPLATES, NOT PROGRAMS

DANA KHOYI AND KEITH D. SWENSON

In other parts of this book, you have seen discussions of templates. This chapter will go into some detail about what a template is. An important point is the difference between a template for an adaptive case management (ACM) solution and a process definition for a business process management (BPM) solution. Since both BPM and ACM use processes, data, forms, documents, etc., it would be easy to jump to the conclusion that an ACM solution is a lot like a BPM solution, but that is far from the truth. This chapter will explore in detail why these are so different and why this is necessary due to the inherent differences between BPM and ACM. What we will find is that a BPM solution is programmed in a very real sense because BPM addresses predictable processes. Conversely, an ACM solution cannot be programmed because the precise work pattern cannot be predicted. Instead, a template approach is used, which requires the active involvement of the case manager. We shall also see that the way a process is described in BPM and ACM is different as well because of the way that the process must be manipulated at runtime by the case manager.

The Purpose of a Template

A case manager can use an adaptive case management (ACM) system without any preparation for a particular case. It is possible for a person to create a case as a blank sheet, give it a goal, and add documents, information, and whatever else is needed to coordinate the case. We have also mentioned that even though a case is not precisely repeatable, there are recurring elements: there are patterns that are followed. Those patterns are based on legal or cultural agreements. Having to manually create the complete pattern every time would be tedious; however, when such patterns exist, it is handy to have some prebuilt components that can be brought to play. That is a template: a collection of prebuilt components. An ACM solution is a collection of templates.

Contrast with BPM

For those familiar with business process management (BPM), you might think of a BPM solution as a collection of prebuilt components as well, but the nature of those components and the way they are used is very different.

Remember that BPM is defined for situations where the process is known. A BPM developer (or business analyst as they are sometimes called) goes through a period known as "process discovery." There are two main techniques for this. The first approach involves (1) studying the norms and customs for the particular domain, (2) interviewing people in the organization who are doing the job now, and (3) interviewing the leaders to know how they would like the process to work in the modified organization. In some cases, systems allow people to collaborate online to create this information. The second approach is known as "automated process discovery" because it mines the information about what an organization has been doing directly out of the history log files for the applications they are already using. This approach provides an ego-free view of how the process really is done today. Either way, after the process is discovered, there usually is a creative period where the most optimal process for the organization is identified, sometimes with the aid of a simulation and optimization tool.

Then the BPM process is programmed. Again, there are a variety of different ways that different BPM systems (BPMSs) do this. In some cases, a high-level diagram from a business analyst is emulated directly by the system or converted directly to an executable form. In other cases, a programmer is hired to take the diagram and write a program that matches it. Regardless of how this is done, the end result is a process that can be executed without modification. The process is programmed.

To say something is programmed is to say that it is automatic and there are no random aspects to it, no whims. The concept of a program is something that is completely defined in order to be self contained and able to take care of every situation. It can have branch conditions, the programmed process can respond to stimuli, but every branch and every response is completely determined by the programming. If it fails to take care of a situation, it is considered a failure or a bug. Programming is the act of completely defining the actions of something.

To say it is programmed does not mean that it is reduced to a computer CPU machine code. Programming can be done in many technologies, starting from a third-generation language that is compiled to executable code and up to scripting languages that are interpreted at runtime. A lot of the focus of BPM is to provide a form of programming that is closer to the conceptual representation of the business process so that the programming can be done by people who are closer to the actual business itself and do not need as many specialized skills. Many argue that the purpose of BPMSs is to provide high-level representations that make it easier to change the processes quickly resulting in a more agile business process. Many organizations like to use business rules within the process because this isolates a certain part of the business logic into a rule form that is (for some) easier to modify quickly.

Even though BPM solutions are designed to be changed easily, they are not designed to be changed by the end user. They are implemented by one person (the programmer, business analyst, or rules expert) and executed by another person (the actual participants in the process). There is no necessity for the participants to know how the process is put together, in fact, many systems purposefully hide what the end users don't need to know. The process must be programmed to execute correctly without modification by the end user. Like most programs, a BPM process is tested extensively to make sure that it does the right things in all the foreseeable situations.

An ACM template, however, is not programmed like this. An ACM template contains components, but the case owner is not simply executing the template; instead, the case owner is using those components to assemble the case file. The components may be modified, or adapted, by the case owner to the specifics of the situation. This gives the ACM template an entirely different flavor. The template provides pieces that might execute when assembled, but there is no guarantee that the template itself is able to execute in any meaningful way.

SMORGASBORD ANALOGY

The best way to understand the difference is to consider the difference between two types of restaurants. One is a sit-down restaurant where you order food and the waiter brings it to you. The other is a smorgasbord buffet, where food is arrayed into displays, and people go there with an empty plate and select what they want to put on their plate.

In the first case, the sit-down restaurant, you order from a menu that describes the dinner that you are ordering. In some cases, you can order a combination of things that will be brought together. In some cases, you have some choices, some options about the meal, that can be specified. Once the food is prepared it is brought to you. At this point, there are specific rules that you will have about how the food will be on the plate. Instead of rules, we should call them expectations. The specific rules, or expectations, depend upon the kind of cuisine, the kind of meal, and may depend upon any number of local customs that may even be peculiar to that restaurant. Let's call those the "rules of a dinner plate." Your expectation is that the rules of a dinner plate must be met in order to properly eat a meal. The chef is instrumental in ensuring that those expectations are met.

In the case of the smorgasbord, you may also have rules of a dinner plate. The diner has a more active role in ensuring that these rules are followed: filling their own plate from the buffet tables. But focus your attention on the buffet table. The chef has prepared and set out food on the buffet table according to a different set of rules and expectations. The "rules of a buffet table" are not the same as the rules of a dinner plate. Instead, the buffet table is designed in a completely different manner, but in a manner that is conducive to helping people get food onto their plate. Then they take the plate back to their table to eat. It is fair to say that the smorgasbord buffet does not present the food in a way that is proper for eating. That is, it does not obey the rules of a dinner plate.

BPM is like the sit-down restaurant: the programmer puts together a complete process definition ready to run, just like the chef put together a complete dinner ready to be eaten. The process definition in a BPM solution is a complete process, ready to run. There is nothing for the end user to modify, and in fact, for the most part, the end user cannot modify anything. However, an ACM template is like a buffet table. A template is not ready to run, and in fact, it probably cannot be run in its natural form. It is designed instead to present to the case owner a set of components that can then be assembled at runtime into a case that runs (to the extent that you can call it running).

CONSTRUCTING A TEMPLATE

A better picture comes from understanding what goes into creating a case solution. As described in CHAPTER 6: *Data Orientation*, the solution designer starts by modeling the business entities—the things—involved in their solution. For the employee onboarding example in CHAPTER 6, we defined the following business entities:

◆ **Candidates**—Represent the people who are under consideration for positions.

◆ **Managers**—Represent the people who are empowered to make hiring decisions.

◆ **Positions**—Represent the positions to be filled.

◆ **References**—Represent the references supplied by candidates.

◆ **Interviews**—Represent interviews that have occurred.

◆ **Recruiters**—Represent the recruiters that supplied candidates.

This would be modeled in an ACM system by creating a template for each of these business entities. A template is simply a predefined case that is copied when creating new cases. The template specifies all the prebuilt things that are available for a new case of a given type.

For example, a candidate case would include structured data to track the candidate's name, contact information, desired salary, references, and previous employer. A case should also be able to manage a set of associated documents. For the candidate case, these could include the candidate's resume, job application form, and copies of their identification, etc.

All of these bits and pieces are elements of the case; we've described two types of elements in this example: structured data and contents. Depending on the capabilities of the ACM platform, there may be many different types of elements that can be incorporated into the template.

Once a case has been created (by copying a template), the participants (the people working with the case) can add additional elements as needed (and as allowed by the permissions they have based on their role in the enterprise).

To better illustrate how this works, let's look in more detail at activities, content, and presentations—some of the most important elements in any ACM platform.

ACTIVITIES

An activity (sometimes called a task or a step) identifies something that needs to be done. Activities have a status (not started, in-progress, waiting, deferred, completed, etc.). An activity usually has an associated action that specifies how the activity is done. Some examples of activity actions are manual, process, and script.

◆ **Manual Activity**—A manual activity reminds participants of work they need to do. For example, a new employee onboarding case may have a "reference check" manual activity. This acts as a reminder that someone working the case is to do the reference check. A participant clicks on the activity to mark it complete asserting that they did the work.

◆ **Process Activity**—A process activity initiates a new process instance in predefined processes. For example, a loan solution case may have a "suspect fraud" process activity. Clicking the activity creates a new instance in the fraud investigation process. This type of activity can be used when there is a well-defined, structured process that may or may not need to be performed as part of processing a case.

◆ **Script Activity**—A script activity invokes a script to perform an automated action. For example, a loan solution case may have an "update customer database" script activity. This enables the participant to make an intelligent decision as to when the customer information in the case is complete and ready to be posted to a database.

An activity can be assigned to an individual making them responsible for its completion. Most systems also enable the assignment of an element to a group, indicating that any member of that group can do the work. Ideally, the system offers several forms of interaction depending on the participant's connection with the solution. For users who access the system infrequently, an email can be sent notifying them of an assignment. For users who interact with the system as their primary job function, a work list UI can be provided that displays their activities enabling them to efficiently manage their work.

Activities can have deadlines and dependencies that specify when the work is to be done. Dependencies are often specified as part of the deadline. For example, a mortgage loan origination activity "credit check" might be specified with a deadline of "eight business hours after the application form is complete." Managing deadlines and dependencies is similar to project planning. The set of activities in a given case can be thought of as a project plan.

Content

Most cases interact with content that is managed outside of the case in order to aggregate all of the information for the case. This includes a list of links to other objects in the case. The case acts as a folder. The number of content elements in a case varies widely between types of cases.

For example, a mortgage loan case is a classic example of a case that has many related objects such as forms and documents collected (the original solution form, plot plans, appraisals, credit reports, etc.). There may also be references to other cases that represent the applicant or the property being mortgaged. In contrast, an auto loan solution case would include few content objects: the application form, credit report, and perhaps a copy of the title.

Often, a content element has an associated or embedded activity. For example, in the mortgage loan case example, the content element "Form 1003" (the application form) would have an associated activity to verify that the form is complete. Some systems simply associate a status to the content element itself.

Some case management systems provide the ability to include links to content in other repositories. Some can make interacting with the linked objects seamless for both users and scripts.

Content is defined in a template by creating "placeholders" for content that is expected to exist in the course of processing the case. Placeholders help participants visualize what content is and is not present in the case. Further, they provide a place to hold deadlines and other rules that define the behavior of the content when it arrives.

PRESENTATIONS

The presentation of a case (sometimes called a form, but it may not appear like a paper form) is the specification of what is displayed (presented) to a user when they open the case. It is important for a case management system to provide the ability to define customized presentations for a case. The presentation of a case should be optimized for each type of user—designed around the way they will interact with the case—so that they can be as efficient as possible. For example, a loan origination case will be accessed by data entry operators and underwriters. A presentation that is optimized for a data entry operator would be less useful for an underwriter. Consider the following:

◆ The data entry operator should see the document containing the data to be entered and the form into which the data is to be entered.

◆ The underwriter should see an interface that provides access to all of the content linked to the case, the list of activities to be performed, as well as providing access to other solutions in the enterprise.

TEMPLATES ARE ADAPTED TO THE SITUATION

Case management systems address the variability in business processes by enabling the case owners to change a case as it is processed. Some may shudder at the idea of participants changing the process, but that is the nature of knowledge work. They are experts in doing their job correctly, and as Drucker (1999) points out, they know their own job better than anyone in the organization. The system should provide case owners with the information they need, so they can use their experience to make informed decisions.

A case owner adapts a case by adding, modifying, and removing elements from the case. For example, an underwriter working on a loan origination case decides they need evidence of a recently paid off loan. They can add a new placeholder to the case to hold the document when it arrives and set up a deadline to follow up if it does not.

When you realize that a situation is really not that exceptional—that a significant number of cases need this support—then one should be able to add the extension to the "template element library." This codifies and streamlines exception situations, bringing them into the normal business process. Some systems may provide a "personal element library" as well as a "team element library."

Permitting participants to add elements "on the fly" enables them to handle unusual situations on their own. However, these elements will not have any associated rules or scripts—they are completed manually. As the system matures, rules and scripts may be added to the elements in the library adding "guardrails" to avoid common mistakes and scripts to automate routine activities.

This process of allowing the system to mature and develop as it is used is called "emergent design." Emergent design is the optimal design methodology because it emerges from the use of the system in the situation of doing the work.

A good case management system includes analytics to monitor cases as they are worked. This provides detail on the way the work was actually done to suggest elements that should be promoted to team or template libraries, places to add guardrail rules, and places where routine activities can be automated.

Further, as new solutions are implemented, it is common to find existing case templates that can (and should) interact with the new solution's templates. For example, when implementing an employee offboarding solution, you will probably find that the manager and position cases templates from the onboarding solution can be reused in the new solution.

Moving Solution Development to the Case Owner

Good case management systems provide features to defer the definition of portions of the solution to the case owners that use it. This may seem risky, but if you empower your users, they will create and enforce their own structure.

A good ACM system might enable participants to modify presentation to fit their needs using direct manipulation of the UI structures. Consider a presentation for an insurance underwriting solution created by a solution designer as shown in Figure 7-1. One of the underwriters notices that they are constantly clicking on a tab in the bottom left panel to access information needed to process the case. She should be able to customize her presentation by clicking and dragging the tab out into its own panel.

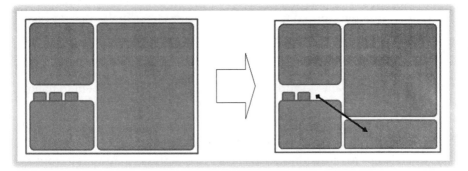

FIGURE 7-1: Direct Manipulation of the User Interface

This capability enables the solution to be finished by the participants after it is deployed. This eliminates the need to communicate requirements to a development team. An initial solution can be created faster, deployed faster, and in production faster. Then we learn from the participants how to improve the solution, and an enhanced solution is developed iteratively over time (i.e., the design emerges).

Once a case has been modified and found to be useful, there should be a way to promote the change to include it in the template that the case originally came from. Promoting elements and presentations to higher-level libraries does not need to be an IT operation—it can be done without significant risk to the operation of the system. The IT organization can allow business analysts to create and modify templates as needed to address the needs of the business.

LESS CODE

Case templates are created using the same interface that participants use to interact with a case instance. Users with permission to create templates see an additional tool in the interface to save the case as a template. This enables any participant with sufficient permissions to create new templates. Case templates may evolve over time by incorporating elements created by participants. None of these activities require any coding.

It would be wonderful to contemplate a world where coding skills were never needed, but the fact is that as a case template matures, it should be enhanced with functionality that can only be implemented with rules or scripts.

◆ Rules should be used to provide guardrails that prevent users from going into territory that you know will produce bad results.

◆ Scripts should be used to automate routine or well-defined activities—reducing the opportunity for errors.

Defining these rules and scripts requires programming skills that are typically found in the IT team requiring interaction between the business participants and the IT team. The important thing to note is that this programming is not required to create the initial case template. Such programming can be seen as enhancements that are added incrementally as the system is used and the need for them becomes clear.

The way that ACM templates are developed causes an inversion of control from the normal way that technology is developed. Instead of the development team driving the process, asking the participants for information, the participants drive the process and ask the development team to add an occasional rule or script to their solution. The IT team can focus on smaller, easily implemented projects that have clear requirements.

PROCESS MODELING NOTATION REQUIREMENTS

We have covered most of what one might need to know about templates, but because the business process field is filled with discussion about how to draw a process diagram, we include here a discussion of how the requirements of the process definition differ between BPM and ACM, and how those differences affect the modeling notation.

It is not a stretch of the analogy to consider the difference between the quality of food in a sit-down restaurant and in a smorgasbord. A chef can assemble an elaborate meal with many specific details. The chef needs a lot of freedom and very precisely prepared sauces and garnishes, and the chef has the skill to compose these on the plate for the diner.

Food from the smorgasbord is somewhat simplified and cannot be expected to be as refined as that in a sit-down restaurant. It is not a matter of ingredients or skill, it is just not practical for a fine meal to sit in a buffet. The buffet is not a collection of ingredients that a chef might have, but instead ingredients suitable for self serving (as well as lasting for a certain time), and so they are necessarily simplified.

Business Process Modeling Notation

Business process modeling notation (BPMN) is a process diagramming language designed to specify a complete process in a standardized way. The goal of the notation is to provide a dictionary of standard shapes that are meaningful to both business users and developers. Regardless of whether the diagram is created by a business analyst or a programmer, the BPMN diagram is designed to be an as complete as possible definition of a process. BPMN has many rules around how things can be connected, what is valid and not valid, and what this all means. Thus, BPMN can be compared to the rules of a dinner plate—you can use it to create a complete and ready-to-execute process.

The problem is that the BPM community, particularly the people involved in the development of BPEL (business process execution language) at OASIS and UML at OMG (Object Management Group), has promoted the idea that BPMN should be a fully complete process programming language. This is supported by the desire to make it possible for a person to model in any tool supporting BPMN and to allow that to be automatically translated to BPEL. Extensions specifically for the support of BPEL have been introduced into the standard for BPMN 2.0. These extensions have the effect of making the language less accessible to an untrained user. The kinds of extensions included for BPEL are the kinds of things that would normally be used only by professional programmers, not business users.

An ACM template, however, follows a different set of rules analogous to the smorgasbord rules. What is important is not that the template is fully defined and it runs, but instead that various pieces are available in a way that they can be easily composed. The rules of how these fragments are made (the rules of a buffet table) are completely different from the rules of a complete process (the rules of a dinner plate).

So with an ACM template, the pieces that you have to compose at runtime are necessarily simplified compared to the pieces you might use in a BPMN diagram. This is not surprising. The person creating the BPMN diagram has available a reasonable amount of time to put the diagram together and to make sure that it works. Extra time spent perfecting the diagram is made up for at execution time with the increased efficiency of the running process. A BPMN diagram is designed to provide flexible and accurate control of the state but with that power comes complexity. A template, on the other hand, must be something that can be assembled by a case owner who does not want to think about the details of putting things together. It needs to just snap into place, and it needs to work regardless of where it is snapped into. The case owner does not want to have the complexity of having to deal with syntax errors and validation errors. The syntax must be simplified.

Anyone experienced with creating a BPMN diagram will know that it is not as trivial as dragging and dropping shapes randomly onto the canvas. A considerable understanding is needed to get a diagram that is valid. There are many unresolved online discussions about whether a particular drawing is valid or about what a particular diagram means. While BPMN promises to be easier than traditional programming and seems to accomplish this, it still is far more complex than a typical case owner wants or needs. What is desired is a formalism that is user friendly (i.e., typical case owner friendly).

Templates represent the middle ground between a completely blank slate and a completely defined process. The template allows the process to be partially defined ahead of time and then adapted at runtime to the situation. How is this modeled?

MODELING FOR ADAPTATION

Early work on graphical notation for collaborative work has been presented in "A Visual Language to Describe Collaborative Work" (Swenson 1993a) and "Visual Support for Reengineering Work Processes" (Swenson 1993b). The prevailing belief at that time was that if you made graphically designed process models, then actual end users would be able to do the modeling. An experimental system was implemented to explore this usage (Swenson 1994). This modeling notation was remarkably similar to BPMN. It is difficult to simulate a realistic business collaboration scenario in the laboratory, but the whole approach got a break when the core capability was incorporated into a successful workflow product. This product exposed the ability to adapt processes at runtime to many thousands of end users around the world. No formal study was done of usage patterns, but informal observation showed that most end users were not comfortable with modeling a process diagram, even with an easy to use graphical modeling approach. It appears that ability to use the tool was not the barrier, nor was the ability to read the meaning of the diagram. Instead, the users were uncomfortable with the kind of abstraction that a graphical model required. In general, business users are not comfortable working through the formal logic required to ensure that a diagram is expressed correctly. Furthermore, the public nature of a collaborative system means that any mistake in this logic is highly visible and potentially embarrassing.

Undeterred by this, Fujitsu proceeded to re-implement the approach in new products that offered an applet-based process modeler that allows any user (with appropriate access rights) to modify a process model at any time, even while the process is running. In spite of the ready availability of a process modeler, that modeler was actually only used by the process analysts, and essentially never the regular end user. The conclusion we draw from this is that a BPMN-style diagram is good for many things, but we should not expect end users to manipulate a process in this form at runtime.

Remember that an ACM template is not a complete process, but instead prepared pieces of a process that are expected to be adapted to the specifics of the situation. The prepared process template might not itself be a runnable process. A template may include instead a smorgasbord of possible activities that are meant to be selected from when the actual situation is known. It may make no sense at all to attempt to "run" the full collection of activities. Thus, testing a template is not at all the same as testing a process execution. A process template is designed to be adapted, and it is not designed to be executed directly.

A formalism for describing processes in a way that is easily modified by knowledge workers is described in "Workflow for the Information Worker" (Swenson 2001). Instead of making a two-dimensional graphical map, a simpler linear list of steps is viewed and manipulated. This representation looks a lot like a Gantt chart, and it often is embellished with a timeline and Gantt-chart-like time bars (see CHAPTER 10: *Innovation Management*).

FIGURE 7-2 displays the process as a list of activities, with check marks indicating completed activities and an arrow indicating the currently active activity. Activities may be added by adding a line and removed by deleting a line. Instead of sophisticated routing logic, activities can be manipulated directly: started and stopped manually. Completion of an activity automatically starts the following activity (if not already started or skipped). CHAPTER 10: *Innovation Management* will cover the idea that a product may be able to switch between two views: a Gantt representation and a more traditional two-dimensional process diagram notation.

Status	Activity	Expected	Actual
✔	Requirements Gathering and Validation	13-Mar-00	26-Mar-00
✔	Release Planning	20-Mar-00	26-Mar-00
✔	Authorization to Proceed	21-Feb-00	27-Feb-00
✔	Feature Planning	27-Mar-00	05-Apr-00
✔	Design	10-Apr-00	26-Apr-00
✔	Development	29-May-00	02-Jun-00
✔	Integration Test	09-Jun-00	09-Jun-00
✔	Alpha Test	05-Jun-00	09-Jun-00
✔	Beta Test	15-Jun-00	30-Jun-00
⇨	Release Approval		
☐	Released	04-Aug-00	
☐	End of Life Notification		
☐	End of Life		

FIGURE 7-2: Activity List Representation of a Process

SKIPPED STEPS

The idea of a skipped step is unique to ACM; it does not exist in BPM. In BPM, if an activity is not needed, it is simply removed from the diagram. Unlike in ACM, the presence of an activity in a BPM diagram that will not be run does not provide any value. In ACM, the idea of marking an activity as skipped is superior to simply deleting the activity because it clearly shows that the activity was considered and that a conscious choice was made to not perform that activity. In a case management system, there is no single official process— every case can have a process that fits the situation. If one person notices that a particular activity that is normally included is missing, this person might assume that the case manager simply forgot to add it. In such an environment, new activities are introduced from time to time, and the knowledge workers learn when and how these activities are to be done.

FIGURE 7-3 displays an activity list of potential steps where step 2 has been skipped in the past (notice the arrow that indicates the currently active activity is at step 4), and steps 5, 7, and 8 are marked to be skipped in the future (a conscious choice was made to not perform the associated activities). Marking an activity as skipped is a remarkably simple way of communicating to others that you have concluded that this activity is not needed for this case. This is just one way that the process modeling requirement for ACM templates diverges from BPMN, which is intended for designing complete processes that do not need modification at runtime.

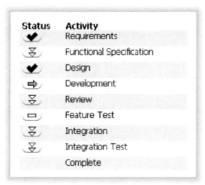

**FIGURE 7-3: Activity List of Potential Steps
Where Some Are Marked for Skipping**

SEQUENCING AND OVERLAP

Because the case manager can directly manipulate the state of an activity in a template, there is less of a need for the sequence to be precisely defined. The process in the template does not need to be exact because minor variations can be accommodated at runtime. A BPM process expected to run thousands of times without modification needs very clear routing logic. This is the nature of programming: define a sequence of actions such that the result is always guaranteed. But if the user is able to modify the process at runtime, a much-looser sequencing of activities is accommodated.

Imagine that sometimes a case manager wants two activities to run simultaneously and at other times sequentially. Using a graphical notation like BPMN, you have to draw an arrow between the activities to indicate that they run sequentially. But to indicate that they should run in parallel is a lot of trouble: you need to draw a parallel split, a parallel join, and a lot of arrows between these. Consider instead that you have a start/stop button on the activity itself. It is far easier to manually start two activities running simultaneously, than it is to draw the diagram that would automatically cause two activities to start running simultaneously. Once again, the mass-production trade-off is relevant: if you are designing a process to be run one thousand times, then it is worth drawing the parallel paths. But if you are drawing a diagram to be run once, it is far easier to simply start the steps in question by direct manipulation.

FIGURE 7-4 displays steps 6 and 10 running simultaneously (notice the two arrows that indicate the currently active activities). This came about because the case owner decided to start step 10 concurrently with step 6. The reason for this could be very complex, and it could be based on information that is not included in the case in a testable form. Specifying the exact logic behind why step 10 needs to be started may be a lot of complex work. Simply starting the activity by direct manipulation is far easier.

Status	Activity	Expected	Actual
✔	Requirements Gathering and Validation	13-Mar-00	26-Mar-00
✔	Release Planning	20-Mar-00	26-Mar-00
✔	Authorization to Proceed	21-Feb-00	27-Feb-00
✔	Feature Planning	27-Mar-00	05-Apr-00
✔	Design	10-Apr-00	26-Apr-00
⇨	Development	29-May-00	
✔	Integration Test	09-Jun-00	09-Jun-00
⧖	Alpha Test		
⧖	Beta Test		
⇨	Release Approval	29-May-00	
▭	Released	04-Aug-00	
▭	End of Life Notification		
▭	End of Life		

FIGURE 7-4: Activity List of Potential Steps with Some Running Simultaneously

Similarly, if the case owner needs a reminder sent to someone that is unique to that situation, it may be far easier to manually compose and send the notification at the right time, than to set up a timer to send the notification automatically. This is not to imply that ACM systems don't need the ability to send preprogrammed notifications. In cases where a time-out or a reminder deadline is well defined and common, the template is going to need such a definition. But in a situation that requires a unique timer, it may be easier to manually send the notice than to set up a timer to do it.

IS THIS PROCESS MODELING?

One might look at the sequence of activities in FIGURE 7-4 and question whether it really represents the modeling of a process. It does not look like the common understanding of a model, which is usually graphical. That question can be answered by the same person who will answer whether business users really want to model processes.

What we do know is that knowledge workers want to accomplish work. They need to do so by giving activities to people. In this chapter, we do not want to say that all ACM systems must produce this exact kind of model, but what we are seeing is that such systems usually include something very much like the simple list of activities displayed in FIGURE 7-4.

This is the curious nature of creating processes in a case at runtime. Ease of use requires that you allow the creation of an activity with just the definitions of the activities and without the overhead of linking it up inside the process. A process definition needs to be extremely lightweight. A sophisticated routing pattern becomes less useful, since for a single case, manually performing that routing may be less work. This chapter leaves you with the following guiding design principle for ACM processes: *Creating an activity at runtime needs to be as easy as sending an email message; otherwise, the knowledge worker will send the email message instead.*

SUMMARY

This chapter has established that it is desirable to be able to create solutions for both BPM and ACM. BPM solutions will consist of process definitions (it is natural to think of these process definitions as programs because they are prepared to be executed without modification by the user at runtime), and ACM solutions, on the other hand, will consist of templates. Templates are not programs that are intended to be run without modification. A template is better thought of as a smorgasbord of pieces that are convenient for a particular situation. The case owner picks and chooses from these pieces and constructs the running case from them. Templates are adapted to the situation.

CHAPTER 8

HEALTHCARE

DAVID HOLLINGSWORTH

This chapter considers the nature of healthcare business as an archetypal example of a professional case management environment. The fundamental attributes of the care process are described, illustrating the importance of clinical knowledge as the basis for decision making and the difficulties of applying a traditional process management approach in this context, where unexpected outcomes may commonly arise. The role of the clinician within such an environment is considered as a "choreographer" of underlying clinical services, coordinating assessment and treatment delivered through a range of potential provider departments and organizations, across a range of care facilities. Potential opportunities are identified for improvement through access to integrated patient data and decision-support information, both facilitating enhanced clinical decision making. These two elements are considered key building blocks in the delivery of integrated case management within healthcare.

Healthcare in Context

Healthcare is the single largest business segment in the world. In the developed world, it accounts for around 10% of GDP (OECD 2009); in the nondeveloped world, it is one of most critical areas for future growth.

Healthcare exhibits a mix of public and private services, delivered through a set of complex distributed care processes, typically involving many different organizations and specialist departments within organizations. These range from local general practitioners, health visitors, and pharmacies through to highly specialized and advanced hospital facilities.

It is also an industry facing unprecedented change and challenges through the following:

◆ Demographic changes (in the developed world, an aging population is forcing a rethink on the most appropriate and cost effective means of delivering care during lengthening old age).

◆ The impact of technology advances (medical progress includes ever-advanced imaging and diagnostic capabilities, more-personalized medical treatments from genetic advances, the introduction of home based telehealth facilities, etc.).

◆ The advancement of public access to clinical information through the Internet and associated opportunities for beneficial personal involvement in prevention and simple problem self-diagnosis.

These changes have significant cost implications, leading to increasing emphasis on efficiency and effectiveness in the care processes. This is a complex task as healthcare processes span multiple organizations and change in one often impacts others in adjacent care disciplines. Common change patterns include the following:

◆ Optimization to make more effective or intensive use of expensive resources (e.g., reducing hospital inpatient time), to reduce administrative costs (e.g., repeat prescriptions), and to reduce wasted resources (e.g., avoiding "no-show patients," etc.).

◆ Increasing emphasis on prevention and early detection through personal information campaigns and screening programs.

◆ Up-skilling (e.g., nursing or pharmacy staff undertaking activities previously performed by doctors).

◆ Transferring care, where possible, from more expensive intensive or acute facilities to cheaper and typically more localized facilities in the community.

KNOWLEDGE WORK WITHIN HEALTHCARE

Healthcare is one of the business segments with a very high number of professional and skilled knowledge workers. They operate in a highly structured context involving many different specializations and disciplines, linking through complex end-to-end care processes. Rigorous training and professional knowledge, in both depth and breadth, are prerequisites for clinical roles—resulting in a workforce well versed in critical decision making in a complex environment.

Medicine is characterized by many professional bodies and exchange of professional information and case studies (both through document distribution and conference events).

Information is gathered and collated at all levels: from the professional as an individual, by departments, by organizations, and by national government bodies through to international organizations and research groups. This aggregated set of clinical data informs decision making within the care process. The Internet has extended the scope and reach of such information among professionals and also, importantly, brought it (at least partially) within reach of the layperson.

While there is recognition of the potential benefits in automating such decision making, there are also many potential problems.

The complexities and individualism of the human organism, coupled with the rate of scientific advancement, means that many treatment decisions are difficult to automate within a care pathway. Clinical assessment and treatment decisions are rarely made with 100% certainty of outcome; numerous complicating circumstances may arise, often not easily predictable in advance. Furthermore, clinicians (as with other classes of professionals) operate in a culture of personal responsibility for decisions made, making it difficult to accept automated, rules-based systems developed by third parties as the primary decision route.

Hence, most of the decision making during assessment and treatment is made by the clinician, supported by the established and continually developing base of clinical data. Business process management (BPM) capabilities, driven through prespecified and automated rules sets, have addressed some parts of the lower-level administrative processes but have made little progress into the core clinical care activities.

Concerns over clinical safety and public acceptance have further limited the scope for fully automated decision making driven through prespecified and automated rules sets.

Thus, a key focus for clinical systems has been to enhance the decision-making process rather than to automate it. Progression toward integrated case management and the incorporation of decision-support capability bring together as much relevant data as possible to assist in diagnosis and treatment decisions.

Case management has historically been handled in a fragmented approach with each organization involved in the care process maintaining its own case records. Integrating the case records across diverse disciplines and organizations provides a holistic view of the patient and his care activities, providing a better context for decision making. New initiatives in this direction are emerging across the developed world.

Decision-support capability may be "hard" (based on formal rules evaluation) or "soft" (presenting suggested or recommended templates as a basis for planning treatment). The former has often focused on drug prescribing, making reference to norms of dosage, delivery method, and established contraindicators, etc., to advise clinicians on the possible complications associated with prescribing decisions. However, taking a broader view of decision support, one can also include the provision of more general ("soft") information on established care pathways associated with particular conditions. (In this context, a care pathway may be thought of as a recommended template for the assessment and treatment options associated with a particular set of symptoms or condition.)

This is not to say that there is no role for BPM within healthcare; there are many administrative processes that are amenable to automation using predefined rules sets. It is the linking of BPM for these elements with the provision of integrated case management and decision-support software that provides the most interesting opportunities for the future.

THE CARE PROCESS

Traditionally, the highest level view of the care process has been seen as a simple five step model: (1) register, (2) assess, (3) treatment plan, (4) deliver treatment, and (5) review (see FIGURE 8-1). At this level, it may be considered applicable to both planned (prescheduled) and unplanned (emergency) care situations. Clearly, the time granularity and detailed underlying activities will be very different between the two situations, but the basic flow of activities can be thought of as similar.

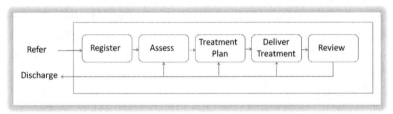

FIGURE 8-1: The Care Process

STEP 1: REGISTER

The patient presents (or is referred) at the appropriate care facility with problem/symptoms. The patient is registered, details are captured, and a current case file is created. This activity is typically capable of automation as it normally comprises standardized activities.

STEP 2: ASSESS

The assessment may include an initial diagnosis or may result in specific investigations (imaging, pathology tests, etc.). Depending upon the complexity of the case, this may require referral to another organization or specialism. The assessment itself is a knowledge-based activity for the controlling clinician. This may be made in consultation with specialist advisers, and it is rarely capable of automation, although valuable supporting information may be accessible through capable IT support systems. Further diagnosis information is added to the current case.

STEP 3: TREATMENT PLAN

Based on the results of the assessment, a treatment or "care plan" is developed for the patient. This is an individual plan, although established care pathways may exist to provide a treatment template for certain types of conditions, these will be generic and will normally need review and tailoring to the particular circumstances of the patient. Again, this is a knowledge-intensive activity.

Step 4: Deliver Treatment

Treatment is delivered—medication, surgery, physiotherapy, etc.—and provided individually or as complementary actions. This may be a single activity (e.g., a defined surgical procedure) or a continuing series of actions including follow up (e.g., physiotherapy). While certain underlying actions may be capable of automation (e.g., admission/theatre bookings and scheduling, or electronic management of prescriptions), the treatment remains a mix of knowledge and skill-driven activities. Case documentation is continually reviewed/updated.

Step 5: Review

Treatment is reviewed for efficacy and impact, including side effects, etc. Steps 2, 3, 4, and 5 typically operate cyclically with feedback between all steps. Again, this may involve consultation and conferencing across several disciplines.

Eventually treatment is deemed "complete" and discharge occurs with the current case details closed and summary information added to appropriate medical case records.

This simple view of the clinical process may be extended to include associated administrative, financial, and reporting/analysis activities proceeding in parallel with the clinical activities (see Figure 8-2).

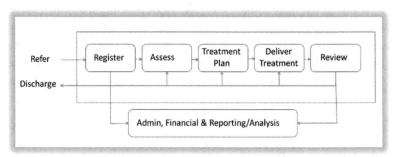

Figure 8-2: The Care Process—Extended

This model can be seen as a simple process diagram where care referral to more-specialized facilities is required, establishing a chain of care. FIGURE 8-3 displays such a referral chain established between different organizations.

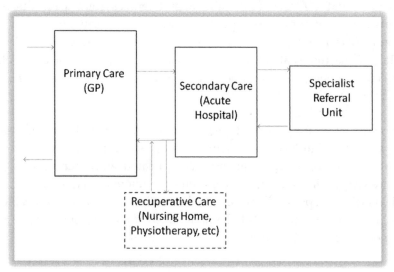

FIGURE 8-3: Referral Chain

In some ways, this may be seen as a care process chain, decomposing the various activities throughout the care process into those undertaken within the various specialist treatment facilities. In this simple model, it may also be viewed as a responsibility chain with immediate responsibility for treatment transferred between organizations.

Normal practice is for each facility to create its own active case to manage the care process within its own domain of responsibility. Summary patient details would typically be transferred between organizations (or departments) at points of linkage (e.g., referral, admission, transfer, discharge, etc.). There are some well-established standards in healthcare, based on HL7 (Health Level Seven International) messaging, that support elements of this linkage between different facilities or organizations.

This includes patient ADT (admission, discharge, transfer) messages, orders, and results (e.g., for pathology or radiology tests) and prescription transfers, etc.

However, these do not really amount to a fully automated, process-driven model. The normal approach to automation is based upon events and actions associated with HL7 messages and defined in each independent clinical system. For example, an admission event—when an inpatient is registered on a hospital patient administration system (PAS)—would typically result in the generation of an outbound ADT message to other departmental systems with admission details of the patient demographics. At each of the receiving systems, the inbound ADT message would typically cause an action to create a new (or update an existing) patient-identity record. This may be followed by other message sequences, for example, placing orders for tests or returning test results, etc.

In practice, the care process depicted in Figure 8-1 may be thought of as a very simple high-level process model. In practice, the flow of work in a healthcare environment is far more complicated with many underlying activities happening in parallel and sometimes without formal synchronization and coordination points. For example, the medical practitioner may call for a number of investigative tests to be undertaken at the assessment stage as in the model shown in Figure 8-4.

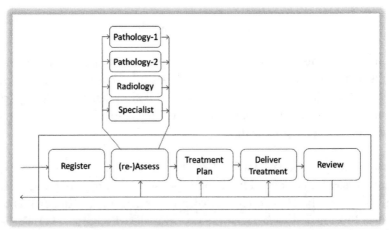

Figure 8-4: The Care Model Focusing on the Assessment Step

More-complex situations often arise where different aspects of care are under the ongoing responsibility of different organizations/departments. This is often the case with long-term conditions—where a patient is under ongoing treatment for a long-lasting problem (e.g., diabetes, arthritis, or chronic pulmonary condition) but may also suffer other related or unrelated problems—that require parallel treatment from other specializations.

In such cases, patients may be treated for multiple conditions, with potentially complex interactions, requiring collaboration between different specialty units. Multiple medical conditions may require treatment in parallel, further increasing the potential complications of multiple care pathways.

In traditional BPM terms, one could think of multiple parallel processes in operation with complex and (potentially) unpredictable interactions between them (see FIGURE 8-5).

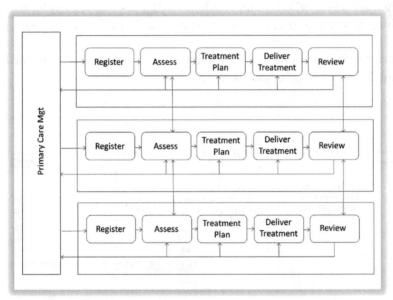

FIGURE 8-5: Traditional BPM View of the Care Process

One of the problems with these types of models is that their primary view is organization and/or procedure centric. This may make it difficult to coordinate assessment or treatment activities happening across different care organizations. Typically, each organization maintains its own case record for the patient (and may well use a different patient-identification code for the record). Formal exchange of information may only occur at defined points: for example, the start of a referral and its completion. Information arising from activities occurring between these points—tests and results, drug prescriptions, discovery of allergy conditions, etc.—may be entered in a local case record, which is often not visible to other organizations with which the patient may be interacting.

In many ways, a more relevant approach is that of a patient data-centric model evolving over time. In the final analysis, the care process may be broken down into, essentially, a continuum of ongoing parallel activities, with review and amendment occurring frequently to assess the implications of the patient's current situation. This requires information sharing between and decision making across multiple departments and organizations. In particular, the provision of an integrated (i.e., cross organization) medical record for the patient becomes a critical element in delivering this form of integrated care. A process-centric approach, while potentially useful for managing some of the underlying detailed activities within a particular facility, is generally inadequate at this higher level where multiple independent organizations may be involved in the care, and the course of care is dynamic and often unpredictable.

FIGURE 8-6 illustrates this style of working—a patient data-centric model using a time-based (or longitudinal) approach.

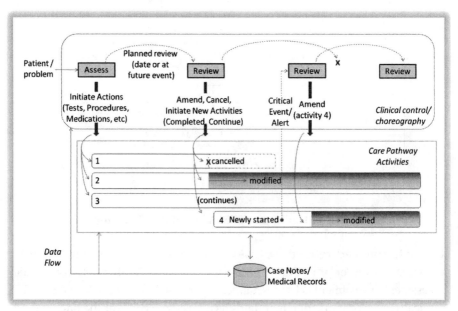

FIGURE 8-6: Patient Data-Centric Model of the Care Process (more representative of the actual working pattern)

Patient care is represented as a series of activities (one or more) that continue as a longitudinal view through time. At any particular point in time, treatments or tests may be in progress and new conditions may arise that are assessed or reviewed. These constitute activities within the patient care pathways.

It is the assessment and review points in which the clinical decisions are made and underlying assessments and treatments are orchestrated that become central to the control of the workflow. In FIGURE 8-6, this is termed the clinical control or choreography function. At such review points, a number of actions may occur. Activities may be as follows:

◆ **Initiated** (e.g., a series of tests to diagnose a new problem).

◆ **Completed** (e.g., a treatment course has successfully concluded).

◆ **Amended** (e.g., a medication course may be amended to a different dosage or an alternative drug or dispensing method).

◆ **Cancelled** (e.g., a particular treatment is curtailed as noneffective).

◆ **Suspended** (e.g., physiotherapy is suspended until a complicating condition is resolved).

Some activities will continue unchanged through such a review point (indeed, some activities may be under the control of a different organization and fall outside the scope of a particular review). Conversely, some activities, particularly related to less serious ailments, may well complete without any formal review point—essentially a presumed successful conclusion. (For example, a course of medication is prescribed and taken, and the patient feels better and has no need to return to the doctor.)

It should be noted that in the bigger picture (e.g., embracing both medical and social care), there can be quite significant separation of responsibilities for different facets of care, emphasizing the importance of collaborative working between organizations in delivering patient-centric care.

As discussed, activities may be discrete action steps or a series of interlinking process steps (in effect, a subprocess). For example, a doctor may initiate a set of pathology tests that break down into a phlebotomist making an appointment to take blood specimens; the bottling, labeling, and transport of such samples to one or more laboratories; and the collation and return of results.

Some of these underlying procedures may be well automated—electronic ordering, appointment making, etc.—but the higher-level clinical workflow control remains essentially a knowledge-based activity.

The review or choreography process may include planned and unplanned events. Examples may include the following:

◆ **Time-based events** (e.g., "I'd like to see you again in three weeks.").

◆ **Planned events linked to some future occurrence** ("I'll let you know when your test results are in—come and see me then.").

◆ **Unplanned events** ("Following complications, this patient needs immediate surgery.").

In FIGURE 8-6, a planned series of reviews is shown as interrupted by the occurrence of an (unplanned) critical event during activity 4. This may result in a planned review point being brought forward or an immediate response being initiated. In general, the exact nature of this orchestration is difficult to predict. It will typically embrace both planned and unplanned events, and the decisions made will be based on a knowledge of the individual patient's situation, the established wealth of clinical practice, and knowledge relevant to this situation. This is the essence of the adaptive case management (ACM) approach.

THE KNOWLEDGE DIMENSION

While healthcare information systems often support automated processes at the underlying administrative level, it is clinical knowledge and decision making that controls the workflow. PASs may handle patient appointment bookings or automate hospital registration, but it is clinical knowledge that assesses the patient's condition, treatment options, and potential complications and decides on the appropriate procedures.

There are a number of reasons it has proved difficult to incorporate this vast knowledgebase into automated, decision-based processes and software, and among them are the following:

◆ The breadth of the subject as healthcare covers a huge knowledge space with very many areas of specialization. It has proved difficult enough even to develop a unifying codification scheme for documenting this space, let alone use it as a basis for automated decision making.

◆ The different organizations, often independent, that are involved in different aspects of healthcare make the development of common, shared processes difficult, and their introduction into established professional working practices potentially problematical.

◆ The complex nature of clinical knowledge and potential interactions between conditions, treatments, and medications. (The human body remains the single most complex system in the world; medical science continues to evolve at a phenomenal rate.)

◆ The fact that few clinical decisions can be absolutely 100% deterministic, and the wide range of possible exception and complicating conditions.

◆ The difficulty in providing a complete and holistic view of all patient data from multiple source organizations in an electronic form.

◆ Concerns over clinical safety, and the difficulties of testing such potential automation and its acceptability to clinicians, the public at large, and regulatory authorities.

Despite all these reasons, advances in clinical software continue, but their focus has been on (1) consolidating and filtering clinical information about the individual and (2) matching that against the continually evolving knowledge about the nature of clinical conditions, treatments, and outcomes. These are the two essential elements of clinical case management.

CASE MANAGEMENT WITHIN HEALTHCARE

Case management may be considered to incorporate two broad elements: administrative and clinical.

Administrative case management covers details such as appointments, visits, ordering, admissions, transfer between wards or facilities, planning and scheduling of facilities (theatres, etc.), discharge arrangements, billing and financial reporting, etc. This information is used actively during the course of the care process, and many of these aspects are becoming the subject of business automation—in whole or part. This aspect is not considered further in this chapter.

Clinical case management is the more challenging aspect. That is, the management of the clinical notes and data sets relating to an individual's medical history, conditions, tests, treatments performed, medications prescribed, etc. This aggregated set of personal clinical data can then be assessed against the wider base of clinical knowledge (including conditions, treatments, and outcomes) to support the development of the most effective care plan for the individual concerned. These two aspects of clinical case management—the consolidated medical record for the individual and the provision of wider information to support clinical decision making—are further considered below.

Historically, an individual's medical records have often been fragmented across different organizations, with each organization, or even department, maintaining its own case data associated with a patient's particular care episode at the facility. One area that is being addressed within the industry is the electronic linking of this different case data into an integrated and comprehensive record for the individual.

In this chapter, the term "integrated case management" refers to this aggregation of patient data across multiple diagnosis and treatment facilities. Common terms within the industry are EMR (electronic medical record) and EHR (electronic health repository), referring respectively to the aggregated medical data set for the individual and the storage facility supporting this for a target patient population. It may be achieved either through copying key aspects of individual records into a separate (real) centralized repository or as a virtual capability by providing indexes and links to the individual record sets within different organizations allowing integrated access to the whole. It should also be mentioned that the most stringent of security regimes are normally enforced to control access to such information.

Integrated case management is not just concerned with collecting together all possible clinical information about a patient. There is the further consideration of summarizing, extracting, and linking the key data to reduce the volume of potential information presented and structuring it into the most significant and appropriate format to support the task at hand. (For example, a hospital may maintain a large quantity of detailed monitoring data during an inpatient stay that may be relatively unimportant after discharge. Whereas, the discharge summary record provides key information on the treatment provided, the patient condition on discharge, a record of drugs administered, and notes concerning aftercare.)

As many care processes involve multiple organizations and/or departments, it is the EMR that becomes the key component in delivering the integrated view across organizations. This may be regarded as data-centric rather than process-centric integration. The ability to link from a patient's current case record in one facility to pick up details from current or historic cases in other facilities is becoming increasingly important to facilitate sharing of critical patient data and improving decision making.

A comprehensive view of the medical record makes it much easier to inform decision making with appropriate and relevant supporting information.

Decision support is normally regarded as the provision of the appropriate information to assist clinical decision making or to provide a cross-check on potential outcomes of the decision. The emphasis is not on automating the decision making, but on assisting the knowledge worker (drawing upon his personal knowledge and experience) through the availability of wider information assembled and presented by the IT systems. This may take the form of a recommended care pathway for a particular condition, rules databases about the impact of certain medications, contraindicators, etc.

The assembling of such information may be at personal instigation (for example, searching the Internet or medical journals for relevant information pertinent to the current case) or may be presented by an IT system as a "recommended" care pathway for the known patient symptoms or condition. Decision-supporting functions may be automatically invoked in electronic prescribing software (for example, as a cross-check that medication dosage and delivery is within accepted norms of the profession or to warn of potential contraindicators).

Each may be considered as a perfectly valid decision-support capability. The aim in each case is to improve decision making through the provision of further relevant information. The result should be clinical decision making that is as well informed as possible, and the reduction of potential risks arising from the decision.

The essence of effective case management is thus to bring together a comprehensive and relevant view of patient data and to support this with as much relevant and useful data as possible from the broader clinical knowledgebase (see FIGURE 8-7).

That having been said, effective decision-support software is not easy to develop or deploy. Quite apart from the difficulties of ensuring correctness and accuracy in any data provided, there is a difficult line between interventionist and informative principles.

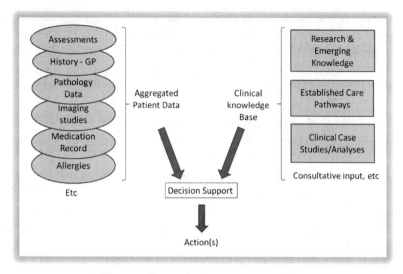

FIGURE 8-7: Bringing Data Together

Some prescribing systems have been developed along the former line (i.e., interventionist principles), where there is clearly the potential to improve patient safety by automatically cross-checking and warning of possible prescribing errors before accepting the order.

In most other situations, the latter line (i.e., informative principles) has been followed—where the clinician is provided with optional access to information (for example, links to related information on the Internet or in-house guidelines, etc.). In the U.K., a set of several hundred care pathways has been developed under the guidance of the National Institute for Clinical Excellence and deployed as an information source for access by medical staff (the "Map of Medicine"). This draws on expert knowledge in various medical specialties with the aim of offering a "recommended" template for more general consumption in dealing with certain presented conditions. In such cases, it is the ability to deal with peer review and incorporate comments and feedback that is often critical to the success (or not) of such endeavors. In this way, the outcomes of individual cases (good or bad) are aggregated back into the ongoing body of knowledge for future use.

Of course many, indeed, probably the majority of clinical decisions are taken directly by the clinician based on personal knowledge and experience without the need for access to deep supporting information. This further reinforces the informative approach—let the clinician decide when additional information would be useful, but in those cases, organize easy and rapid access to appropriate material.

This draws out a further important consideration in terms of the authority for the use and accuracy of such electronic sources of medical data. Most professional, knowledge-based workers have their own professional body of recognition, often incorporating an associated code of conduct. Many, although by no means all, are self-employed or part of a partnership with their own direct line of responsibility for the outcome of decisions made. This means that in many cases, the introduction and use of decision-support software is the responsibility of the professional concerned, with any coordination in wider usage and updating being influenced by the professional body.

An important facet of case management systems in the healthcare industry is the provision of a full audit trail, embracing the provenance of data (who originated or updated the information and under what role?) and its subsequent access (who read the data and under what role?). This provides irrefutable linkage between the clinician and the data of a particular patient (or group of patients).

In complex cases, decisions may be multidisciplinary, involving dialogue between several professionals or departments.

Finally, there is also an increasing requirement to involve the patient in the process of case management. In some situations, it is the patient who is well placed to provide coordination across different disciplines by injecting his personal knowledge into consultations and discussions. (This cannot apply in all circumstances, of course. For example, where the patient is unconscious or in some cases of mental illness.) Furthermore, the trends toward improved self-diagnosis and monitoring (including for example, telehealth initiatives) will require more active involvement of the patient in case management activities.

CONCLUSIONS AND SUMMARY

Healthcare is in many ways unique, but it also displays many of the typical characteristics of knowledge-based working. It is based on many professionals working in a multidisciplinary, multiagency environment with complex decision-making responsibilities.

The key workflows within the care process are built around clinical decision making—assessment, care planning, treatments—involving frequent review and re-assessments. This is a knowledge/experience/skill-based activity, with the clinician's role essentially one of choreographing the underlying detailed activities: initiating and undertaking tests and examinations, deciding on the detailed approach to treatment, and ordering/coordinating its individual strands, etc. (See Figure 8-8.)

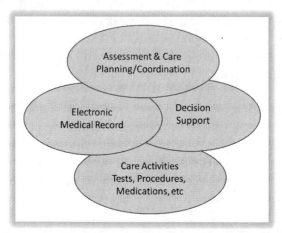

Figure 8-8: Integrated Clinical Case Management

Case management within healthcare is long established, and there is a strong industry trend toward delivering a more integrated, patient-centric approach to this, identified in this chapter as integrated case management.

Important aspects of this include the ability to consolidate key elements of medical records into a unified record for the individual, and to complement this with information access systems to support decision making.

Most of the detailed care activities are human-centric tasks. Process automation has a role to play in the management of parts of this, but it is effective primarily in the underlying administrative and ordering activities. Common processes and associated standards exist in some areas to support this, particularly in communication between diverse systems for specific messaging actions.

However, it is the patient-centric view (rather than the process- or organization-centric view) that is increasingly recognized as paramount. Hence, the primary focus in healthcare remains case management and its integration.

CHAPTER 9

IMPROVING KNOWLEDGE WORK

FRANK MICHAEL KRAFT

Elsewhere in this book, the challenges facing an increasing number of knowledge workers is discussed. This book is about how information technology can leverage the abilities of individual knowledge workers. This is not about individual tools; it is about a holistic approach: adaptive case management (ACM). But the approach will only work if individual knowledge workers draw immediate benefit from it. In this chapter, I argue that knowledge work will become easier, more fluent, if the right technology is provided. This is the basis for success within a network of knowledge workers, which in turn will yield the return on investment for the companies they work for. To accomplish this, the characteristics of knowledge work must be directly reflected within the information technology so that the use of such technology feels natural. I will discuss the technology needed to achieve this goal. In closing, I will sketch the full long-term potential for ACM.

The Struggles of Knowledge Work

Leona works in the engineering department in a company of about one hundred fifty employees. Her regular job is to design new functionality for the telephone system they sell. This includes requirements for hardware components ordered from a supplier and software components developed by their software development team. This week, it's her turn to provide second-level support: she takes customer calls that cannot be solved by first-level support to ensure that the more difficult cases are solved. Although it is not her favorite job, she recognizes how important it is.

Leona frequently gets hotline calls from customers asking about the progress of their problem. These calls interrupt her work, so it is hard for her to concentrate on the problem analysis she needs to do. It is particularly difficult to answer questions about problems reported last week when she was not on hotline duty. The colleague that received the call last week remains the case owner. She has to run around in development and find the person that is working on the problem, if there currently is one. Even more troublesome are the frequent calls to the supplier to determine the status of resolutions. This takes much of her time. Somehow she feels that this time is wasted and could be used better.

Leona feels that she is overloaded. Some customer cases require a lot of attention that she has to balance against the challenging deadlines of the development projects. When her manager, Dan, wants her to do additional work, she finds it hard to explain her inability to take on new tasks—it is hard for her to account for all the different things she has to do.

Leona has day-to-day challenges that she needs to solve as well. A constant flood of emails keeps her inbox full. Occasionally, she overlooks an important email. When collaborating on a document, it is often exchanged via email making it hard for her to determine the latest version and to reconcile different changes. She knows that it is better to edit the document on a file share, but it is still difficult to determine who is editing what and when. Did she accidentally miss an important change by someone else? Sometimes, her requests to others to make changes do not produce the expected results. She wonders whether a new technology like Google Wave might be a solution.

She occasionally makes a list of tasks. So many tasks accumulated that they were hard to manage. The constant reminders of missed due dates did not help either. She has found that a project planning system works for some of her projects. But she can't plan too far into the future because so many unexpected events occur making it hard to predict what will happen next week. Clearly, the kind of work she does is different from a project plan such as that needed for building a house. Her work is unique, less predictable, and emergent: it unfolds while it is being done.

She would occasionally like to delegate some work to John, the new team member. But sometimes it turns out that he does the work quite differently than she would have expected.

There is a growing stack of papers she wants to read. Somehow she has to catch up with latest developments.

At the start of the day, Leona wants to focus on the most important and most urgent tasks. How can she keep her deadlines? How can she organize the urgent tasks? How can she delegate work to John and be comfortable about his implementation plan and progress? How can she find time for self-education? When Leona leaves the office in the evening, she wants to feel that she has everything under control—at least somehow. She wants assurance that she achieved results this day. Although she feels uncomfortable with the errors, she knows that all progress in knowledge work is made by trial and error. She knows that she has to take the good with the bad and that all knowledge workers share this experience. Leona is part of many teams: her department team as well as some project teams. One project is a standardization project with participants from different companies around the globe. She often wonders whether the teams have a clear status about their work and fears that others might have lost focus on the goal.

Then the telephone rings and a customer is on the line describing a problem with dropped calls under certain conditions. Leona asks some questions about when the problem occurs, what the circumstances are, and whether it is reproducible. Her knowledge of the design of the system guides this line of questioning.

Imagine that Leona has an adaptive case management (ACM) system available now. She would create a case, take notes about the symptoms, and try to estimate for the customer how long it will take to close the case.

She knows that their product should never drop calls, so she writes as a goal of the case: "Close case only after problem is resolved." She promises this to the customer and ends the call. The goal of the case defines the frame for all subsequent activities; however, it is not specific enough to estimate how long the case will take.

She remembers that three weeks ago there was another case where she linked the documentation. So she searches the ACM system for that past case and gets the link to the documentation. After reading it, she determines that the new version, released two months ago, addresses the problem. She also knows from that case that the delivery takes three working days. Leona updates the case with the more specific goal ("Close when new module 1-3252-3 has been delivered"), planned completion date, and instructions for delivery (see FIGURE 9-1).

She knows that Dick is responsible for the delivery, so she assigns Dick as the responsible processor of the delivery. She triggers a notification email from the case to the customer informing him about the current status and the planned completion date. The customer may follow the link in the email to see the case in his browser. At least she is relieved from frequent customer calls now.

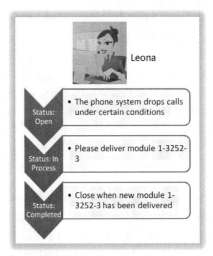

FIGURE 9-1: Representing this First Example Case in an ACM System

Later, Leona gets a call from another customer who complains that in certain situations calls cannot be forwarded. She creates a case for this and searches again for an existing solution, but in this case, no preexisting solution to the problem can be found. This will take much longer because the problem cause must be analyzed and mitigated. She writes the new goal: "Close when call forwarding is enabled under all conditions." (See FIGURE 9-2.)

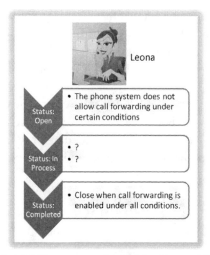

Figure 9-2: Initial Representation of the Second Example Case

Leona needs to involve different parties. Because of the nature of the problem, she is quite sure that some software checks and hardware checks are needed. The software check can be done by their own personnel, but the hardware check needs to be done by the supplier of the module. She knows that it can take around two weeks to get the supplier's service technician onsite, so she defines an expected solution date of three weeks. In addition, she sets a reminder: Remind three days before the estimated completion date is reached to check the progress.

Now she needs to plan the next intermediate goals. She breaks the goals down.

It is obvious that before the problem can be mitigated the problem cause must be identified. So the first intermediate goal is to "Find the problem cause." This is done by two measures (two subgoals): (1) remote software check and (2) onsite hardware check. She is not completely sure if both will be necessary, but to not lose any time, she plans both now. There is no definite sequence for both subgoals. She thinks that if the remote software check identifies the problem, the onsite hardware check may not be necessary. But since it is always difficult to get the supplier's service technician, it is better to schedule the visit and cancel it if it is not needed.

After she has done this, she assigns the supplier company as the responsible processor for "On-Site Hardware Check" and sends the supplier company a notification email from the case. Then she can use the time to better plan the remote software check. She knows from her experience that most probably Checks A–C are needed. She can perform Checks A and B herself, but for Check C she must involve a colleague from development; therefore, it is better to plan this now. She might start the checks tomorrow.

The next day, Leona gets a notification email from the case that the supplier has updated the service visit date. She sees that it is scheduled for tomorrow, so she can update the expected completion date of the case accordingly and notify the customer of the updated completion date. (See FIGURE 9-3.)

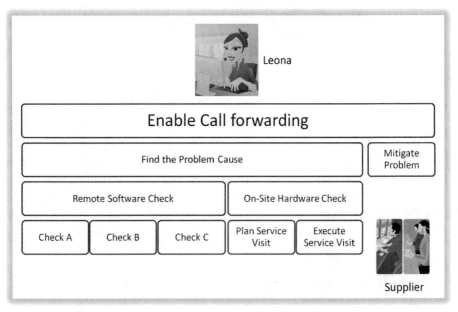

FIGURE 9-3: Planning to Determine the Problem Cause

By the next week, all of the checks have been performed. The problem turns out to be more complicated than assumed, so a conference call is needed between the customer, the supplier, and development. Leona is not on duty taking calls this week, but she is the case manager for this case since she took the initial call last week, which is an efficient way to handle these types of cases because one person (i.e., the case manager) can take the case through all of the steps. So Leona updates the case and the expected completion date accordingly (see FIGURE 9-4).

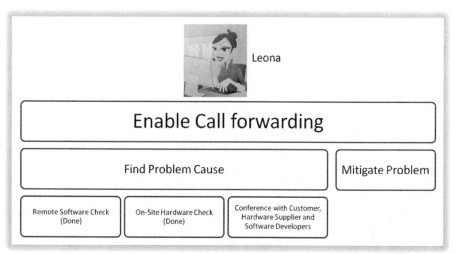

FIGURE 9-4: Plan Updated with Conference Activity

During the conference call, they determined that it is a combined hardware–software problem. This allows the problem mitigation to be planned.

In this example, it turned out that the hardware must be changed, which breaks down as follows: negotiate with the supplier, create a specification for the new functionality, and test the new device from the supplier. The software problem must be fixed by her own development team. Since it is Leona's area of expertise, she takes over the software problem but delegates management of the hardware problem to Steve—however, she remains the overall case manager. Steve will detail the hardware part of the case, while she details the software part of the case. They collaborate on the case for about two months. The customer is kept up to date on the progress. (See FIGURE 9-5.)

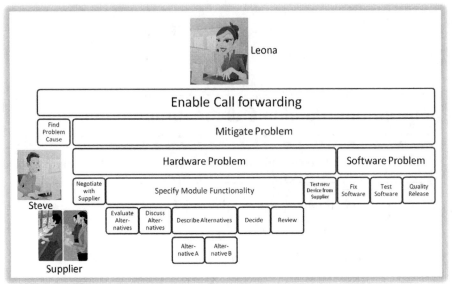

Figure 9-5: Plan Updated to Include Problem Mitigation

In the eighth week, the customer calls asking about the status of the case. Leona can drill down the case and can see that there is a delay in testing. She determines that the responsible tester is on leave and locates a replacement.

Finally, the tested solution is delivered, the case is closed, and the customer is satisfied. The case remains in the database for future reference for similar customer problems.

Characteristics of ACM

The case we just examined has several characteristics that distinguish it from common approaches resulting in several advantages that I want to discuss in more detail.

The characteristics/advantages of the approach taken are as follows:

◆ **Goal Orientation of the Case**—The stream of work of the case is best described in a goal-driven way.

◆ **The Unpredictability of the Work in the Case**—The resulting stream of work is not able to be defined in detail ahead of time.

◆ **Guidance by a Case Template**—There still should and can be guidance for the stream of work.

◆ **Constraining by a Case Policy**—It is desirable in some cases to constrain the stream of work by policies.

◆ **The Community Library**—A mechanism that promotes the sharing of templates between team members can have a big affect of productivity.

◆ **Burndown of Remaining Effort**—Tracking of work that remains to be completed for the goal is an effective way to stay focused.

◆ **The View of the Manager**—Providing some visibility of the work to managers and coworkers can help a team be more effective.

◆ **Accomplishing Day-to-Day Tasks**—Time is freed up for more creative tasks since much of the organization of the stream of work is done automatically by the system.

GOAL ORIENTATION OF THE CASE

I explained that Leona would first define the goal of the case. This has several advantages such as the following:

◆ It helps in estimating a date for the completion of the case.

◆ It guides the planning of activities to reach the goal.

◆ It makes it possible to prioritize the activities in relation to their contribution to reach the goal.

◆ Goals remain more stable, even if the activities vary.

Estimating a completion date aids communication with the customer. Since the goal is connected to the status "Completed," the system is able to watch that date and escalate or remind if necessary. Of course the estimated completion is not definite, but it is the best of knowledge at this point in time. It is even possible to track how the estimated completion date changed over time. Goal orientation is a large advantage because it allows for tracking, monitoring, and alerting.

Once the goal is determined, activities to reach the goal can be defined. It is not necessary, or even desirable, for one knowledge worker to do all of the planning. Often, specialists should be involved in detailed planning. These specialists might come from within the company or maybe from partner firms, suppliers, the customer, and even—depending on the work—experts from a social network. Since this is knowledge work—not routine work—the planning itself is already a decisive part of the work and critical for success.

The knowledge worker must continually reevaluate the priorities of activities with regard to the goal. During reading, researching, thinking, discussing, and designing, new findings are discovered. These findings influence the prioritization of activities planned to reach a goal. The activities are not predefined. The knowledge worker plans the activities toward the specific goal. Because of the constant realignment of the activities to current goals, nonessential activities are withdrawn, postponed, or given a lower priority. This provides the necessary agility.

I want to emphasize an important difference between a goal that is broken down into detailed goals versus an activity within a modeled process that is broken down into detailed activities. At first glance, they look similar. But an activity that is broken down into detailed activities is automatically completed once the detailed activities are completed. This is the common understanding. A goal, instead, is a definition of some result that must be achieved. The completing of the main goal is independent of the completing of the detailed goals.

When planning the problem identification, Leona did not know whether the problem could be identified by performing tests or not. This was determined only after a conference call with all participants. If "Problem Identification" had been an activity, it would have been completed automatically after the tests had been performed. This is not what is needed in knowledge work. Therefore, planning with goals is a better fit to the way knowledge workers work. Goals remain stable, even if the means to achieve the goals change. Of course, sometimes goals also change, but they change less frequently than the means to reach them do. Lower-level goals change more frequently, while higher-level goals remain more stable.

It matters less how the goal was achieved, than the fact that it was achieved. There are two notable points:

◆ The way to reach the subsequent goals depends on the result of the preceding goals. In our example, it is obvious that the way to repair the problem cause depends on the problem cause that had been identified previously.

◆ The ways in which the preceding goals have been reached are largely irrelevant to the succeeding goals. What is relevant is the achievement of the preceding goals.

These characteristics are common to many more types of knowledge work. A lawyer would first assess a case before she decides about further legally relevant steps, depending on the result of the assessment. However, she may as well rely on the assessment that another specialist has done. In fact, as knowledge becomes more specialized and the methods to assess are innovated, this becomes more common.

So goals tend to be more stable than the means to reach those goals. Planning the intermediate goals gives a handle on the stream of work, even if the details of it are planned by a specialist. For example, it is possible to use this to define service-level agreements. There could be a standard time for completion of problem identification. If the case is especially difficult, it would be possible to assign a prolonged deadline.

Goal-oriented planning accounts for the freedom of the knowledge worker to define different alternatives to the means to reach a goal. It is typical for knowledge work that the way to the goal is not so clear in the beginning so different alternatives need to be considered. That leads to the discussion of unpredictability.

THE UNPREDICTABILITY OF THE WORK IN THE CASE

Let's continue our example to make clear why the stream of work in knowledge work is not predictable. Given the problem description of the incident, Leona created a first list of tests. Subsequently, the tests are executed to either confirm or exclude problem causes. These tests might be executed by different groups of technical experts. In complex cases, even coordinated tests are necessary. During test execution, a new insight—a different possible problem cause—might come to mind. This insight can lead to a new possible problem cause description necessitating a new test.

This is not the case with first-level support. In first-level support, we have mainly routine processes. But since the second-level support gets all the difficult cases to solve, and since systems that are compiled from many components become more complex, it is not unusual for Leona—and many knowledge workers with her—to face these difficulties.

It is possible that the problem cause identification goal cannot be reached easily. In this case, it was necessary to plan the conference call, as already discussed. It is even possible that the problem cannot be identified at all. In this case, a different intermediate goal would be to achieve a different compensation method with the customer. Still, the final goal remains the same: the case must reach status "Completed," even if the intermediate goals change.

The same flexibility can be necessary for the problem repair. Just imagine that the repair of one problem causes another one—a phenomenon commonly known in software architecture for example. Or the repair of one problem reveals that there already was another problem that was obscured by the previous problem.

I established earlier that the stream of work is not predictable *a priori* in knowledge work. The needed steps emerge as we go and largely cannot be predefined. Subsequent steps depend on the results of previous steps. In addition to this, the discussed example shows that changes to planned steps become necessary as the stream of work progresses because of new insight gained on the way.

This is typical for knowledge work. Since the area to be explored is complex and the knowledge of individuals is limited, the work must start with certain assumptions. Later it turns out that the assumptions were wrong or partially wrong or that important facts were missed. This means that the plan must be adapted. Knowledge workers are familiar with this and find it sometimes difficult to explain to their manager what they do and why they do it. The nature of their work involves a lot of experimentation that often has to be abandoned. So they find themselves in situations where they try to explain why the plan is different today than it was yesterday, which is quite natural if yesterday's plan did not work as expected. Changing the plan is clearly superior to sticking to a plan that has been shown to be unfit.

Knowledge work is an exploration into how a goal can be reached. Therefore, the intermediate goals emerge along the way instead of being predefined. Also, I want to mention that there are many unpredicted or unpredictable outside events that influence goals. These can be economical, political, and scientific, and they can stem from competitors, partners, and customers.

However, there are shades of gray. There is not only predictable and unpredictable, but also semipredictable. This leads me to discuss how guidance can still be given for a case within knowledge work.

GUIDANCE BY A CASE TEMPLATE

Since I have established that cases are unpredictable, let us have a look at whether parts of it can still be predicted and how the predictable parts and the unpredictable parts can be assembled.

Parts of the stream of work are predictable as of the best knowledge. These may be overall goals, intermediate goals, or individual procedures.

The list of possible software checks would not be reinvented for each incident report. A template might provide a predefined list of software checks; however, the knowledge worker is not restricted to what is on the software check template. Indeed, the knowledge worker might (1) add problem causes, (2) delete problem causes, and (3) mix checklists from several different templates.

In our example, Leona might find it useful to bring in Check A and Check C from a template, but not Check B. Additionally, she adds Check D, which is not in the template. (See FIGURE 9-6.)

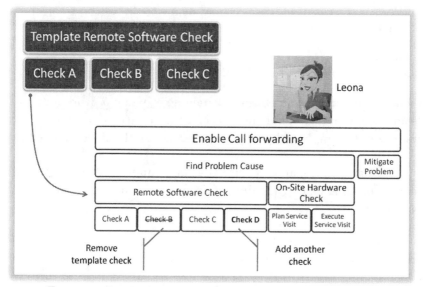

FIGURE 9-6: ACM System Templates Provide Fast and Easy Case Creation and Ongoing Flexibility

In addition, there might be templates for test procedures that describe step by step what typically would be done—without the requirement to follow every step of the procedure precisely.

It is very powerful to be able to choose which parts of a template will be used in a particular case. Work items within the template cannot have a status like open or completed. After being copied into the case, they can be marked with the right status with each progression. For example, if a test cannot be completed in one day, only the test items that have been completed will be marked. Testing will continue the next day where it left off, even if a different person is involved.

Therefore, ACM does not require that a case receive a complete copy of a template. Instead, a case consists of its own distinct goals and work items plus parts that have been copied from different templates as required and merged into the case. In the end, each individual case will be unique, unlike any another individual case, even if it is assembled partly from predefined templates.

The case owner decides which template he wants to merge and which not. Thus, the templates give guidance, not constraints. It remains possible for each individual case to be sensibly shaped as needed.

However, in certain areas, the company or department might want to selectively enforce some parts of the case. This leads me to discuss how constraining would work.

CONSTRAINING BY A CASE POLICY

There are certain areas in which constraining a stream of work for a case is desired: either to help guide novices of a subject matter, as obligatory best practice, or to comply with corporate governance or legal requirements.

In our example, the company might decide to apply best-practice problem analysis in certain areas. The different ways this could be accomplished are as follows:

◆ A template might be declared as obligatory, leading to the enforcement of it.

◆ The company might choose to enforce some basic checks and give freedom with the rest.

◆ It might be enforced that if one certain check will be executed, another one must be executed as well.

◆ It might be enforced that if one certain check will be executed, another one must not be executed as well.

◆ Checks might be enforced for inexperienced knowledge workers, while particular tasks are left optional for senior experts.

◆ It could be required that a certain set of checks be at least considered thereby enforcing that the check is either made or consciously marked as skipped for some reason.

The important message is that unpredictable parts of cases do not preclude the use of policies that are made obligatory. The detailed definition of what is obligatory is defined by the individual application area.

Governance of knowledge work requires some defined processes. Typically, they define some milestones and reviews. It is just the same with engineering change management as well as with audits. The art is to balance the necessary constraints with the unpredictable parts—and of course, to allow deviations from the strict process—that in my experience are inevitable.

But where do the templates and policies come from? That leads me to discuss the community library.

The Community Library

If we establish a technology that supports the management of individual cases, then it is quite natural to extend it to a community library for templates and policies.

Once in place, a community library is one of the most valuable assets of a company in the area of knowledge work. The unique practice to achieve goals—that is, to provide products and services—is what characterizes a company. If that invisible asset is made visible and accessible for daily work within the company, the company yields even more profit than before.

BPM promises something similar for routine work. But BPM never aspired to cover emergent processes like the ones needed for knowledge work.

There is a world of difference between the classical approach of modeled process analysis and the way a community library will be built up.

In the classical approach, typically, a modeled process is analyzed *a priori* by process analysts and implemented later. After the implementation, the process is executed for the first time. It is then that practical problems arise that had not been foreseen by the process analysts during modeling because they lack the practical knowledge. At that point, mitigation of these problems is expensive, if possible at all, resulting in the following:

◆ Suboptimal processes through lack of system support.

◆ The constant struggle of knowledge workers against the system.

◆ Working around the system by the knowledge worker.

◆ Inexperienced staff being led astray. They don't think about the best possible ways to solve a problem.

I am aware that BPMSs ease the burden to a degree. However, the pattern remains the same: process analysis and modeling, modeled process implementation and execution, problem identification, and problem mitigation by going through the cycle again.

Even if the cycle time with BPMSs is smaller than with development projects, problems can only be mitigated by going through the cycle again. This prevents many from using BPM for the purpose we discuss here.

In the new approach, case instances emerge as they are necessary. This means the knowledge worker can start the work without any templates: just with the empty ACM system. A knowledge worker enters the first case, just as the working day requires from them. If they want, they can work in that way forever adding case by case.

At the beginning, one case looks different than all the others. As work becomes repeated, the individual knowledge worker identifies snippets of cases that he might want to convert into a personal template and reuse (see FIGURE 9-7). So from now on, the work for him has become even easier. Later, templates of individual knowledge workers might be shared with other knowledge workers of a group, so team members can benefit from the knowledge, and the delegation of repetitive tasks becomes easier, while still some guidance in how the work shall be performed can be passed along. It is better to share a proven method than a theoretical construct that has never been executed before.

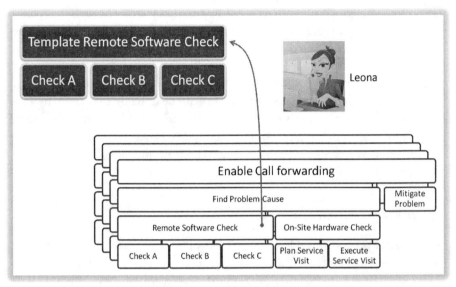

FIGURE 9-7: A Case Template Can Be Created from Existing Cases

In our example, after having several similar cases, Leona recognizes that some checks for the software appear regularly, so it would be best to include them in a template. She thinks that if she can make the template available to John, a new colleague, she might ask him once in a while to perform the checks for her so that she saves some time. Therefore, she searches for the case that contains the checks she has in mind, copies the part that she wants into a new template, and edits the template with instructions so that John will be able to follow them. Then she publishes that template in the community library's section for their group. John can now access the template. If John is on duty and he has a similar case, then he can copy the template into his case. And if Leona is on duty and has a similar case, she quickly copies her template into her case but assigns John to perform the checks. So in effect, Leona has saved some time for herself, while still giving guidance and instruction to John.

Users of templates can rate them, tag them, and make suggestions for improvements.

A template can be promoted to a policy. Here, it makes sense to establish a review of templates within a group. This means that a template is only promoted to a policy after it has been reviewed and accepted by the relevant participants and parties. The same can happen with the discontinuation of templates/policies.

As a result, only practically proven cases become templates. The set of templates is constantly improving: new templates are created as needed and obsolete templates are discontinued.

As an effect, the template library's content can adapt to new processes and new business situations as the need arises. This can be done by the company that uses the technology themselves—no consultants are needed; no implementation projects are needed. Still, the community library can adapt to ever-changing conditions that a company, project, or department finds itself in. That is true adaptability.

Burndown of Remaining Effort

We have not yet addressed Leona's problem of feeling overwhelmed with work most of the time. However, if Leona manages her cases as described, she can find it easier to estimate her workload. All she has to do is to maintain effort estimation for each of the goals. She finds out that she can use the ACM system not only for her customer call cases, but for her development activities as well. The kind of work she does in development is similar. Sometimes, the customer cases directly result in development activities, so that fits well together. She creates cases for development goals and estimates the effort, and the ACM system aggregates the remaining effort for her. First, when she sees the result, she is shocked by how much work she actually has. So she thinks about priorities and prepares a proposal to her manager, Dan, to postpone some of the work and to get the documentation department more involved to take over some work, and Dan agrees. So Leona can reduce her work by this measure.

As a second measure, she sees that the ACM system offers the possibility to define sprints and to assign packages of work to them. So Leona defines some milestones for herself and slices and dices the work she has according to the milestones. Of course she knows the company milestones but would also want to have personal milestones. The ACM system is capable of preparing statistics of how much work she had each day and how she succeeds in burning down the work. (See Figure 9-8.)

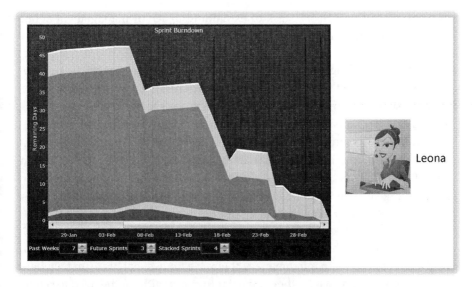

FIGURE 9-8: Sprint Burndown Statistics Using ACM System

The sprints help her to stay focused: even if new work is added for later, she would still concentrate on finishing the sprint at hand, if possible. Over time, she sees that she needs to add new sprints or remove old ones. For the first time, she feels that she has a clear picture of how much work she actually has to do. It helps a lot in her discussions with Dan.

The other team members have also shown an interest in the sprint functionality, which they haven't used yet. Dan is all for it because the ACM system is also able to aggregate the remaining work for the whole group. So if all group members participate, he will have a strong foundation of solid, credible data from which to argue with senior management. He does not want to dictate his group to use it because he wants the group members to find it useful for themselves. So he asks Leona to present her experience to the group, and he is quite confident that this will convince the others because at this point she is very positive about it.

THE VIEW OF THE MANAGER

Dan, Leona's manager, has his own view of the whole situation. He's constantly struggling to get transparency on what the members of his group are doing. Dan hates the feeling that he does not have control of what is happening. At times, he worries that everybody is just doing what they please. Dan has the unpleasant and unwelcome task of explaining to senior management about the plans and the changes in plans.

Dan wants to reach agreement about goals with each team member, or with the team as a whole, and track the achievement progress of the goals. Furthermore, if circumstances change, he will need to realign goals to the new circumstances, and for this, he wants a clear picture of the implications of these changes before they are done. In some urgent cases, he needs to quickly identify why a goal has not been reached or why it is in danger and clarify the situation. Once in a while, he needs to reassign responsibilities within the team to balance the load, and he also needs to handle the situation when a team member moves on or a new member joins the team.

Dan is also aware that his team members don't want to be micromanaged; neither does he want to micromanage them. He knows that his team members need a security zone where they can try things out without the need to report every detail of their work or reveal it to their peers prematurely.

Dan is aware that he cannot predict the cases of customer service in detail—they just occur. Of course, he knows if a new version of a phone system module is shipped, customer service cases increase, and he knows which parts of the module are new. Once in a while, he needs to help Leona or another team member with a difficult case or even get another department involved.

Mainly, he wants to make sure the engineering work milestones are kept, and the promised functionality is provided. He knows that a certain quality is expected.

Dan thinks that using the ACM system for his own work will benefit him in the same way that it benefits Leona's work, but he wants to do more than that. After he has reached agreement on goals with the team, he wants to track them in the system the same way that Leona tracks her goals. He wants to define team sprints that each team member would use. In other words, he needs a team workspace that contains team goals and team sprints/milestones, while the personal goals and milestones of his team members remain in their individual workspaces that he cannot see in detail. This is just fair because the team members would not see his personal goals either.

Even though knowledge work is constantly changing, managers need to have a means of analytical evaluation of case data. In all the changes, it is especially interesting to know how many goals have been achieved, what percentage of goals have been changed, where bottlenecks or areas of high goal volatility are, and the like. Managers need to quickly find out the reasons that a given case does not progress and who is responsible. So mining the goals and cases has great potential for managers.

The key for analytics is to make the case data available. If it is not available, you can't analyze it. The knowledge worker is not inclined to make it available if it does not directly benefit and speed up their work. Software technology that does not account for the unpredictability of cases is not fit for the purpose. Naturally, a level of mutual trust is prerequisite for sharing the data. Workspaces, though, offer the right means to protect data, while at the same time share what is needed.

Dan finds the ACM system practical to manage team member changes. Past shared cases—for example, the customer service cases—are continuously available. Even best practices are still available in the form of templates and policies. This makes his life much easier when bringing new team members up to speed.

Dan realizes that it is not enough to have a workspace for shared goals only for his team; projects are constantly changing too and require workspaces as well. These project workspaces, however, are linked to the team workspace, and he gets positive feedback from the project managers about the ACM system.

ACCOMPLISHING DAY-TO-DAY TASKS

Once Leona has organized her work using ACM, she can more easily clear her email inbox. With each email she asks herself: Does this have to do with any of the goals that I pursue? If yes, she attaches the message to the case. If not, she can most probably archive the email, or if it is really important, start a new case, however, this is rare.

Leona browses through the stack of papers she has been wanting to read. She assigns some of the papers to cases that she has where she thinks it benefits the goal, and she estimates the effort to read it. Most of the papers she has assigned to cases are in PDF form or she has a link for them, the other two papers she can scan and put them in the case attachment. But she is very clear that she cannot read everything, so the rest—and this is most of the stack—goes to the wastebasket. If it does not have something to do with one of her goals, then it can be neglected—after all, that's exactly what goal driven means.

Her desk and her inbox are clean. Sure, she still gets many emails, but some of them she answers writing friendly but clearly that she currently has other assignments. So the email flood decreases as well.

If there is a document to edit, she creates a case for it and can break down the work with the other authors. Responsibilities are assigned and sprints are as well. She recognizes another feature of cases: repackaging work—which makes work somewhat more efficient.

Leona had different customer cases that required documentation updates. Instead of doing each update separately and starting the review of the documentation change separately, Leona found it more practical to cluster the changes into a user documentation release and review it collectively. She could reassign these user documentation update work items into the case for the user documentation update. However, the link to the source cases would still exist, so it will be easy for the customer cases to determine when the documentation is finished (see FIGURE 9-9). By clustering work, overhead for each change of the documentation is minimized, and again, time is saved that can be used for more important things. This is also a good way to collaborate with the department that helps in the documentation because they can take over more of the work.

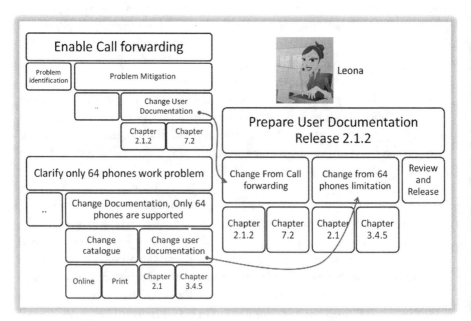

FIGURE 9-9: Efficiencies Gained by Repackaging Work
While Retaining the Link to the Source Case

After half a year of using the ACM system, Leona suddenly realizes that she is not so overloaded anymore, and perhaps it is time to start that small research project or to write that scientific article and publish it—and there is no doubt that whatever she chooses, she will create a case for it.

Enabling Technology

Is there a technology today that supports all of the needs discussed in this book? What we have is a conglomeration of email, file share, spreadsheets, documents, RSS feeds, online conference services, maybe wikis and forums, and yes, Google Wave. These technologies exist individually and will continue to be useful in that way. But what is missing is the managing part that binds all of them together. What is needed is the case with related goals, work items, information items (documents, links, scans, feeds, forums, etc.) and participants that are necessary to reach a predefined goal.

Requirements to Technology

Clearly, a solution such as software as a service (SaaS) must be provided. SaaS means that software is provided by one provider to many organizations through the Internet. The reason is very simple. Yes, there are cases that are possible to solve solely within one company or government agency—but this is the rare exception. An ever-growing number of cases includes participants from several organizations. They can only collaborate by a solution using a multi-enterprise business application (MEBA) architecture that lives in the cloud. Any other approach clearly falls short of what is necessary. Of course, this presupposes mechanisms for separated workspaces and controlled sharing mechanisms, so the only templates shared within a project are those that are needed there, and all other templates remain private. And mobile devices like smartphones should be supported as clients.

Effective system support for cases is needed with the following features:

◆ Creating cases with goals

◆ Storing workstream-related information (goal driven)

  ◇ Decide about information structure as you go

  ◇ Decide about required information as you go

◆ Plan about next steps as you go

◆ A clear status of the case and all parts of it

  ◇ Reporting about the remaining work

  ◇ Drilling down capabilities to identify blocking reasons

◆ Merge/split cases as you go

◆ Collaboration and communication over the information

  ◇ Decide about groups as you go

  ◇ Decide about access as you go

A community library is needed with the following features:

◆ Possibility to define templates and snippets

◆ Depending on progress and decisions

  ◇ Merge template snippets into a running case as you go

  ◇ Merge own case snippets with templates as you go

◆ It must be possible to define constraints in templates

◆ Governance

  ◇ It must be possible to declare templates as mandatory or voluntary

  ◇ The scope of template enforcement must be possible to declare based on groups/departments

  ◇ Sharing, tagging, evaluation, and feedback functionality

  ◇ Review functionality integrated in the library

  ◇ Deviation analysis

USE OF THE TECHNOLOGY

The ACM portal would be accessible through the Internet. Individual knowledge workers can apply for users and workspaces inviting co-workers and colleagues to work with them on individual projects. This is independent of the fact if they are within one company or a project team across companies. Also, it might be the decision of a department or of a company to use ACM as a whole. In this case, users and workspaces would be designed to fit the needs of the individual organization. But like all of knowledge work, the structure of the workspaces will most probably change. Adaptations in the structure of workspaces and users are a natural part of the use of the ACM portal.

BENEFITS

The information about a case is at one place and can be accessed by each participant, be it within the enterprise or cross enterprises. Thus, the work can speed up. Instead of hunting for the most current information and sending emails back and forth, the information is there. But it is not just information (as with a wiki) because it is clearly goal driven, which helps to find the needle in the haystack.

Clearly defined responsibilities support the organization. Goals can be reorganized as needed but still are related. Thus, it is possible to adapt to decisions, either planned or unplanned, and to events or new facts that emerge on the way.

It is possible to adapt working group members as becomes necessary. Thus, experts can join or leave the case as needed. Today, experts often are part of a working group but only needed sporadically—thus, they waste their time. If they join only when they are really needed, they can concentrate on what is necessary. Priorities of the work are clear and can be adapted as necessary.

Best practices can be identified and made available for a greater community. Thus, experienced personnel are released from repetitive tasks, and inexperienced staff can be guided. Company policies can be enforced, if needed.

The reporting gives transparency about the workload and the progress, whether it is an evaluation for yourself or for a manager. This is performance management. It is possible to use the intelligence and analytics to get the insight to guide the course of action and report back on whether it's working or not.

Problematic cases can be nailed down by drill-down analysis and solved. If team members leave, their results are preserved for future team members who can be brought up to speed quickly by the available information. Furthermore, it is possible to get better insight into the data by using analytics to predict developments and trends that could impact the goals of the company, department, or project in a positive or negative way.

DIFFERENCE TO EXISTING TECHNOLOGY

I briefly want to discuss the main differences between existing technologies and ACM technology.

BPM vs. ACM

The main differences between BPM and ACM are as follows:

◆ In BPM, a process is first designed and later executed. In ACM, the planning is done during the execution.

◆ In BPM, the designer and the one who executes the process are typically two different people. In ACM, it is typically one and the same person.

◆ In BPM, the general process is designed before the first instance can be executed. In ACM, the general process is compiled after many case instances have been executed.

◆ In BPM, a major top-down project and significant investment is needed before the return on investment is reaped. In ACM, even one knowledge worker can start right away and will already have benefits. However, the benefits of ACM are not limited to that. The more knowledge workers that participate in the collaboration, the more benefit is achieved.

◆ In business process modeling notation (BPMN) there exists ad hoc subprocesses. But they are embedded within a meta model for predictable process models. ACM, in contrast, is built to capture the unpredictable from the beginning. The details of it may be part of succeeding scientific analysis.

Project Management vs. ACM

The main differences between Project Management and ACM are as follows:

◆ In project management, the whole project is preplanned. Therefore, it applies only for mainly predictable domains. Applying it to unpredictable domains has been tried, but often ends up in a mixture of pretending and hard-to-explain delays. In ACM, it is clear from the beginning which part of the case is already clearly planned and which part cannot be planned at this stage.

◆ In project management, the plan often is on a high planning level. This defines the boundary conditions. But the plan often is not immediately actionable. The plan needs to be broken down into many details. This work is done by many knowledge workers. ACM would be capable of reflecting the result of this detail and linking it to the overall project plan.

Web-Based Collaboration Tools vs. ACM

The main differences between web-based collaboration tools and ACM are as follows:

◆ Web-based collaboration tools solve parts of the problem like document sharing, task management, and communication. But they are not case focused and goal driven like ACM. Especially, web-based collaboration tools would not support a community library for templates and policies with an integrated governance process.

◆ Web-based collaboration tools often are hard-coded for a specific purpose like organizing a conference or tracking software package defects. ACM, in turn, is a general-purpose method and tool, and it contains the ability to specialize by means of the community library for templates and policies.

FUTURE PERSPECTIVES

The insights and technology described in this chapter so far are standing in their own right. Thus, they can be realized and will yield the benefits they promise already. That does not mean that the possibilities are limited that way. Instead, it opens up a whole new world of possibilities that should be mentioned.

Probably in the intermediate scope, we would not only have an ACM system, but an ACM platform as well. This means that there would be the possibility to add or define new business objects that are related to ACM like decision, decision outcome, problem, need, idea, and others, as need arises in this young discipline.

Possibilities exist for the integration of ACM with other enterprise software systems. Enterprise resource planning (ERP) systems already present in many companies might be integrated with ACM. One possibility would be to link to a transaction of the ERP system to guide how it should be used in a certain situation. For example, if an employee gets a new company car, there could be a template describing the necessary steps in a case and a link to the transactions shown in Table 9-1 with some emails and approvals in between.

TABLE 9-1: Integration of ACM with ERP System

TRANSACTIONS REQUIRED SCENARIO: EMPLOYEE GETS A COMPANY CAR		
	TRANSACTION	PERFORMER
1	Order the Car	Self-Service for Employee
2	Approve the Order	Employee's Manager
3	Purchase the Car	Purchasing
4	Create a New Asset	Finance
5	Update the Payroll	Human Resources

One might argue that this is a routine process that could be predefined. However, there would be an advantage to using a single technology for a wide variety of types of work: routine and knowledge work. A technology able to deal with unpredictability, can deal as well with predictability (which is not true the other way around). The advantage is the ability to include unpredicted parts into a running case. It would be able to handle, for example, the exceptional case of an employee who leaves the company while the company car is being purchased. It is unlikely that this would be part of a predefined process model but inclusion into the running case when it happens is easy.

When the information structure of the case is defined in forms, that information can be mapped to a web service that performs an automated update of the back-end system. For example, if there is a case for the company car example, the "Create New Asset" step could be a web service call mapping data that has been entered into the case using a form.

If we open up the world of web services for cases, the possibilities are virtually unlimited. For example, you might want to create a case for performing a training class. There is one step to invite participants using a social network web service—or several. There is another step to check for available training rooms—you might want to use a web service from a favorite business center provider. Then order training material from an online bookstore in a next step using a web service!

This technology, in principle, already exists in BPM suites (BPMSs), and therefore, it can be ported to an ACM system giving it additional flexibility.

Furthermore, it is conceivable that future ERP systems will be built differently than today. They would have ACM technology integrated into their core, so their business objects would seamlessly integrate with the case, and of course, with the outside world. This is quite possible given, as an example, that cloud-based ERP systems have entered the market already.

There is no reason why case templates could not be products or services, or contain products or services. For example, if there is a best-practice library containing industry-specific or topic-specific how-to guides, this would be a great opportunity to offer the content to the market. Because it is not only text, but it is a template that can be converted into a case by a user of that portal, the user of the portal would maintain the status of the progress of the how-to guide for his case. That functionality is better than a written text. If the case gets stuck due to some unexpected deviation from the description in the how-to guide, the user can call for help. For example, if it is a how-to guide for the installation of a software package, it might unexpectedly get stuck because the installation prerequisites are not completely fulfilled on the user's computer. In this case, the user has to solve the question of what to do in this case. He might call for help in the running case instance. Then experts may offer their services and probably even bill for them. The advantage for the experts is that the case already contains much of the information they need to analyze the problem—that is, which installation steps have already been completed successfully or with which result. There might be templates that already offer paid services at certain stages. For example, there might be steps in the best-practice case that guide the creation of a document like a proposal, and then the template might contain a step to take advantage of a paid consulting service that ensures the quality of the proposal. If the customer somehow followed the previous steps of the template, the consulting service might be relatively efficient and thus inexpensive. The customer might even start bidding for a consultation between different suppliers at a certain stage. And—this is the nice thing—it is always possible to deviate.

This should, all in all, be only a relatively small functional extension of an ACM portal.

ACM technology will—this is my conviction—first make the life of the individual knowledge worker easier because it will release the limits of what software is able to do today. Then applications will emerge that are not possible today because current software and models are so limited as to be unable to master the unpredictable.

CHAPTER 10

INNOVATION MANAGEMENT

HENK DE MAN, SHIVA PRASAD, AND
THEODOOR VAN DONGE

As innovation work and management of innovation are extremely knowledge intensive, analysis of innovation provides a good opportunity to demonstrate adaptive case management (ACM) characteristics and to analyze and suggest practical ways of formalizing ACM, so businesspeople can share the same understanding of it and appropriate technology support can be developed. In this chapter, we will analyze and demonstrate how an ACM system, as an integral part of a broader business operations platform, can make management of innovation productive and innovation better sustainable.

THE NEED TO INNOVATE

Innovation is central to the success of a company, and the only reason to invest in its future.

Sawhney (2006) defines business innovation as "the creation of substantial new value for customers and the firm by creatively changing one or more dimensions of the business system." He defines his "innovation radar" based on twelve dimensions that are grouped into four main areas, as depicted in FIGURE 10-1. Innovation can be about "what" is offered to customers, "how" internal processes are managed, "where" a company is present in the market, and ways to serve customers better ("who"). As shown in FIGURE 10-1, product innovation is a part of business innovation: business innovation focuses on all twelve dimensions and product innovation is a subset of it focused on four dimensions.

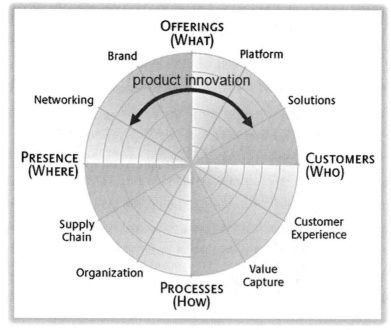

FIGURE 10-1: The Innovation Radar (Sawhney 2006)

Hertle (2007) builds on Sawhney (2006) and analyzes how business innovation typically follows four overlapping phases whereby each phase relates to a main area in the innovation radar (see FIGURE 10-2).

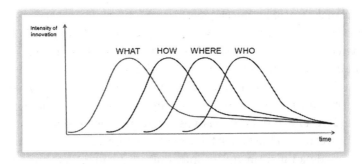

FIGURE 10-2: Phases of Innovation (Hertle 2007)

These phases are very recognizable for technology companies. Typically, these companies first bring a major new technology to the market (what). As soon as the technology has emerged, companies focus on process innovation (how) to produce cheaper, faster, and with higher quality. As soon as company processes are lean and effective, scale, in terms of market footprint, becomes essential (where). This is followed by a segmentation phase in which offerings and customer interactions are differentiated, for example, with focus on niches and vertical markets (who).

The world is undergoing major technology shifts, not the least of which is in IT. New technology waves are following each other faster and faster. Many new vendors enter the market. Consequently, there are many companies today that feel the need to move from what-focused to how-focused and beyond. In other words, many companies wanting to bring product innovations to the market are facing the challenge of improving their product innovation process. They have to make their product innovation process more productive and predictive, generate higher levels of quality, better manageable, etc. As soon as these companies have learned how to do this, they will have to broaden their innovation focus from product innovation to the total of business innovation. In this chapter, we will particularly focus on technology companies that try to make the transition from what-focused to how-focused and to continuously innovate from there onward.

STATE-OF-THE-ART IN MANAGING INNOVATION

The heart of technology (or product) companies lies in their R&D organization. The technology that these companies create is often, and per definition, high tech. Their processes are often extremely knowledge intensive. Engineers and related personnel make use of high-tech tools to support their work, such as computer aided design (CAD) systems, product lifecycle management (PLM) systems, integrated design environments (IDEs), and other systems that focus on team collaboration. Nevertheless, most R&D work is executed and managed in an ad hoc and manual fashion. Some of the tools just mentioned do have some means of sharing documents, routing documents through a workflow, sending emails, and tracking the status of issues and requirements. But normally, these means only relate to a fraction of the work that engineers do, are not integrated, do not provide an instrument for integrally managing R&D and its related areas, and are not adequate as a basis for continuous business innovation. For example, sometimes tools are used to help break down requirements into tasks and estimate these tasks. But as these tools do not actually manage anything—they merely serve an administrative purpose—their use is often seen as a burden: they keep knowledge workers from doing their work.

In manufacturing companies, the actual product manufacturing is often well managed and based on enterprise applications such as enterprise resource planning (ERP) and manufacturing execution systems (MES). However, R&D, a knowledge-intensive area, is not managed based on ERP or MES simply because these systems have not been designed to manage knowledge work.

In nonmanufacturing technology companies—such as software development companies and research departments in healthcare, telecom, and academia—technology support for process management never became a mainstream initiative. While the technology that is embodied in their products is often very mature, the way they manage and innovate their own business (and processes) is not mature at all.

In this section, we analyze in more detail the typical problems that such companies struggle with by analyzing an archetypical situation, which the authors believe is close to the state-of-the-art in managing innovation in many companies today, both in manufacturing and nonmanufacturing businesses. This is not to say that there aren't companies that do better than this, but that there are many companies that are equally struggling to manage their innovation processes. There is major room to improve!

On the basis of a recent survey of 630 vice presidents, directors, and executives at large U.S. and U.K. companies across a broad range of industries, Accenture (2009) observed the following:

◆ Despite efforts to add structure to innovation, current management practices and processes have numerous shortcomings. Fewer than half of the respondents (44%) said their company had an effective, holistic approach to new product or service development and introduction.

◆ To raise the return on innovation investment, companies need to treat innovation with the same discipline as other functions. The most successful companies are generating profitable revenue year after year by managing innovation as a business process.

The following discussion focuses on many issues with respect to the management of product innovation; however, as far as we know, there is no framework that can be used to analyze and structure these issues, therefore, we grouped the issues in an ad hoc way into the following areas:

◆ Management information and participation

◆ Capacity planning

◆ Execution management

◆ Management of performance, priorities, and objectives

◆ Cost control

◆ Quality control and security management

◆ Worker productivity

◆ Continuous improvement

MANAGEMENT INFORMATION AND PARTICIPATION

Management faces a lack of transparency into what is going on throughout the product innovation process. Consistent and complete audit data in terms of who has done what, when, why, etc., is missing. There is a lack of information for after-the-fact business analysis. When someone is moved to a different project or position, it is not immediately clear what the impact of that is and what other actions may have to be taken. There is no clear overview of roles, responsibilities, and authorities in an organization. There are no explicit and actionable rules of engagement in terms of who does what, when, etc. There is no explicit and system-supported process.

There is no productive way to track delegated actions. Communications aren't managed or tracked effectively and efficiently. This is also due to the fact that almost all communication is just based on email. There is no guidance of managers and workers in terms of recommendations and reminders. There is no framework that enables empowerment in terms of organized, structural, and transparent delegation of handling escalations, issues, and related decisions and prioritizations. This puts a huge burden on management and underutilizes the potential of employees. Handling escalations is very costly and disrupts the normal flow of work.

Customers and partners can't actively participate in development proceedings (e.g., in the case of issues, changes, delays, decision points, approval points, etc.). Since there is no system-supported process in which they can participate, they don't get instant status feedback and cannot provide their suggestions, sign-offs, etc.

There is no productive support for impact analysis of issues, delays, scope changes, priority changes, etc., and hence, no productive way of proactive action taking. Product changes often cannot be traced back to original issues and needs, and there is no way to formally establish the extent to which product objectives have been reached.

CAPACITY PLANNING

There is no insight into planned and actual capacity requirements from initiatives such as product releases, customer projects, etc., on teams and employees. Basically, there is no adequate support for capacity planning. Analysis of planned versus actual capacity, both time-wise and competency-wise, is not supported. As the process is not explicit, it is almost impossible to adequately plan capacity, work distribution, employee competency development, etc. A formal and sufficiently precise administration of available versus required competencies is not available. This makes adequate process change management, task allocation, and work planning difficult to do.

EXECUTION MANAGEMENT

There is no way to integrally and productively manage and monitor status, priority, throughput, and lead time (flow). There is no real-time feedback and proactive monitoring of milestones. Initiatives aren't managed end to end in a productive way. For example, a release including product launch includes a tremendous set of activities—training, translation, preparation of marketing material, webinars, partner involvement, etc.—but there is no system supported oversight and no means of productive management. As there are no explicit process models, there is no adequate handling of releasing work to the teams and to accept and promise customer-driven development work.

MANAGEMENT OF PERFORMANCE, PRIORITIES, AND OBJECTIVES

There is no explicit notion of priority of the various initiatives, and there is no means to accommodate that everybody is driven by the same priorities. Neither managers nor workers have the necessary oversight of priorities of activities. There are many activities, communicated verbally or via email, from all kinds of directions throughout the company, but it is not clear how they depend on each other, where they contribute to, and what their priorities are.

Explicit performance measurements are not available, at least not based on the monitoring of the actual work performed. Employees are unclear about how their work contributes to reaching corporate objectives. There is no meaningful business metric feedback to employees regarding their own work performance, the performance of their team, etc. They are also unclear about their team and personal objectives. Work execution performance results aren't fed back to and aligned with employee competency management and appraisals. Work execution monitoring and human resource performance management are basically disconnected.

Business plans, as far as they exist, aren't actionable or monitored. There is no real-time feedback and proactive monitoring of objectives.

COST CONTROL

Adequate support for managing based on costs is lacking. There is no insight into how the many activities contribute to the cost of the product, product updates, fixing issues, and customer-driven development projects. There is no monitoring of costs based on the actual execution of processes. Cost calculation of quotations for customers is labor intensive, and as explicit process models and related process statistics are not available, the calculation is inaccurate.

Hours and labor accounting is very rough, after the fact, and disconnected from the execution of the actual process. As there is no real insight into the structure of costs in relationship to the actual activities, activity-based costing

(ABC) analysis is not supported. There is no insight into the impact of process changes on cost and cost structure.

QUALITY CONTROL AND SECURITY MANAGEMENT

There are no built-in quality controls such as system-supported and system-enforced inspections, approvals, nonconformance procedures, activity and template recommendations, built-in checklists, etc. There are no suggested, enforced, and monitored code reviews and sign-offs. There are no designated roles for such sign-offs, and there is no productive and secure participation of such designated roles. There is no means to involve the business in the sign-off of critical-to-quality requirements.

Responsibility and authorization for activities and deliverables aren't defined formally. Basically, authorization is only defined at the file system level, which is cumbersome to maintain. In reality, everybody can do everything, and there is no guidance. There is no adequate check on competencies, authorities, etc.

Information, such as communication with customers and partners, can easily get lost. There is no formal management and tracking of all related information in combination.

These and other related issues also cause the management headaches in productively and adequately managing compliance with regulations in the various industries in which the company wants to be active.

WORKER PRODUCTIVITY

The system doesn't suggest activity or supporting documentation to workers, which is especially a problem to inexperienced employees. Information (activity or initiative context) is too loosely coupled to the activity or initiative or is even missing. Workers often have a need to see examples, similar cases, documents that deal with their topic of concern, etc., but there is no recommendation by the system and no productive way to get that information on the fly.

There is a massive influx of defects and enhancement requests, but there is no means to process them productively. Their content is unstructured, their correlation is unknown, there is no means to process them in real time, there are no meaningful notifications, and related metrics are too high level. And because they aren't processed adequately, there is no proper and timely indication of capacity requirement.

As activities are basically only managed by email, and at best, administrated in stand-alone tools such as project management systems, there is no proper integration between activities and the various tools that are used by engineers and others. There is no system-supported enforcement of standard layouts and templates. Basically, people have to sort things out for themselves, and if they don't know, they just have to go around and ask others, which is very unproductive.

There are several situations in which manual entry or reentry of data is required, which is, in fact, pure waste. For example, hours accounting is done manually and after the fact. This is unproductive and generates data that is inaccurate. Hours accounting should ideally be driven from the actual monitoring of work by the system (see the discussion on cost control). As discussed above, there is no status feedback from milestones in, for example, customer-driven development. Many activities, such as billing, that could otherwise have been automated are executed manually therefore. There are several situations of manual hand-off between parties. Automation would allow people to be involved only when they are needed. Examples are hand-off between support and product management and hand-off between teams and the ones responsible for merging product changes into the central build.

There are also situations where automated procedures are in place, but they are executed in batch mode causing long runs. More interactive and participative processing would be much more efficient and productive. Examples are the daily build process and automated test runs in large scale software development. When problems occur during a run, the run will often continue and problems are identified late. Many tests will still continue even when nasty problems are detected. This is pure waste. It would be better to identify the kind of problem and based on that take action on the fly to fix it or notify the right people about the problem, rather than running further on the wrong basis for hours. There are very similar problems in, for example, exchanging product design data between different engineering teams in automotive and aerospace companies.

Continuous Improvement

As there are no explicitly defined process models that are managed throughout their lifecycle and used to manage activity in the organization, it is difficult to continuously improve the processes. Changes aren't visible, improvement efforts aren't productive, and improvement results aren't sustainable. Next to this, there is no regime of auditing and building statistics, and therefore, no good basis for and productive means of establishing norm times, planning percentages of tasks, etc.

As a consequence of all these problems, the organization is facing the following:

◆ Late deliveries.

◆ Cost-full operations.

◆ Insufficient quality.

◆ Difficulty in growing organizational and process maturity.

◆ Innovation at a too-low pace.

◆ Low responsiveness to trends in the market.

◆ Insufficient capability to scale.

The need to improve this situation is clear to everyone. The question is: how to do that? It would be best to explicitly (and visually) define all processes together with their purpose, ownership in the organization, performance measurements, and participating roles and to manage all activity throughout the organization based on these explicit process models. This would, of course, not directly resolve all the issues, as discussed above, but it would be a fundamental enabler to directly resolve many of them and to indirectly resolve others. However, process models that are based on existing process modeling standards, such as BPMN (see BPMN 2009), do not fit the needs of product innovation management. BPMN-style process models are adequate to define procedures that can be automated. Predefined workflows, such as a sequence of approval steps or a workflow to automate transaction processing across multiple systems, can typically be defined in BPMN. But knowledge workers, such as engineers, product managers, and other related businesspeople, do not behave like robots. They have to be given the freedom to improvise and decide how to best achieve their objectives. When BPMN is used for knowledge-work processes, the result is an overly complicated mess that is difficult to understand

and maintain. Modeling would become a burden rather than a means to improve the management of knowledge work. So it is clear that a different paradigm for process management has to be developed to support innovation management and knowledge work in general.

In the next sections, we will take a closer look at innovation management and suggest a framework for it. Based on that, we will discuss how such a framework can be made actionable in the sense that it can actually manage innovation activity and participation of knowledge workers. We will discuss characteristics of processes that fit in the framework and serve that purpose, and we will see that these processes are based on a new paradigm that is called adaptive case management (ACM).

Case management is a method or practice of coordinating work by organizing all of the relevant information into one place. A case is a specific situation to take care of. The representation of the case in the case management system is thought of as holding all of the information and processes, and it coordinates communications necessary to accomplish the goal for that particular situation. The case becomes the focal point for assessing the situation, initiating activities and processes, as well as keeping a history record of what has transpired.

Case management has specific meanings in the healthcare, legal, and social services fields. In this book, case management is considered a technique that could be used in any field of human endeavor, including the subject of this chapter: innovation management. This book adopts the term adaptive case management (ACM) to abstract the generic and fundamental notion of case management from the domain-specific connotations. The term also suggests that it is a technology-supported capability for business users to configure their own models and templates to use as the basis for managing their particular situations as cases rather than having to depend on predeveloped niche applications in specific domains.

ACM differs from traditional business process management (BPM) in that the case information is the focus and the thing around which the other artifacts are organized. And it is the case information that persists for the long term. On the other hand, we can consider ACM as a new dimension that enables BPM to become a broader discipline. Note that although we talk about process and process management, in this context, the notion of process should not be taken as narrow as "processes like the ones that can be defined in BPMN." We need the term "process" in a much broader sense as in "everything that happens comes from a process." We deal with processes that are not just transaction based, but especially the ones that involve or are driven by knowledge workers. Consequently, BPM should be taken in a broad sense as well, as Jeston (2009) defines it: "a holistic management practice that requires top management understanding and involvement, clearly defined roles and decision processes as part of BPM governance, appropriate BPM methodologies, process-aware information systems, educated and well-trained people, and a culture receptive to business processes."

A FRAMEWORK FOR INNOVATION MANAGEMENT

As FIGURE 10-3 indicates, business innovation involves management at the following three layers:

1. **Strategic Planning or Strategic Management**—Strategic planning is an organization's process of defining its strategy, or direction, and related goals and objectives, making decisions about the initiatives to be undertaken to achieve the objectives, and establishing priorities in relation to both objectives and initiatives.

2. **Transformation and Change Management or Tactical Management**— Transformation is about the actual redesign and re-implementation of (parts of) the system, which might be the product (e.g., IT system), business system, or both in combination.

3. **Continuous Improvement as Part of Operational Management**—This is about continuous monitoring and fixing of issues as they occur within the span of control of an area of operational management.

Product innovation as an integrated subset of business innovation might then be associated with the following:

◆ **Strategic product planning** as an integrated part of strategic business planning.

◆ **Research and development** (which is actually management of product transformation and related changes).

◆ **Product maintenance** (which is actually continuous product improvement).

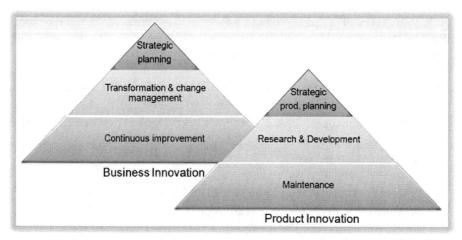

FIGURE 10-3: Levels of Business and Product Innovation

FIGURE 10-4 represents the main concepts or entities of the innovation framework at the three distinct levels of innovation management.

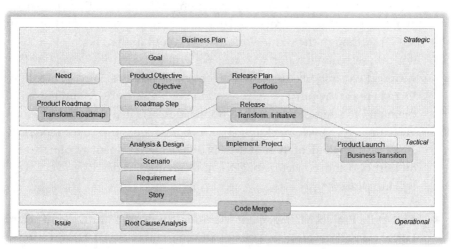

FIGURE 10-4: Innovation Management Framework

Most concepts are universal and are equally applicable to both product innovation and business innovation management. Sometimes, concepts in product innovation and business innovation are similar, but they carry a more-business-oriented name in business innovation management. In these cases, in FIGURE 10-4, the business innovation management counterparts are shown overlapping their product innovation management counterparts. A few concepts might just be specific to product innovation management, such as "Story" and "Code Merger" (also known as continuous integration).

The framework depicted in FIGURE 10-4 is based on common sense and practical business experience, but it reflects important elements from various published management frameworks and methodologies, such as the following:

◆ **The Business Motivation Model (BMM) (see BMM 2008).** This is probably the only industry-wide standard that formally defines strategic planning concepts. BMM provides some good definitions (goals, objectives, etc.) but is yet insufficiently specific to serve as the basis for an actionable framework.

◆ **Project Portfolio Management (PPM).** PPM is about balancing a set of proposed initiatives to achieve an organization's goals and objectives. A good explanation of PPM is provided by Morris (2004).

◆ **Lean and Six Sigma Management Systems.** Lean and Six Sigma Management Systems spanning the levels of senior, middle, and front-line management and making use of techniques such as policy deployment (Hoshin), A3 management, DMAIC (define, measure, analyze, improve, control), Kaizen, and quality function deployment (QFD). Although the framework that we adopt in this chapter is in line with these management systems, we will not dig into details of the various Lean and Six Sigma management techniques. We just mention them here for the purpose of recognition by those who are familiar with them and to suggest referring to publications such as from Ballé (2009), Hutchins (2008), Womack (2008), Morgan (2006), and Liker (2004). A successful implementation of the Six Sigma management system, based on portfolio and project management techniques, is described very well by Harry (2006).

◆ **The Agile Project Management Methodology Scrum (Sutherland 2007).** Later, we will discuss elements of Scrum in more detail. Scrum comes from the world of agile software development, but it can be applied very well to product innovation and even business innovation in general. Iver (2009) suggests: "Agile methods such as Scrum can offer inventive solutions that can bring order and reason to otherwise chaotic environments. Focus the team on the true business goal, position the team to organize their work in ways in which the meaning of "done" is clearly understood, measure the team's progress in terms of attaining some portion of the business goal, and free the team to seek and react to feedback that will help continuously improve both its performance and its processes in order to meet the real business objective." Sutherland (2009) presents a case where Scrum was successfully applied for the purpose of enterprise transformation. The authors of this chapter are aware of manufacturing companies that recognize the opportunity to manage their product engineering processes the Scrum way.

◆ **Evolutionary Project Management (Evo).** Evo is another agile project management methodology, which partly overlaps Scrum. It is also used to complement Scrum with techniques for prioritization of objectives, initiatives, requirements, etc., and it is based on performance criteria from the stakeholder perspective and cost criteria collaboratively with stakeholders (Gilb 2004) and (Gilb 2005). In this chapter, we will not further focus on Evo details.

◆ **A Recent Study on Business Transformation by Jeston (2009).** This study is interesting because it starts from BPM, and it concludes that focus should shift to management processes and a framework for business transformation.

We will shortly explain the various entities at each of the levels of innovation management framework.

STRATEGIC PLANNING LAYER

Business plans typically cover a one-year horizon. Normally, there are different business plans for different but related management areas, and these business plans are mutually aligned based on collaboration and consensus, or in Lean management terms policy deployment or Hoshin Kanri (Hutchins 2008) and (Morgan 2006). There will typically be corporate business plans, business plans for specific managerial areas, such as product management, as well as business plans for specific lines of business or teams. For example: "Corporate Business Plan 2010," "Product Management Business Plan 2010," and "ACM Framework Development Business Plan 2010."

A business plan covers strategic objectives or goals. A goal is broken down into SMART (specific, measurable, achievable, realistic, and time-constrained) objectives. Product objectives are a subset of business objectives. Objectives address needs that reflect the voice of the customer (VOC) or the voice of the market (VOM). They also might reflect regulations.

An objective or a set of objectives is associated with a roadmap, which might represent a product roadmap in a product innovation context or a transformation roadmap in a business innovation context. A roadmap consists of a series of steps whereby each step is reached via a specific initiative. In a product innovation context, an initiative might be a product release, service pack, etc. In a business innovation context, transformation roadmap steps are reached via transformation initiatives. Specific methodologies often have their own specific variations of such initiatives, such as A3 projects, Kaizens in Lean, and DMAIC projects in Six Sigma (see [Ballé 2009] and [Harmon 2007]). Initiatives might also be defined to resolve operational issues that can't be handled at the operational level itself.

A company might define many possible initiatives to reach various objectives and to resolve issues. However, initiatives require resources, which imply costs or delays in operational business. They also may increase risk. There might also be a significant difference in the impact that initiatives have on performance (the extent to which they contribute to reaching objectives) and therefore on returns. It is essential, therefore, to manage a portfolio of initiatives and to continuously reprioritize initiatives based on consensus. This determines roadmap timelines. In product innovation, such a portfolio, essentially, is a release plan.

Transformation and Change Management Layer

At the tactical level, the actual transformation and change is performed through execution of initiatives. Initiatives will be started based on priorities and planned dates as defined in the portfolio (or in product innovation, defined in the release plan). Initiatives can typically be decomposed into one or more "pre-games" or analysis and design projects; a series of "games" or the actual implementation projects; and a "post-game" to actually launch the product or new product version in the market, or in the context of business innovation, to roll out the resulting business changes enterprise-wide (business transition).

An analysis and design project translates the VOC (a set of related needs) into specific change specifications in the solution domain (requirements). Requirements are normally decomposed into more granular requirements. Requirements are the perfect instruments to track and coordinate changes across components (or business areas in business innovation) and teams. As requirements may imply cross-team dependencies, a specification is required of what a team is supposed to contribute to a particular requirement. This can be done by "stories," as are commonly used in Scrum-based projects. A story is a testable piece of functionality that can be handled by a single team. A need can be decomposed into stories, and stories can be linked to requirements. Specification of requirements based on needs is typically based on an analysis of scenarios. Scenarios might be described in text, but will still be quite explicit and structured. In product innovation, such scenarios are typically use cases. In business innovation, it is common to use value networks or value stream maps, such as product development value stream maps (PDVSM) as suggested by Morgan (2006). The Object Management Group (OMG) is currently developing a specification for value delivery modeling for this purpose (VDM 2009).

Requirements are subject to analysis of impact in terms of performance (and return), risk, and cost, and based on consensus, they are selected for actual implementation. Methodologies such as Lean and Six Sigma have formalized this into QFD (Hutchins 2008), and Evo uses a similar technique called impact estimation (IE) (Gilb 2005). In product innovation, the set of selected requirements (with related stories) is often called product backlog.

Implementation projects are defined for the various teams, requirements (and stories) are linked to them, and required capacity is estimated for the requirements (and stories) collaboratively with the teams. It is the teams' responsibility to execute the implementation projects. Specifically, in software product development, it is required to frequently and incrementally "merge" changes into the product-in-progress. The "Code Merger" entity in FIGURE 10-4 denotes the corresponding area of responsibility for and management of that. In manufacturing product design, there is design integration activity as well. Of course, all change increments as merged into the product are traced back to requirements. The product is then launched to the market, which implies such activity as hiring new people, training people, preparing marketing material, organizing marketing campaigns, lining up partners, etc. In business transition, there is similar activity, like hiring and training people and lining up partners.

CONTINUOUS IMPROVEMENT LAYER

After having implemented all changes and following product launch (or business transition in business innovation), the operational system continues operation based on the new baseline. In product innovation, this means service and delivery sells and installs the new product or product version in hosting centers or onsite with customers. In business innovation, in general, this can also mean that the business operations now run based on a different work organization, different processes, etc. Operations will identify and report issues (e.g., defects). These have to be fixed or further analyzed by means of root-cause analysis. This is the area of continuous improvement. When issues are too big to fix locally, new initiatives might have to be requested for triggering activity at the strategic level, etc. Innovation management is about a closed-loop and continuously iterating system.

Case Management to Make the Framework Actionable

In this section and the next, we focus on product innovation. In later sections, we revisit the broader concern of business innovation. All concepts and related activities that we discussed in the context of the innovation framework can be grouped in a set of main areas, each of which can be represented by a main entity, in Figure 10-5 called case (following the terminology introduced earlier in this chapter). Cases can be considered undertakings, endeavors, or micro-enterprises as well: there are goals to reach, certain means that can be considered for use, certain rules that guide further action and decision making, and there is major room for knowledge workers to plan how to actually reach the goal.

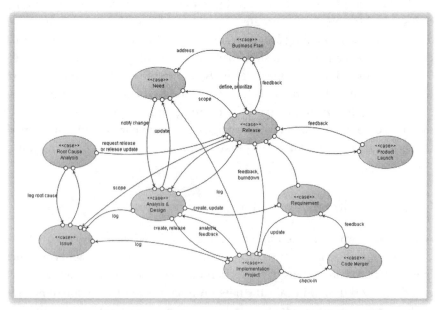

Figure 10-5: Product Innovation Ecology

For instance, in Figure 10-5, the "Business Plan" case is responsible for and coordinates any activity that is required to define a business plan, and it does that in concert with and continuously interacting with other cases. The "Requirement" case will carry responsibility for coordinating and tracking change from the definition of it until it has been fully implemented and administrated, and it does that concurrently with other cases, such as implementation project cases, a release case, etc. Figure 10-5 also shows the kind of collaboration and communication that takes place between these cases. For instance, analysis and design is not a one-time deal; during the execution of implementation projects, problems might occur, such as doubts on stories as they have been defined and estimated and based on feedback, new activity is triggered in the "Analysis & Design" case, etc.

Figure 10-5 represents something that can be qualified as an innovation ecosystem. Ecology is the discipline that studies interactions between organisms and their environment. Ecosystems are webs or networks of relations and related interactions between organisms and organisms and their environment. Ecology is the discipline that studies ecosystems. Innovation management literature uses the terms ecosystems and ecology metaphorically: it talks about business ecosystems, innovation ecology, innovation ecosystems, and engineering business ecosystems. (See [Brown 2008], [Dai 2008], [Janner 2008] and [Marín 2008].) These studies also focus on infrastructural support for making such innovation in the context of such ecosystems actionable. Basically, they suggest distributed infrastructures that support the collaboration of agents. Agent technology is currently gaining more momentum. OMG is busy creating a standard for it (AMP 2008), and it defines an agent as an autonomous entity that can adapt to and interact with its environment. An agent can be human, machine, software, or any other entity that acts as an agent. It is autonomous in the sense that it can decide how best to achieve certain goals. Note that the concept of an ecosystem with cases as collaborating agents resonates well with the definition of a case in this book (as referred to above): A case holds all of the information and processes, and it coordinates communications necessary to accomplish the goal for a particular situation.

This observation brings us a bit further in analyzing a new process paradigm for managing cases: a case autonomously interacts in its environment and with other cases until it has sufficiently reached its goals. Interaction between such cases can be formalized and be made explicit (modeled) in terms of specifying possible interactions. Whether and when, or under which conditions such interactions happen is subject to the autonomy of the agents. In that sense, interactions are still unpredictable—even interactions emerge. Achieving goals is also about creating deliverables. Creating deliverables requires inputs, which are, for example, deliverables of other cases in the ecosystem: certain inputs are required to create certain outputs. Normally, there are dependencies of outputs on inputs. This implies that there is a logical ordering of interactions. Note that dependencies of outputs on inputs are very different from sequence-flow dependencies between activities.

We can think about reaching goals as assembling outputs from inputs. In between inputs and outputs, it might be useful to consider subassemblies. Inputs or information about inputs, as well as intermediate results or information about it, and outputs or information about outputs has to be captured and tracked during the lifecycle of a case. In the remainder of this chapter, we will talk about a case file, as a complete collection of documents relevant to a case and that can contain information of any type and according to any format, such as form data, electronic documents, scanned hard-copy images, audio and video files, photographs, etc. A case file consists of case file parts, which are individual items that with others make up the case file. It normally contains a document as well as other related data, such as attributes and annotations associated with the document (CMPM 2009). So, inputs and outputs and any relevant information about them are captured in a case file via its case file parts.

In the next section, we will zoom into some of the cases of FIGURE 10-5 to analyze patterns of how cases can autonomously reach goals and create outputs based on the interaction that they do in their environment and the evolution of their case file. We will particularly focus on the implementation project case, which is also in the heart of Scrum.

Demonstrating Case Management in the Context of Scrum

Sutherland (2007) provides a thorough explanation of the Scrum methodology. FIGURE 10-6 represents the basic pattern of it. Note that the full Scrum methodology relates to almost all cases in FIGURE 10-5, but its core is most related to the analysis & design and implementation project cases, whereas most of Scrum specifics are related to the implementation project case.

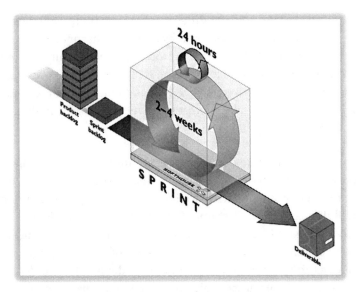

FIGURE 10-6: The Scrum System (Sutherland 2007)

When applied on a large scale, this pattern is not just occurring within a single team but in a more distributed fashion. In the context of this chapter, product backlog can be considered the set of requirements and related stories that have been defined for an initiative, such as a product release. The product backlog is developed in the analysis & design case and is its core deliverable. As discussed above, requirements and stories from the product backlog are distributed across the various implementation teams. Each implementation team, in the context of its implementation project case, will develop and maintain a sprint backlog by defining tasks for the stories that are assigned to that team. This will not be done once for the entire project, but it will be done incrementally and iteratively. An implementation project will be executed in phases, or iterations, called sprints in Scrum. Sprints typically take two to four weeks' lead time (but fixed in a certain situation). The number of sprints may be predefined but normally is not. The team might just start planning and executing the first sprint and only during sprint review decide with their stakeholders that a next sprint is required. Meanwhile, new issues might come up and requirements and stories might have to be redefined that will trigger concurrent activity in the surrounding cases in the product innovation ecosystem. In its most agile form, tasks (for stories) are only defined one sprint ahead and only roughly defined at that. During so-called daily stand-up meetings, additional tasks can be defined, tasks can be adjusted, etc.

As Damiani (2007) states, a major difference between traditional development processes and agile ones as prescribed by Scrum, is that analysis, design, and development activities during a Scrum process are intrinsically unpredictable. However, a distributed control mechanism is used to manage unpredictability and to guarantee flexibility, responsiveness, and reliability of the results. This observation makes Scrum-like management very interesting in the context of ACM: mastering the unpredictable!

We will now focus in more detail on how an implementation project case is managed. Figure 10-7 presents a diagram for that purpose. The diagram (model) is defined such that it lends itself well for technology support (automation), as we will discuss below. First note the similarity between Figure 10-6 and Figure 10-7. Figure 10-7 shows the same pattern as Figure 10-6, and it is easily understood by businesspeople. Representations of case management like the one in Figure 10-7, can stimulate common understanding and a common language among all businesspeople involved. We will first explain the model in Figure 10-7 in more detail and then discuss what its purpose can be in the context of an ACM system.

First note the phasing of the case: there is an initial phase (or state), and then there is a series of sprints whereby each sprint is followed by a sprint review phase, during which it is decided to do another sprint or to close the implementation project (case). This reflects the main pattern of Scrum. Activities are related to the phases. Note that it is quite common to define agile projects in terms of phases and activities that make up the phases. Damiani (2007) presents a model based on a metamodel that is, in a sense, similar to the one presented in Figure 10-7. Figure 10-7 adds more detail to make the model actionable, and it really supports the knowledge workers, as we will discuss below.

The implementation project case itself (or an instance of it) is created from the analysis & design case. The implementation team together with the product manager, etc., is involved in the analysis & design case as well to assign and estimate stories. Together with the team, "done" criteria are defined per story. Done criteria define a sort of checklist containing such items as "properly documented," "unit tests defined and executed," "outstanding issues resolved," "customer sign-off collected," "all changes checked-in," and whatever is appropriate to include. Once the implementation project is sufficiently prepared, it is released. This is reflected in Figure 10-7 by the phase "Waiting for Release." When the release trigger (event) comes, the implementation project case itself becomes active entering in its first sprint phase, as represented by the entry event in the sprint phase. A sprint planning meeting is automatically organized, represented by the follow-up relationship as marked with "A" (automatic).

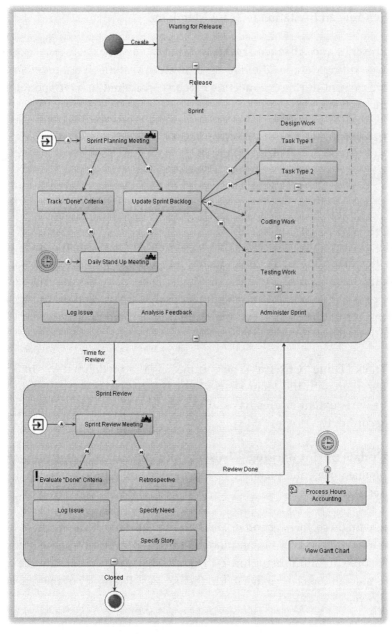

FIGURE 10-7: **Managing the Implementation Project Case**

Note that the meeting activities in FIGURE 10-7 (marked by a meeting icon) are all prescribed by the Scrum methodology. A meeting activity ideally comes with out-of-the box meeting support (by the ACM system), such as the following:

◆ **Sending an Invitation to Team Members.**

◆ **Presence and Absence Tracking**—This can also be used to collect hours accounting data for the hours accounting system. Team members that are present during the meeting can be considered to have spent time in the meeting.

◆ **Recording of Meeting Minutes**—Meeting minutes can serve as a preformatted case file part of the case file, which in this instance, is of the implementation project case.

During the sprint planning meeting, various activities can be done (considered for execution) but nothing is prescribed. These activities can be done anytime during the meeting, as far as people are authorized to do them. There are two activities that can only be done during this meeting and the daily stand-up meeting, but not outside of these meetings. These activities are related to the meeting activity via follow-up relationships that are marked as "M" (manual), which means that people can manually select them or leave them. These activities are as follows:

◆ **Track "Done" Criteria**—The ScrumMaster (a predefined role in Scrum) together with the team checks which tasks have been executed and to what extent stories have been covered. Done criteria are checked accordingly.

◆ **Update Sprint Backlog**—This is about checking the status of already planned tasks and planning new tasks. We will elaborate on that in more detail below.

Along with these, there are other tasks that can be done at any moment during these meetings and also at any moment during the sprint phase (provided that people are authorized for it). These tasks are drawn inside the sprint phase but shown as unconnected in FIGURE 10-7. Examples of these tasks are as follows:

◆ **Log Issue**—When people observe problems or defects that have to be fixed, they can log issues that will then automatically lead to the creation of issue cases to handle them (as indicated in FIGURE 10-5).

◆ **Analysis Feedback**—It might be required to reconsider or improve stories or requirements, and by providing this feedback, the analysis & design case will be triggered (see FIGURE 10-5).

◆ **Administer Sprint**—This is work for which only the ScrumMaster is authorized. For example, the ScrumMaster is responsible for providing sprint burndown data to the release case (see FIGURE 10-5). This data, as prescribed by Scrum, is the basis for release managers and product managers to check progress in terms of estimated versus actual capacity spending.

There are also tasks that can be done at any moment during the entire lifecycle of the implementation project case. These tasks are drawn outside of the sprint phase, but they are still part of the implementation project case model. They also show as unconnected in FIGURE 10-7. We discuss examples of these later in this section.

Note that above, we used the term follow-up a few times. This is a common term in case management. It means given what has happened, and typically triggered by an event, someone has to decide what's next. That person decides on follow-up activities. Basically, the follow-up relationship is a planning construct, as will become more clear below.

By the way, the model in FIGURE 10-7 can also be used to drive user interface behavior of tasks in the ACM system. For instance, when tasks become eligible for selection (such as the ones mentioned above during the meeting activities), an authorized person (here the ScrumMaster), can select them on the user interface of the activities (here the meeting activities), and based on that, hyperlinks (to URLs) automatically might show up on the user interface so that the corresponding tasks can be done.

According to Scrum, during a sprint, a stand-up meeting has to be organized daily. Such meetings should not take longer than fifteen minutes and are scheduled at a fixed time of the day. All team members have to be present. This is indicated in FIGURE 10-7 by a time-triggered meeting activity. During this meeting, team members share their progress (in terms of tasks), tell what they are going to do next, and share their problems. Consequently, during this meeting, the sprint backlog can be updated, done criteria checked, issues logged, etc.

We will now focus on a very essential part of Scrum: updating sprint backlog (see FIGURE 10-7). The actual work to be done by the team members, such as engineers, architects, and testers, has to be done outside the team meetings but during the sprint phase. These tasks, sometimes denoted as tickets in Scrum, are planned during the sprint planning and daily stand-up meetings. Nothing is predefined in terms of a BPMN-like process model, but instead, there are possible task types defined that act as a sort of task template. These task types might be categorized in groups, in FIGURE 10-7 called clusters. There might be clusters for design work, coding work, modeling work, testing work, documentation work, etc. A few of them are included in FIGURE 10-7 indicatively.

Note that any phase, activity, cluster, relationship, etc., in FIGURE 10-7 is just content: people in their own business organization are defining them. In IT terms, the ACM system would come with a metamodel and on top of that a modeling user interface (typically a graphical diagram editor with related property forms) based on which the organization can create its models, such as the one in FIGURE 10-7.

The design work cluster might typically contain such task types as "Draft concept note," "Create user interface mockup," etc. The coding (or maybe modeling) work cluster might contain tasks like "Create application schema," "Implement interface," "Implement method," "Create web service," etc. The task types will also specify the tool to use, for example, to create the corresponding deliverable (kind of open with, via a URL, for example). The task types will also define norm times. Based on these task types, the ACM system will record statistics based on monitoring the actual execution of tasks that are planned, and it should be self-learning: based on such statistics, it should be possible to periodically update the norm times.

As FIGURE 10-7 indicates, the update sprint backlog activity has manual follow-up relationships to the task types in the clusters or even to the clusters directly. This means that at any moment during the meetings, the ScrumMaster, when sitting together with the team leads, can add one or more instances of the related task types to the case, or can add one or more instances of one or more tasks types from a related cluster to the case. Adding actually means planning. Here's where the process is actually planned. In traditional BPM, like with BPMN-style processes, processes are predefined, which means process planning is performed prior to executing the process (as a procedure). This is different in the agile world and in ACM: the activity of process planning is part of executing the process. Process planning is interactive!

Note that the term process planning has nothing to do with scheduling in terms of determination of start dates of activities, etc. Process planning is a well-known term in industrial process engineering. Schlenoff (1996) provides the definition of NIST, as follows: "Process planning is the development of a set of instructions which describe a linear or non-linear sequence of tasks to achieve a specified goal." And in ACM, this is what happens interactively during process execution, at least partly.

The specificity of a task in the planning model might vary from tasks that are fully specified to tasks that merely act as task templates and for which specific task data is specified during interactive planning. When a task (instance) is planned, the following data can still be specified for the task:

◆ **A specific description.** "Create concept note for case modeling for ACM," being a refinement of "Create concept note."

◆ **Work content (in number of hours required to do the work).** A task type can provide a norm time, as suggested earlier. Per task, one can deviate from the norm time, if appropriate.

◆ **A specific due date or duration.** Note that duration and work content are different, although both are a measure of time. A relative due date (or duration) might also be set per task type (task definition), such as "two weeks." In this example, this would match the company-adopted sprint duration of two weeks. In the task (instance), an absolute due date might be specified, if wanted, or one might deviate from the task type due date or duration.

◆ **Work assignment or task allocation to a specific role or member of the team.** Note that work assignment or work distribution might be designed in relation to the case definition, but a specific assignment can also be done when the particular task is planned.

◆ **Relationships between the tasks and specific case file parts to use or produce by the task (see FIGURE 10-8).** For example, a "Create concept note" task "must use" one or more requirements and stories, "must produce" the concept note, and "may produce" some other material if appropriate. The ACM system should support design of case files, tasks, and the management of cases in a coordinated and integrated fashion.

◆ **Typical project management type of constraints and dependencies.** We will elaborate on that in more detail below.

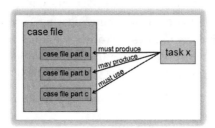

Figure 10-8: Integrated Case File

Note that the ACM system will provide an interactive user interface to manage this kind of interactive planning as driven by the case management model (such as in Figure 10-7).

So far we have considered a case management model (like in Figure 10-7) as a means to drive or guide interactive planning. The result of such planning is an incrementally growing, or emergent case (or case process). But where is the actual case (process) and how to visualize it? The most adequate representation of the actual case process is a Gantt chart, as depicted in Figure 10-9.

Number	Task	Resource	Start	End	Duration	% Complete	January 23 24 25 26 27 28 29 30 31	February 1 2 3 4
1	Investigate state machine in UML		1/23/2010	1/25/2010	1			
2	Investigate events in UML and AMP		1/23/2010	1/25/2010	1			
3	Create prototype for Pub-Sub		1/26/2010	1/27/2010	2			
4	Create basic state machine prototype		1/26/2010	1/27/2010	2			
5	Test Pub-Sub		1/28/2010	1/28/2010	1			
6	Test state machine		1/28/2010	1/28/2010	1			
7	Create rule based routing prototype		1/28/2010	1/29/2010	2			
8	Integrate the prototypes		1/30/2010	2/3/2010	3			
9	Extend event service on the service bus		1/29/2010	2/1/2010	2			

Figure 10-9: Gantt Chart View of the Implementation Project

A Gantt chart should be an integral part of the ACM system. The ACM system keeps track of the actual case (instance) with all its tasks (task instances), and it is continuously emerging, and the Gantt chart provides the most appropriate view of that. The tasks in Figure 10-9 are also proper examples of tickets as can be planned based on the interactive planning model of FIGURE 10-7 (tasks being instances of the task types).

Note that implementation project team members might want to have a look at the Gantt chart at any moment during the course of the case. For that reason, FIGURE 10-7 contains an activity called "View Gantt Chart," showing unconnected and drawn outside the sprint phase and other phases. People that have the authority to do so can look up the Gantt chart at any moment.

The activity "Update Sprint Backlog" might make use of the Gantt chart view as well. In that case it has to be editable: through the Gantt chart, task details can be edited.

As FIGURE 10-9 indicates, the tasks might also have dependencies on each other. The interactive case management planning model (such as the one in FIGURE 10-7) can be further advanced by the possibility to specify constraints and dependencies between tasks. As the tasks are only defined at runtime, so too are the constraints and dependencies, and the case management planning model might contain the parameters to support that (these aren't visualized in FIGURE 10-7, but a further refinement of that model might do so). Such parameters might be defined at the phase level, task cluster level, or even per task type indicating that certain dependencies might be specifiable between task instances of that type. The type of dependency might be fully specified in the model, or it might be left to the choice of the person who will interactively plan the tasks. When tasks are planned interactively, the ACM system might provide an interactive user interface that suggests which types of constraints are possible between which tasks (task instances), whereby tasks might be both already planned ones and the ones that are newly planned.

Various types of constraints and dependencies can be supported, which we will not define in detail here but just mention them, assuming that most people are sufficiently familiar with commonly used project management tools like Microsoft Project and others. Also refer to the project management standard SPEM (2008).

Some examples of possible constraints and dependencies are as follows:

◆ Task dependencies, such as: Finish-Start (FS), Start-Start (SS), Finish-Finish (FF), and Start-Finish (SF). For example, an FF dependency means that the two tasks are planned as finishing simultaneously.

◆ In relation to these: overlap and delay (or lag time) between them.

◆ Flexible task constraints, such as "as soon as possible" and "as late as possible."

◆ Semiflexible task constraints such as "start not earlier than," "start not later than," "finish not earlier than," and "finish not later than."

◆ Hard task constraints such as "must start on" and "must finish on."

The notion of phases, such as those in FIGURE 10-7, might also show up in the Gantt chart via the often used milestone icon. In addition to that, it might be useful to specify certain milestones interactively. It might be useful to refine the interactive planning model further, for example, by activity properties that could drive milestones at a more refined level.

The concept of interactive planning is further highlighted by FIGURE 10-10.

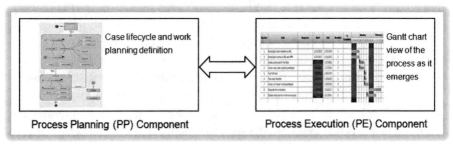

FIGURE 10-10: Interactive Planning

As FIGURE 10-10 indicates, the ACM system can be thought of as conceptually consisting of two interacting components both supported by a graphical user interface.

◆ **Process Planning (PP) Component**—This is the left component in FIGURE 10-10. It is driven or guided by the graphical case management model, like the one in FIGURE 10-7.

◆ **Process Execution (PE) Component**—This is the right component in FIGURE 10-10. Its status can be followed, and its details can be updated through the Gantt chart view. The PE component also handles the dispatching of tasks to the work-lists of teams and workers.

Based on interactive planning actions in PP, the process as visualized in the PE emerges. When the emerging process is executed, events can be raised—such as based on inserts, updates, or deletes of case file parts in the case file, or of attributes and annotations of the case file itself. Other events might be caused by the completion of a certain task, the start of a certain task, the reaching of a certain milestone, the reaching of a predefined time, or a message coming from the ecosystem. Such events typically trigger new planning decisions in PP.

We now revisit the implementation project case in FIGURE 10-7. When a sprint takes two weeks (by choice), a time event might be defined to trigger the transition to the sprint review phase after two weeks (time event).

Note that several tasks that were planned for the sprint might not have completed yet during the sprint. That is a natural thing in Scrum, and these tasks should not be unplanned or terminated but kept in the system as a starter of sprint backlog, possibly for a next sprint. It might be possible, however, that this is different in other case management situations. It might be required to terminate tasks-in-progress in a phase when that phase is exited. If required, such difference in behavior can be specified via properties in the model.

Regarding the implementation project case, the entry of the "Sprint Review" phase will automatically schedule a sprint review meeting (prescribed by Scrum methodology). During this meeting, stakeholders, who may even be customers, will typically be involved as well. Sprint results are reviewed, demos given, etc. It is required that done criteria are evaluated formally. This activity can be done at any time during the meeting (manual follow-up), but the red exclamation mark on that activity indicates that it has to be done (see FIGURE 10-7). The product manager might also consider doing a general evaluation of the sprint, in terms of "how did it go?" and "what can we do to make sure that we do it better next time?" In Scrum, this is called a retrospective.

It is also very common that during the sprint review, stakeholders bring up new insights, which might result in logging issues, specifying new stories or updating them, or even specifying new needs. This is reflected by the unconnected activities in the phase "Sprint Review" in FIGURE 10-7. These can be done at any moment during that phase. When the sprint review meeting is over (activity done), the ACM system will let the implementation project case exit the sprint review phase, and depending on whether done criteria are met (checked via a rule on the transition, often called a guard), the case will either close or enter a new iteration (sprint).

The model in FIGURE 10-7 contains an element that we did not discuss so far: the activity "Process Hours Accounting." Knowledge workers, such as engineers, product managers, and ScrumMasters, can provide progress feedback to the ACM system. For example, by entering or updating a percentage-complete figure per task. Or they enter actual worked hours per task or case directly. It is sometimes also possible that the ACM system concludes on hours spent itself, as has been explained in relation to the meeting activities. This data can be processed automatically as hours accounting data and booked into the hours accounting or ERP system automatically. Note that the activity is not included in one of the specific phases, which implies that it can run anytime. It is triggered by a time event, for instance, daily. It represents the use of a predefined process defined in BPMN. This also shows a way to integrate ACM and predefined processes: in the context of a case, predefined processes can be involved. It will also be possible to initiate cases from predefined processes, although that aspect is not further highlighted in this chapter.

Note that the integration of ACM with predefined processes also allows companies to grow maturity of their process management, whereby they start managing their processes as cases, and whereby they turn subareas of it into predefined processes, where appropriate. Case instances may first evolve based on case worker decisions. Exploring (mining) case instance history as recorded in the ACM system might reveal certain recurring patterns. Sometimes, procedural workflows (predefined processes) might be abstracted from these patterns, which can then be incorporated as case activities in the overall case management models. In this way, case models might evolve over time.

So far we have analyzed in detail how the implementation case is managed, whereby we centered the discussion on the diagram in FIGURE 10-7. We will now highlight a few more aspects of ACM in relation to some related cases in the ecosystem as indicated in FIGURE 10-5.

FIGURE 10-11 represents the management of a fragment of the analysis & design case; specifically, the creation of implementation project cases for the various implementation teams, during a preparatory meeting. A few aspects of it have been referred to above already. In Scrum terms, such a meeting is called an estimation meeting. During the meeting, implementation projects can be created, as is indicated in FIGURE 10-11 by the follow-up relationship to the activity that represents the use of the implementation project case. And because these are cases and cases behave autonomously, they start running and following their own lifecycle, during which what will (or can) happen is specified in FIGURE 10-7. During the estimation meeting, stories will be linked to the implementation projects and are estimated accordingly. The implementation projects will also be released. This detail is not depicted in FIGURE 10-11, but it could either be an explicit part of the estimation meeting activity or could be more explicitly depicted (it's a matter of taste).

We also discussed that from an implementation project case, analysis feedback could be passed back to the analysis & design case to trigger further activity in that case. That is indicated in FIGURE 10-11 by a handler of the event "New Analysis Feedback." When that event is received, the ACM system will automatically ("A") trigger the "Analyze Feedback" activity, during which it might be decided to also plan a next estimation meeting (to reconsider and update the estimates).

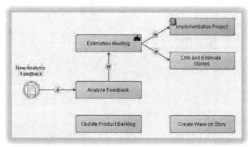

FIGURE 10-11: Management of a Fragment of the Analysis & Design Case

It might be useful to refine behavior around planning follow-up even further. As discussed, in Scrum, planning follow-up activities typically happens during an activity, like in the various meeting activities. Note that sometimes it might be wanted that follow-up is planned upon completion of an activity. The difference in behavior might be controlled by an additional parameter in the model. Generally, follow up can also be planned (follow-up decisions taken) upon any event. For example, on receipt of new information or when a new document is inserted in the case file. If wanted, manual follow-up relationships can also be drawn from an event handler like "New Analysis Feedback" in FIGURE 10-11. The ACM system will then involve someone to make a follow-up decision.

Remember what has been discussed in the previous section: During the lifecycle of a case, while working toward a goal a case file is assembled, and when new case file parts are added or case file parts are changed or deleted, events can be raised, which triggers case workers to decide what other activity is needed in follow-up to that, etc. Clearly, ACM isn't about executing predefined procedures: it's about a continuous process of interactively planning what's to be done next based on what happens, and the case file, as it progresses, is the basis to measure how far a case is off from its goal.

It might happen sometimes that some activities can be planned whereby it is left to the discretion of the case worker to actually plan them or not. This provides good flexibility, but sometimes there is a need to guide the decision maker. In certain situations, it is possible to define rules over the case data (information in the case file) based on which applicability of activities can be controlled dynamically. These applicability rules will then act as a filter for the decision makers that decide on follow up activities.

An example of this is given in FIGURE 10-12, which contains an incomplete fragment of the "Issue" case in FIGURE 10-5.

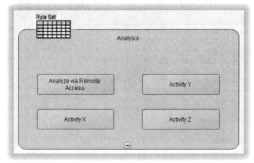

FIGURE 10-12: Controlling Activity Applicability Through Rules

Think about an issue of type defect. Assume that the defect is analyzed in more detail during the phase "Analysis." When a defect is logged and people look into it, they might conclude that they can reproduce the issue based on their simulated data set. They can then indicate and specify that by updating the case data. There might be an applicability rule that determines applicability of the activity "Analyze via Remote Access" (which means logging on to the customer system remotely). If the defect is reproducible, this activity is not applicable. But if it is not reproducible, the activity is applicable and the issue handler can then decide to actually perform it (plan it). The fact of reproduceability might be dynamic: during further discussions and attempts to resolve the issue, it might be that the conclusion is that it is not reproducible, or actually yes it is, or based on new facts, it isn't after all. This implies that the applicability of the activity is controlled dynamically. There might be more activities of which applicability can be controlled by rules. And there might be multiple rules to do that. It is common for business users to have a set of such rules depicted via a decision table. Such a rule set might apply to the entire lifecycle of the case or only to one or more phases of it. In the example of FIGURE 10-12, a particular rule set is only applicable while the case resides in the "Analysis" phase.

So far we have analyzed and discussed the concept of ACM and ways to formalize it as the basis for technology supported ACM in the context of innovation management, and in particular, product innovation management. We'll just round-up that discussion by means of a summary of the main ingredients of the definition of a case (case model or ACM model), as indicated in FIGURE 10-13.

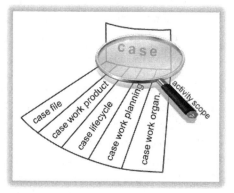

FIGURE 10-13: Case Activity Scope

A case model or case definition conceptually consists of the following:

◆ **The definition of a case file.** From the discussions above, it is clear that the case file plays a crucial role in ACM. It provides evidence of what has happened and especially in the context of innovation management the set of related case files also serve as the basis for tracking changes and providing full transparency from motivation to implementation of change. Case files also actively drive management of cases by means of raising events and serving as context for evaluation of business rules.

◆ **The definition of a case work product or a set of work products.** Note that work products are deliverables or subdeliverables. They will normally be associated via case file parts but might have to be indicated specifically. For example, a well defined and estimated set of requirements and related stories is the work product of the analysis & design case. A well tested and documented product update is the work product of the implementation project case.

◆ **The definition of a case lifecycle.** A case might transit through various phases, might revisit phases, etc., during its lifecycle. The phases and their relationships in FIGURE 10-7 are an example of this. The lifecycle definition can be used as the basis for phasing case work, act as the basis for defining milestones, and can serve as appropriate means to phase the handling of events and evaluation of rules over the case lifecycle. It is optional to define phases. Some cases might not need them. For some cases, the entire case lifecycle is, in fact, a single phase.

◆ **The definition of case work planning.** After the discussion of the model in FIGURE 10-7, and the interactive, model-driven, planning concept, the reader will understand what that means. Note the difference between a "case work plan" and the definition of "work planning." Essentially, what ACM should support is the definition of work planning.

◆ **The definition of case work organization.** This is on the edge between ACM and organization modeling. We briefly discussed work organization and work distribution in this chapter. Work distribution might deserve a definition on its own related to case definitions. It can be as simple as statically linking a type of task to a role or team. Above, we have discussed how during interactive planning tasks can be assigned to specific roles or teams. But eventually, people might need more work balancing support by design and might want to define alternative scenarios of work assignment given different volumes of demand. This will require a more refined and dedicated definition of case work organization. We will not elaborate further on that in this chapter.

Case activities might require a scope that involves some or even all of the ingredients of the case, as shown in FIGURE 10-13. Activities in the case might have the entire case definition as possible scope, although some activities might focus more on some aspects than on others. For example:

◆ Almost any case activity is concerned with updating data in the case file. At least for one or more parts of it.

◆ Many case activities will directly contribute to a case work product.

◆ From certain case activities it will be required to make decisions that influence the further progression of cases in its lifecycle. This could be done indirectly, by updating case data based on which events are fired or which rules evaluate, but it could also be done directly, for example, by pushing a button that marks a decision to have the case make a transition to a certain phase.

◆ From certain case activities, it will be required to plan follow-up activities.

◆ Activities that are concerned with planning follow-up activities might also be concerned with assigning them to certain roles or teams.

Note that not all activities deal equally with all of these aspects. The scope of activities can be defined in the model.

In terms of providing technology support for ACM, one can imagine that phases and their transitions and related event handling will easily map on so-called state machines (Wagner 2006). But this chapter and this book are not the place to focus on implementation technology aspects of ACM. For the same reason, we will not discuss how entities (cases) in the business innovation domain model, with their related cases and information in case files, can best map on persistent storage models in databases and content management repositories. Obviously, the ACM system will have to fully support that, preferably in model-driven ways, but the discussion of that goes beyond the scope and purpose of this book.

Until now, the discussion focused most on the application of the actionable framework to product innovation. In the next section, we will go beyond that and look again to the broader concern of business innovation.

FROM PRODUCT INNOVATION TO BUSINESS INNOVATION

Once product innovation is managed in the way outlined above, we will have turned product innovation into a repeatable and managed process. And with that, we are in the middle of the how-phase of innovation (see FIGURE 10-2).

We can expect further "innovation of innovation" in two dimensions as follows:

◆ Moving on to the "where" and "who" phases in which R&D and sales and delivery will be heavily involved, with focus on customer- and partner-facing processes, dealing with related cases—such as to manage

RFPs, sales contracts, and customer-driven development—together with related cases in the areas of legal, finance, etc.

◆ Having established an innovation management baseline, process driven, and ACM-centric, the company is in a position to start continuously improving and raising the level of maturity of innovation management.

In the business improvement context, it is common to consider maturity models. These are abstractions of the typical stages of improvement companies go through. It is a way of benchmarking based on best practice and industry knowledge.

There isn't a dedicated business innovation maturity model yet. When writing about innovation, Fingar (2009) states: "It is time to develop an innovation maturity model." Therefore, we just look at the business process maturity model (see BPMM 2008), as depicted in Figure 10-14.

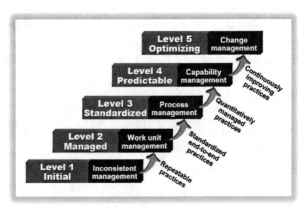

Figure 10-14: Business Process Maturity Model (BPMM 2008)

According to BPMM, after having established repeatable (Level 2) and end-to-end managed processes (Level 3), the next step is to start managing based on measurement and metrics (Level 4) to finally arrive at Level 5 where continuous improvement is ingrained into the management system.

In the context of innovation management, measurement is more than just taking measures and monitoring ongoing activity. Measurement hooks into many elements of the innovation management framework (see Figure 10-4). Figure 10-15 represents the various roles of measurements (metrics) in the context of innovation management.

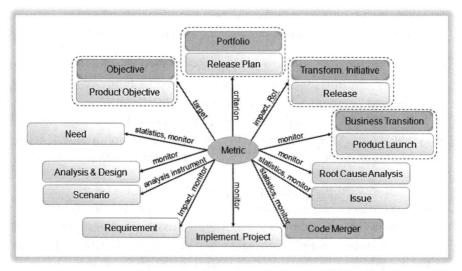

FIGURE 10-15: The Role of Metrics in Innovation Management

In this chapter, we discussed how technology-supported ACM serves as the ideal basis for making innovation management actionable. Support for integrated and real-time measurement is an essential part of it. Activity in relation to the various cases can be monitored continuously, making measurement productive. Metrics are essential to specify objectives (targets for innovation). Comparison of monitoring results with targeted performance will identify performance gaps. When initiatives are defined to reach objectives, again, metrics is essential as the basis for estimating impact and return on investment (ROI) of initiatives and to prioritize them accordingly. When as-is scenarios are analyzed in a root cause analysis case, or when to-be scenarios are analyzed in an analysis & design case, metrics serve as the primary performance analysis instrument.

Obviously, performance monitoring of innovation management related cases will lead to insight into cost, lead-time, and quality related performance aspects of these innovation management cases. For example, implementation projects might take longer than wanted, capacity utilization might not be optimal, the pace and quality of needs analysis or issue management might be insufficient, etc.

Logically, the next step will be defining initiatives not just to innovate the product, but to improve the process of product innovation, or generally, business innovation. The portfolio of initiatives will then also include business transformation and improvement initiatives, such as Kaizens, etc. And this will put business innovation management in full action. Business innovation management has now become the engine for continuous innovation, not just of the product, or the business, but also of business innovation itself.

Note that in business innovation (or process innovation), the number of improvement initiatives, such as Kaizens, can be huge. We have seen average-sized companies that conduct hundreds of initiatives a year. But there are also large companies that run thousands of initiatives in parallel at any point of time (for example, see [Harry 2006]). Business innovation, if taken seriously, becomes a business on its own and a company within a company.

This is also why proper balancing of a portfolio of initiatives in the context of managing business plan cases (see FIGURE 10-5) becomes crucial: since product innovation initiatives and process innovation initiatives will compete for the same scarce resources and funds, and one initiative might increase the level of risk for others. This also says that when moving on to the next phases of innovation (see FIGURE 10-2), the different aspects of innovation, such as product and process innovation, can't be separated from each other but have to be managed in a coordinated fashion. And this, again, stresses that all business innovation has to be managed based on the same integrated framework.

TOWARD A NEW CLASS OF TECHNOLOGY

An important question is: which technology to use as the basis for actionable business innovation management?

Note that some aspects of product innovation are addressed by dedicated and niche tools, such as JIRA by Atlassian (2010) or Bugzilla (2010), an open source product (for example, see [Doar 2005]).

However, these tools lack essential capabilities such as the following:

◆ Some do have support for workflow, but such workflow still follows the paradigm of predefined processes.

◆ Given the notion of the innovation ecosystem as discussed above, real-time collaboration and the integration of people, process, and technology (including such applications as ERP, enterprise content management [ECM] systems, etc.) is essential. But these tools are off-the-shelf end-user applications. They aren't platforms that serve such enterprise wide or even extended enterprise-wide integration needs.

◆ The process in such tools is still implicit and invisible. The processes (or cases) are not model-driven and are not tangible and visual artifacts that can be continuously improved.

◆ These tools are specifically geared toward the specifics of software development and can't adequately satisfy the broader needs of business innovation management.

◆ Some elements of innovation management are addressed, but the scope of the innovation management framework goes far beyond what these tools can handle.

Some of these tools might still be reused, for example, as data stores for issues, etc., but a broader technology platform is required to satisfy the needs of business innovation management.

Business process management systems (BPMS) are more likely candidate platforms for business innovation management. But many of these platforms still focus on modeling and managing predefined processes (BPMN-like), don't provide the means to manage knowledge work, and don't support the full closed-loop management that spans the levels of strategic, tactical, and operational management that are involved in business innovation.

However, there is a growing awareness in the market that a next generation technology platform is needed that covers the needs of full business innovation management. Fingar (2009) is one of the first to start writing on this, and he talks about a business operations platform (BOP) as this next generation technology. According to Fingar, a BOP is a next generation BPM solution delivered in one single platform that allows organizations to design, execute, monitor, change, and continuously optimize critical business processes and operations wherever they are deployed. A BOP manages applications, especially people-intensive applications; decouples the process from the application; allows processes to change over time; and puts the process into the hands of the business user.

A BOP is the ideal platform to roll out business innovation programs. A BOP has to support multiple process management paradigms including, and in particular, ACM in such a way that predefined and emerging processes are fully interoperable.

A BOP typically supports model-driven development of service-oriented architecture (SOA)-based and process-based applications. When ACM is part of BOP, case file parts of cases can smoothly integrate with work products such as application artifacts (including models) and other related case data that is handled in the BOP itself. There is also a tendency to further extend the business modeling footprint of BOP beyond processes. BOPs are expected to come with integral support for modeling and analyzing business organizations, business capabilities, value chains (or value networks), as well as related analysis of performance and risk metrics. BOP will not only support design, deployment, and management of applications but also more and more of the business (or business system) itself. When ACM is an embedded part of BOP, case files of business innovation related cases can readily include work products, such as all the modeling artifacts that are involved in business analysis, implementation, and monitoring. This way, BOP will eventually support the definition of as-is and to-be scenarios of the business, as well as the management of innovation around transforming and continuously improving the business.

In this context, it is interesting to point to the Business Ecology Initiative (BEI 2009) that is a manifestation of this trend. Its mission is to foster the evolution of application development platforms and related standards and practices to business ecology platforms and related standards and platforms. BOPs, or if it sounds better business ecology platforms, will emerge or continue to emerge that focus on supporting management and innovation of business in all of its facets.

Fingar (2009) also associates a BOP with cloud-based deployment, whereby cloud stands for on-demand IT resources at low cost via the Internet. The term "cloud-based" normally indicates low cost of deployment, and this will also enable small- and medium-sized enterprises (SME) to make full use of a BOP. The cloud is also the natural place to position the business arena, and the natural place for collaborating in the context of product and business innovation. Note that business innovation management is collaboration intensive, and the best place to bring distributed and remote stakeholders and partners together is in the cloud (see FIGURE 10-16).

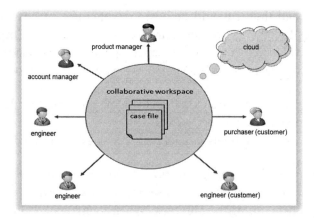

FIGURE 10-16: Collaborative Innovation, Ultimately in the Cloud

Collaboration is best served by the sharing of information (documents, artifacts, etc.). This is preferable over exchange or "federation" of information, unless organizational policies prohibit sharing. Innovation processes can best be enforced when they are shared. Cloud-based deployment of a BOP facilitates this well. The concept of open innovation is becoming very popular today (Chesbrough 2003). Open innovation is a paradigm that assumes that companies can and should use external ideas as well as internal ideas. As far as innovation is concerned, the boundary between an organization and its environment becomes porous. The renewed interest in open innovation is also due to the rise of the cloud as the ideal place to deal with the VOC or VOM. It is noteworthy that technology that is developed to support open innovation is typically cloud based.

Note also that collaboration service and technology providers, such as Google, bring new ways of human collaboration, such as the recently announced Google Wave platform. A BOP smoothly integrated with such capabilities will be the best "bed" for integrated ACM, and the best basis for business innovation management.

THE VALUE: PRODUCTIVE AND SUSTAINABLE INNOVATION

In this chapter, we started by articulating the struggle to manage product innovation in an environment where almost all activity is conducted manually, and any overview of the process and integration of its many parts is only based on the understanding and discipline of the individual knowledge workers.

We then argued that it would be best to explicitly (and visually) define all processes together with their purpose, ownership in the organization, performance measurements, and participating roles and to manage all activity throughout the organization based on these explicit process models.

This does, however, require a paradigm to define processes that do full justice to the way knowledge workers, such as engineers and their managers, work. Traditional workflow models (predefined processes) aren't adequate for this.

We demonstrated how the innovation management environment can be considered an ecosystem of related cases that collaborate with each other and their environment during their lifecycle. When zooming into some of the case areas, we discussed how the typical patterns of innovation work follow the principles of ACM very well. We also demonstrated how the management of these cases can be explicitly defined in ACM models that can serve as the basis to plan, manage, and monitor most, if not all, innovation management activity.

This paves the way for a new class of technology whereby ACM becomes an essential and integrated part of a BOP that will be a major enabler to overcome the typical problems in innovation management as discussed earlier.

As a first step, the new system will enable companies to adequately manage and monitor the product innovation process based on a new and technology supported baseline for innovation process management. This provides management full transparency and will make the product innovation process productive for both managers and knowledge workers. It enables the organization to scale, makes change transparent and managed, and collects any performance management metrics as needed. This paves the way for the next step: a continuous, strategy driven, improving this baseline whereby the system, as implementation of the generic innovation management framework, will equally manage and monitor all activity involved in improving the baseline. Actually, the process of innovation is a process itself. The system will support management of both innovation and innovation of innovation.

Innovation has then reached its critical mass. In the context of innovation theory, Rogers (2003) defines "critical mass" as the point where there are enough adopters that further diffusion of innovation becomes self sustaining. Or more specifically in the context of our chapter, as Rogers (2005) states: critical mass is the point at which the random activity of unrelated elements in a system suddenly becomes more complexly structured and ends-oriented, as self-organization takes over. At criticality, an innovation ecosystem's actions are no longer random, but rather take on a certain degree of predictability.

And this is exactly what we are reaching here with respect to ACM-driven and BOP-based business innovation: business innovation has become productive as well as sustainable.

Chapter 11

ACHIEVING AGILITY

DERMOT MCCAULEY

In the face of increasing global competition and rapid changes in technology, legislation, and knowledge, organizations need to overcome inertia and become agile enough to respond quickly. Organizational agility might indeed be one of the most important skills of a successful enterprise. Adaptive case management is shown to provide the right kinds of support to help an organization become more agile.

Most large corporations are at risk of capture by inertia—the force that holds back progress and often seems to overcome once-successful organizations as they grow. The organization captured by inertia is characterized by lumbering, ineffective processes. Even the most successful and effective organizations are subject to some degree of inertia's dragging effect.

But there is an effective weapon against inertia for organizations that retain their determination to succeed and to be on top of their game: agility. Agility is a key attribute of successful public and private organizations in the modern world, and the need to increase agility is a top and urgent priority on most management teams' agendas.

The challenge for organizations is to embark on a journey that traverses the space from "inert" to "more agile" and to do so continually. A new and practical approach to achieving greater agility—the adaptive case management (ACM) platform—is emerging for organizations that want to escape inertia's grip. The journey is an evolution and the ACM platform is an essential tool for corporations as they steer their course.

WHY AGILITY MATTERS

Agility has been thrust more urgently onto "must-do" lists everywhere because the challenges organizations face today are more pressing than any they have previously known.

Arguably, the most significant of these challenges is the ever more widespread impact of globalization. The world of competition is increasingly "flat" (Friedman 2006). Competitors can, and do, appear from anywhere. Today's competitor could be a company from across the world that you have never previously heard of. Competitors, in this sense, include challenges to the way the public sector operates—governments are increasingly outsourcing back-office functions to suppliers with facilities in developing nations.

Old barriers that slowed or stopped new competitors from entering a market— such as geographic distance, the quality of communications connections, legislative constraint, or supply-chain frictions—have rapidly disintegrated. The move to a "friction-free" global economy is now well underway. To survive and prosper, all organizations must adapt faster today than ever before.

Companies need to be open to global opportunities, in terms of sourcing raw materials and services and in supplying new markets. Public agencies need to consider radical options to cut costs. Organizations may need to consider the outsourcing of the delivery of back-office and core services. They need to see competitors and partners in a new light—a company that may be a competitor in one context, can be a partner in another.

Compounding the globalization effect into a "double whammy" has been the global recession that impacted every organization at the end of first decade of the new century. The necessity to become more efficient, more responsive, more attentive, more cost conscious and to work faster than in the past has become more urgent as a result.

These dynamics contribute to an ever more rapid pace of change in the way all organizations operate. Fast change externally must be matched by fast change internally. Contexts in technology, legislation, knowledge, and innovation are all moving quickly.

Only agility enables organizations to respond quickly and positively to a more demanding commercial environment and to higher expectations of personalized service from corporate and individual customers and clients.

WHAT IS AGILITY?

For every organization, we can define organizational agility as follows:

> An agile organization is one that can sense opportunity or threat, prioritize its potential responses, and act efficiently and effectively.

An agile organization is like a successful sports team. Consider the excellent basketball player and his winning team. He is continually able to sense what is happening, prioritize his best next actions, and then act effectively. And he does this within a team and in a highly constrained time frame. In the NBA, each team has twenty-eight seconds to make its play and score. Every player must sense, prioritize, and act quickly for the team to win. An agile organization behaves in this fashion. Let's further examine this sensing, prioritizing, and acting.

Sensing

An agile organization excels at recognizing opportunities and threats. It must be aware not merely of its own organization, but also of its operating environment. It needs to understand its customers' demands and how these change; its competitors' capabilities and how these change; and the macroeconomic environment and how this affects its operation and those of its customers and competitors. Its own performance capability needs to be transparent within the organization, enabling it to respond to changing external realities.

Prioritizing

An agile organization has a clear purpose, which is clearly articulated and widely and deeply understood by its people. The organization's destination is known. It ensures that the organization's entire population is aware of corporate priorities at the enterprise, department, function, and individual levels. It has a set of goals that are coherent and connected, and the achievement of these goals is pursued in a joined-up fashion across the business. The joined-up goals of the organization are used by its people to make the best choice of action in any circumstance.

Acting

Agility culminates in people taking appropriate, timely action. In an agile organization, people execute existing business processes exceptionally well, and crucially, they also adapt those processes quickly as business needs change.

Few organizations excel at sensing, prioritizing, and acting. Even fewer excel at all three at the same time. Those that do are the successful agile organizations. Take a few moments to answer the following two simple questions and write down your answers in Table 11-1.

◆ How agile is your organization today?

◆ How agile must your organization be in twelve months' time?

TABLE 11-1: Agility Assessment and 12-Month Goal for Your Organization

	AGILITY TODAY (SCALE: 1–10)	AGILITY NEEDED ONE YEAR FROM TODAY (SCALE: 1–10)
Sensing	?	?
Prioritizing	?	?
Acting	?	?

Now take some time to respond to this question: Do you have a plan and the right tools in place to ensure that your organization will achieve the agility goal you set for it in TABLE 11-1 for twelve months from now? Let's discuss the relevance of case management to agility and then consider the case management platform your organization will require for its agile journey.

AGILITY AND CASE MANAGEMENT

The need for agility when placed in competition with the dragging, constraining effect of legacy structures results in tension. Frequently, this tension is uncreative. We are all familiar with cultures where statements such as "we can't do it that way" and "it would be too hard to change our process to allow for that" are commonplace. Rather than being a creative tension that inspires innovation and drives continual improvement, too often the tension is uncreative, resulting in entrenched and ineffective processes, many unmet customer needs, and widespread failure to exploit opportunities for improvement.

While this uncreative tension is widespread in organizations, it is perhaps most acutely felt in the detailed workings of the relationship between the organization and its customers. It is usually the customer who suffers first. Eventually, the organization that cannot exploit this tension positively suffers also.

At the core of this tension, we find knowledge work in which customer and client interactions (such as complaints, orders, claims, appeals, service requests, incident reports, and investigations) are received, analyzed, and responded to; or, from our new agile perspective they are sensed, prioritized, and acted upon. When this tension occurs in the midst of the case management process, it has the potential to be "creative tension" or "uncreative tension." An agile organization has the capability to make the tension creative and to benefit from it.

This knowledge work is typically both central to an organization's operations, and also, paradoxically, the reason it is unable to operate more dynamically. The knowledge work juxtaposes set procedures (e.g., the this-is-how-we-operate-around-here rules in a customer complaints process) with a seemingly limitless range of potential variations in emerging facts for any particular case. The result is frequently very expensive for organizations to deal with, and for many, it presents an insurmountable challenge.

When a customer complaint, for example, presents a challenge to an organization's set procedures, the result can be an ineffective response that leaves the customer unhappy and frustrated. The organization fails to satisfactorily meet customer demands as a direct result of its inflexibility.

Some inflexibility is deliberate—the result of conscious policy choices by the company. But much, perhaps most, inflexibility is not the result of choice by the organization, rather it is the result of a failure to adopt ways of working that enable the organization to be more responsive. The organization lacks agility.

As if this were not bad enough, there is frequently also a lost opportunity to spot a potential improvement that if implemented would not only make a particular customer happy, but would improve customer service (or case management) more generally. Yet it is rare for an organization to be equipped with case management practices that are capable of helping the organization learn.

Opportunities to improve based on the lessons that emerge from cases occur every day, in every organization, in multiple contexts—customer service, sales, product development, investigations, and many more not limited to "customer-facing" processes. Yet the means to take advantage of this creative tension is lacking or weak in most organizations. The ability to sense, prioritize, and act is low, and as a result, case management is often very poor.

Through agility, knowledge-work corporations can overtake their competitors and public bodies can better serve their citizens by responding more quickly and more appropriately, generating higher customer satisfaction, and being more efficient.

The agile organization is one that, like the excellent basketball team, senses what to do, prioritizes its options, and then acts appropriately, player by player. The organization might be pursuing a new sales opportunity, bringing a new client onboard, responding to a customer complaint, or processing an insurance claim. Whatever the particular situation, organizations that are agile in their knowledge work win more new deals, keep more customers happy, operate less wastefully, and spot more opportunities for improvement.

I hear an objection rising in the minds of the skeptics among you: Surely all the basketball team (or organization) needs to do is prepare a very thorough playbook. The team should figure out all the right plays to make and all the situations that such a play should be used in. The players need to sense the situation, prioritize their options, and make the right play at the time in accordance with the playbook. Once the playbook is finished (correctly), it can be set in stone, right?

Really? What about the competitor? Was there ever a winning team that had the game all figured out ahead of time and didn't have to adapt midgame? I don't think so. Yes, good teams revise their playbook after each game, and this intergame learning is important. But they also, crucially, adapt their strategy in the midst of a game. It is this all-around agility—in the midst of the game, as well as between games—that distinguishes the winners. For the knowledge worker, the playbook, if there is one, is at best a guidebook—the plays are adapted to what is occurring in the midst of the action.

WHAT IS CASE MANAGEMENT?

Knowledge work is common in almost every type of organization. A small selection of examples of knowledge work by organization type is shown in TABLE 11-2.

TABLE 11-2: Knowledge Work by Organization Type

ORGANIZATION TYPE	KNOWLEDGE WORK
Law Enforcement	◆ Firearms licensing
	◆ Investigations
	◆ Forensics management

ORGANIZATION TYPE	KNOWLEDGE WORK
Government	◆ Social welfare benefits applications
	◆ Licensing and permits management.
	◆ Freedom of Information Act requests
	◆ Planning applications
	◆ Industrial health and safety enforcement
	◆ Immigration applications
	◆ Regulatory monitoring
Financial Services	◆ Corporate customer onboarding
	◆ Regulatory compliance management
	◆ Insurance claim processing
	◆ Trade settlement exception management
Telecommunications	◆ Customer provisioning
	◆ Fault reporting and resolution
	◆ Billing issue resolution
	◆ Order processing

There is knowledge work even in something that might seem substantially automated, such as customer provisioning in the telecommunications industry. Have you ever called to find out what happened to that extra broadband line you needed? to query your bill? to ask for digital TV? or to get extra minutes on your kid's cell phone this month?

Some knowledge work, such as investigation work in law enforcement or compliance organizations, is highly unpredictable. While in other knowledge work, such as Freedom of Information Act requests, that unpredictable work is constrained by clear procedures, policies, and regulations to be followed. Knowledge work exists in almost every organization.

Why not take a few minutes and write a list of processes in your organization that are similar in character to the examples above.

Knowledge work always requires some degree of agility. Organizations need to enable their knowledge workers to adapt what they do as they deal with cases: sensing, to understand clearly the circumstances of each case; prioritizing, to ensure that the case management choices fit with organizational objectives and the best means of resolving each case; and acting, so these choices have the right result.

In any of the examples above, the knowledge worker is faced with a wide variety of circumstances that differ on a case-by-case basis. This variation leads to tension between "standard procedures, practices, and policies" and "what needs to be done to resolve this case." This tension will be creative if the organization is agile, uncreative if it is not. Let me be clear—when I use the term "creative," I don't mean to encourage "creative accounting" or any other behavior that is not compliant with law, regulation, good policy, or an organization's agreed goals. By creative tension, I mean tension that leads to beneficial innovation, either in a particular instance of a case (e.g., finding a better way to do the right thing in a benefits claim situation) or in general (e.g., finding a better way to process benefits claims overall). Supporting the beneficial innovation of knowledge workers by improving their ability to sense, prioritize, and act is a good thing! The organization benefits by enabling knowledge workers to be more agile.

Some of you might be thinking that this tension exists only in "nonroutine" cases. But consider a "routine" case where one of your colleagues could decide to do something extra for a client. For example, an insurance company processing a claim might see a significant benefit if it was able to ask the claimant: Why don't I schedule a call with one of our representatives, since we've discussed how your latest insurance claim has highlighted that you really ought to consider increasing your coverage? Even in insurance companies that can do this today, it's likely to have taken a long time for this idea to surface, longer for it to be considered and ratified, and even longer for it to be enacted. For most organizations, this kind of impromptu idea could not emerge and be acted upon quickly. The organization is constrained by inflexible processes, noncollaborative organizations, and other factors that unwittingly conspire to constrain agility and, with it, beneficial innovation.

Throughout this book, the concept of case management is explored and varieties of definition are discussed. In light of the examples and discussion in this chapter, and bearing in mind your organization's case management processes, consider now the following more complex definition of case management:

> Case management is the management of long-lived collaborative processes that require coordination of knowledge, content, correspondence, and resources to achieve an objective or goal. The path of execution cannot be predefined. Human judgment is required in determining how to proceed, and the state of a case can be affected by external events.

Let's dig below the definition and expose some of the common characteristics of all case management processes and how a better case management platform can increase the agility of your organization.

CHARACTERISTICS OF CASE MANAGEMENT

Knowledge work appears to vary substantially across organizations. In practice, however, case-handling practices are usually very similar. Knowledge workers need to manage a complex set of steps from the start of a case through to its completion. This usually involves interaction with others in their organization or external agencies, and it requires the generation of and complex interaction with correspondence, documents, and records. The key characteristics common to most case management processes include the following:

◆ **Goal Driven**—Every case is pursued for a purpose. Without a purpose, the effort would be groundless, directionless, and impossible to deem a success on conclusion.

◆ **Knowledge Intensive**—Typically, processes require the intervention of skilled and knowledgeable personnel. Staff acquire their knowledge through their experience of working on similar cases and through collaboration with more experienced colleagues, becoming thoroughly familiar with the tacit and explicit rules governing how cases should be managed.

◆ **Highly Variable Processes**—While a particular type of case will share a general structure (e.g., handling benefits applications), it is not possible to predict the path that a particular case will take. A case can change in unpredictable, dynamic, and ad hoc ways. Basic procedures may be fixed, but there can be considerable variation in how steps are executed according to circumstances.

◆ **Long Running**—Cases can run for months or years—much longer than the short interaction cycles handled by standard customer relationship management (CRM) systems, for example. Because a case is long running, it changes hands over time, different people work on different aspects, and often, no single individual has a persistent view of the case all the time.

◆ **Information Complexity**—Knowledge work involves the collection and presentation of a diverse set of documents and records. Emails, meeting notes, case documents, and correspondence related to a case must be easily accessible. This can be difficult for knowledge workers to organize and manage efficiently, with the risk that an important record, note, or file will be unavailable, lost, or overlooked when it is needed. Retrieving the correct information required at a particular decision point may depend on the knowledge of the case worker and the effective linking of electronic and physical filing/storage systems.

◆ **Highly Collaborative**—Knowledge workers usually need to coordinate interviews and meetings among interested parties (e.g., the applicant, colleagues, legal representatives). Many cases require a team-based approach, with different specialists working on different aspects of a case or acting as consultants to their colleagues. Team members need to access case information and discuss it. And people outside the organization, such as clients, third-party experts, loosely interested parties, and others must be part of the case community. Increasingly, with the advent of social networking and other community-enabling technologies, the community of parties that a case can engage is expanding.

◆ **Multiple Participants and Fluid Roles**—Many people mistakenly assume that organizations are stable and that people rarely change position or role. Clearly this is untrue—try calling your insurance company today; it is unlikely that you'll be able to speak to the same person you spoke to last time you called, even though you'll be speaking to a person in the same role. Staff members leave or case workers' roles may change in the course of a case. There may be several parties involved directly or indirectly, and they may play different roles in the case at different times.

◆ **Inter-related Cases**—The outcome of separate cases may have an impact on each other. For example, an application for citizenship by an individual may be affected by the success or failure of an application by a spouse or immediate relative. Cases can be explicitly linked, or they may be linked by inference and conducted with this inferred link in mind.

◆ **Juggling Fixed and Flexible Timescales**—While cases may vary in how they are conducted, they may be subject to the same inflexible requirements for case completion such as legislation or service-level agreements (SLAs).

◆ **Sensitivity to External Events**—External events and intervention can change the state of a running case (e.g., a phone call from a lawyer, the unscheduled arrival of compliance documentation, or the enactment of new governing policies while a case is in progress).

◆ **Cross-Organizational Visibility**—It can be difficult for supervisors to monitor progress or for case workers to do so after handing cases to colleagues in other departments or organizations to undertake specific steps. For example, when onboarding a new client, the client onboarding manager may lose sight of the case when it goes to the legal or KYC (know your customer)/compliance department.

◆ **History**—Every action performed, every decision taken, and every piece of correspondence received has to be tracked, not just for audit purposes, but also to provide guidance for future similar cases. Workers need access to this history when making decisions, while auditors and compliance officials need the history to ensure policies are adhered to. The case history is the organization's defense mechanism and a key learning tool.

◆ **Demanding Security Requirements**—Strict control is necessary to protect access to sensitive information. The scope of this security challenge is unusually wide in case management processes, enveloping many pieces of information/data, many documents and other artifacts, a wide range of case participants in multiple roles and organizations, and many related information systems.

◆ **Isolated Pockets of Automation**—Case management is usually only partly automated and there is a disjunction between those pockets of automation. Legacy systems automate slices of the processes, but the end-to-end management of a case still relies heavily on paper documentation, physical folders, and multiple artifacts that are not able to be automated (e.g., original signature copies of legal agreements).

This list of characteristics is not exhaustive, but it captures the essential common aspects of case management work. So, is there today an ACM system that you can buy and deploy that will enable the agile practices that your organization needs?

SUPPORTING ACM WITH TECHNOLOGY—SO FAR

A range of technologies has been deployed with varying degrees of success to support knowledge work. These have been partial successes because the characteristics common to all knowledge work present a considerable challenge to automation.

Let's review some of the barriers that have been particularly challenging to attempts to support knowledge work to date.

◆ The extent to which human judgment is required at various stages is a difficult challenge for traditional automated systems. It is simply not possible to automate all human decision making, hard though many technology vendors may have tried. An ACM system needs to support human decision making, not replace it. But the human decision making at issue is highly complex and wide-ranging, and hence, it is difficult to support. For example, the human decision might be to do something completely new that the organization has never done before, or to act in contravention to normal policy for a perfectly good reason, or to create a new way of working that needs to immediately supersede prior practice.

◆ The "right information, right person, right time" problem is especially challenging in knowledge-work contexts. Perhaps the single biggest cause of case management ineffectiveness is the need to put the case on hold because a case participant cannot access the right information, see the right document, or talk to the right person in a timely fashion.

◆ So many systems, so little communication. A typical knowledge-work scenario (pick any of the examples in TABLE 11-2) transcends multiple organizations and needs to draw on information, documents, and other artifacts from many different information systems. The challenge of bringing all these systems together coherently in the context of managing a case has been too difficult or too expensive for many organizations to address.

Of course these challenges have not deterred the intrepid solution seekers in every organization. They have bought and deployed a great deal of computer hardware and software in their attempts to support case workers.

Various platforms have been proposed for supporting knowledge work, including business process management suites (BPMSs), enterprise content management (ECM) systems, and CRM systems. While these technologies play a role, no one of them alone is sufficient to address the complete requirements.

The ACM platform that successfully supports an organization's needs is a combination of these technologies and of others that support human collaboration (e.g., email, texting, instant messaging, online chat, social networking, etc.), personalization (i.e., allowing individual case workers and other case participants to customize their electronic desktop to meet the needs of their role), etc. A fully effective ACM platform must do all this, or to make the challenge a little simpler, it must at least enable all these technologies to work effectively together in support of the knowledge worker.

CAPABILITIES NEEDED FOR ORGANIZATIONAL AGILITY

> "The trick…is to introduce bits of automation that will fit into the work and do useful things, and then make it possible for people to work with those bits of automation embedded in the systems while leaving them the discretionary space to exercise the kind of judgment they need to exercise to really get the work done."
>
> —Derek Miers
> *Process Innovation and Corporate Agility (2007)*

The five essential capabilities that must be provided by an effective case management platform are (1) goal management, (2) empowerment of case participants, (3) adaptability in execution, (4) effective availability of information, and (5) enablement of continuous improvement.

GOAL MANAGEMENT

◆ The case must be governable by explicit goals, targets, milestones, etc. These will be provided by the organization or the case participants, or they will be required by, for example, company policy, SLAs, or governmental regulation. Even in one-off cases (as distinct from a single instance of case, such as a particular insurance claim), there is a goal and the platform must allow the governance of case progress to be driven by the need to achieve that goal.

◆ While maximum flexibility in the "disposition" of a case (i.e., how it is progressed) must be maintained, this must be done within the discipline of required time, budget, and other constraints.

Empowerment of Case Participants

◆ The primacy of the case must rest with the knowledge workers and case participants. While the ACM platform is active in the case, people are the critical determiners of the outcome.

◆ The case participants must be able to assemble an electronic workspace, similar in concept to the desktop with which software users are now familiar, that suits their needs as a role player in the case management process. Information and data must be organized and presented to all case participants in a useful way to avoid them being overwhelmed or confused and to assist their efficient and effective participation. Such a workspace might provide instant access to a prioritized to-do list, a calendar displaying key case deadlines, a document folder containing all relevant case documents, a buddy list indicating availability and allowing instant contact with people relevant to the case, etc.

◆ The case management process and the progress of each individual case must be visible to all case participants. This visibility must allow participants to understand the case goals/objectives, constraints, roles (and who is acting in the role for each case), deadlines, current status, etc.

◆ Collaboration must be easy, widespread, productive, and appropriately secure. Meetings among parties to the case need to be easily scheduled, coordinated, managed, recorded, archived, retrieved, etc. Case workers and participants need to able to share everything related to a case, including its history, discussions, correspondence, and previous decisions. Correct information must be available to team members at the right time, without losing the context or current state of progress of the case. The platform must know who needs what and when, must not supply irrelevant information, and must not release confidential information to those not authorized to access it.

◆ Participation of people in the case must be intelligently and productively driven. Work must be routed to participants at the time and sequence required to meet the goal of the case work. This requires sophisticated workflow routing and synchronization, ensuring overall milestones are monitored and met, identifying delays, anticipating issues, and escalating where necessary.

ADAPTABILITY IN EXECUTION

◆ The end-to-end activity flow of a case does not have to be fully determined in advance. The case must be allowed to "unfold" or "emerge" over time, either as a variant of standard practice or as a completely new and potentially one-off practice.

◆ As the case emerges, it must be possible at any time to add new tasks and processes, include new participants, change the roles of participants, alter the rules/policies that apply, etc. These changes must be achievable by human intervention and choice. They must also be achievable as a result of state-aware automated intervention. For example, to accelerate the remaining steps of a case management process if the previous steps have taken longer than planned, and the case must nonetheless meet a statutory deadline for completion.

◆ At any time, the case worker must be able to "step back" or "jump forward," to redo previously performed steps, or to skip standard steps that he deems unnecessary in a given case instance.

◆ The state of a particular case may be changed by unpredictable external "out-of-band" events, such as the result of an unexpected phone conversation, and the case must respond appropriately (for example, by bypassing some or all steps that may have been laid out as standard case procedure). Each organization must make its choice about where the "official" state of the case is held. Some will choose to make the ACM platform the "system of record," and indeed, the platform must provide this capability. Others will recognize that the "true life" state of the case may lead the state as recorded in the case platform (i.e., it may take the case management platform time to "catch up" with reality, even though it is treated as the system of record).

◆ The outcome of a case can be affected by progress in other separate but related cases. For example, the granting of a visa to a spouse may trigger automatic approval of a partner's separate visa application.

◆ Predictive analytics must be available to guide case workers and participants to prioritize their actions to achieve the case's goal. These analytics are based on intelligent consideration of historic patterns of case execution performance, case goals, required or expected deadlines and milestones, and on knowledge of the availability of resources, data, documents, etc.

◆ Many cases are, in effect, a combination of predictable case fragments (e.g., commonly used steps in a customer complaint process) and emergent case fragments (e.g., a one-off information demand or unique action required in a given case instance). The case management platform must bridge the gap between predictable and emergent case fragments, reusing elements of predictable processing where an emergent process can or should do so.

EFFECTIVE AVAILABILITY OF INFORMATION

◆ All case documentation, including emails, meeting notes, correspondence, records, etc., must be organized and readily accessible to participants working on the same case. Content and case artifacts may reside on multiple supporting automated and manual systems, including databases, content management systems, electronic record management systems, and offsite, secure physical storage facilities.

◆ Complex case information should be structured and presented to case workers simply, intuitively, and in a context-sensitive manner.

◆ Multiple automated information sources must be orchestrated quickly to provide fast access to the relevant information required in each case context.

◆ Security controls must allow access to case information and documents by a wide range of case participants in multiple roles and organizations, while also enforcing necessary restrictions on visibility in compliance to organizational policy, legal requirement, etc.

◆ Case history, audit trails, and associated records must be retained for specific periods, if required by legislation or organizational policy, and made readily available when needed.

ENABLEMENT OF CONTINUOUS IMPROVEMENT

◆ Case participants must be able to take part not only in the execution of cases (on a case-by-case basis), but also in the proposal, discussion, and decision making of ideas that improve case management effectiveness overall.

◆ An intuitive, graphical modeling environment should be available to allow case participants to understand the current design of the case management process and to engage in its redesign and optimization. The design should include definition of tasks, roles, goals, SLAs, milestones, data and document requirements, policies and rules, etc. The modeling environment should allow participants to "kick the tires" on new ideas, conduct "what-if" analyses on improvement ideas, and compare the performance of multiple versions (including several "old," the current "as-is," and several "to-be" versions) of a case management process.

◆ Case execution data must be captured in detail on a case-by-case basis and tools for historical and real-time analysis of that data must be available. This data provides an evidential basis for assessing performance against goals, identifying bottlenecks, and driving continuous innovation. This case execution data must include details such as who did what when, how long each task took, which data and documents were viewed/changed in that task, how the case status varied over time, which case milestones were met and when, etc.

◆ Learning from experience must be supported. Since similar problems often have similar solutions, the platform must allow case workers to process new cases based on the solutions of similar past cases. Four steps in this case-based reasoning approach must be supported: (1) look at a given case and search for previous cases it might match; (2) consider how the solution to the previous cases could be applied to the current case; (3) test the solution on the existing case and revise it if necessary; and (4) record the new case and the solution that eventually worked, for future reference.

Some of the capabilities just discussed are available today, usually in separate technologies. However, the complete ACM platform is now beginning to emerge as a commercially available suite.

ACM Platforms Support Greater Agility

We began with a discussion of the agility imperative—the urgent need to increase every organization's ability to sense, prioritize, and act. We drew a contrast between the inertia that impairs so many organizations, and the agility that enables a top basketball team to win the NBA title.

We have seen in this book that much of the day-to-day operation of organizations of all types involves knowledge work. Whether the case in question was a social security claim, the onboarding of a new customer, the pursuit of litigation proceedings, or the arbitration of a customer complaint, the approach to dealing with cases shared many common characteristics.

At the heart of the difficult challenges that case management must overcome, we identified the need for agility in managing individual cases, and the need for continuous improvement in case management approaches. And we have described at a first level of detail the five critical capabilities of an ACM platform that can support the effective practices of an agile organization.

An agile organization is one that when managing cases, like the excellent basketball team, senses what to do, prioritizes among options, and then acts appropriately, person by person. Organizations that increase their agility by embracing an ACM platform will win more new deals, keep more customers happy, operate less wastefully, and capitalize better on opportunities for improvement.

CHAPTER 12

THE NEXT EVOLUTION OF CONTINUOUS IMPROVEMENT

CAFFREY LEE AND JULIE MILLER

You've outsourced down to the core, now what? This chapter discusses how some organizations will improve business processes quantitatively, while others will make qualitative improvements with dramatically different results. A detailed example of how a new product is developed shows that this kind of work is hard to predict. Such work can be supported through the use of regular email, but the advantage of using adaptive case management is that it makes what is happening visible to everyone, allows team members to coordinate their work better, and helps new members of the team come up to speed quickly.

Businesses like to measure themselves against quantitative measures, benchmarking performance against the same metrics as others in their industry—metrics such as the following:

◆ Reducing Days Sales Outstanding in their receivables processes.

◆ Leveraging discount opportunities in their payable processes.

◆ Increasing on-time deliveries in their shipping processes.

◆ Reducing defects to improve quality in their manufacturing processes.

These tactical operational metrics are easy to formulate, well-understood, and measurable. And they don't deviate much from the "norm," meaning that the impact of failure is mitigated but so too is the impact of success. Achieving a 5% reduction in Days Sales Outstanding minimally benefits overall cash flow, but it won't revolutionize the way you do business. Compare this with failure to achieve a critical merger opportunity, for example, or the success of being first to market with an innovative product. Organizations on the cutting edge—the ones that continuously outperform—don't spend all of their energy squeezing water from a cactus. Best of breed organizations simultaneously seek new ways to make it rain. While other organizations are competing to outsource or automate yet another noncore, tactical function, goal-oriented organizations are investing in the productivity of their most strategic and valuable asset: their knowledge teams. This is the difference between "quantity-focused" and "quality-focused" organizations.

Quantity-focused organizations remain fixated on tweaking the results of already well-defined processes and procedures: procure to pay, order to cash, expense approval, time tracking and services billing, employee onboarding, and so on. These processes are mature; often highly automated within enterprise resource planning (ERP), customer relationship management (CRM), supply chain management (SCM), and product lifecycle management (PLM) systems; and repeatable and executable within predictable deviations from expected outcomes. Quantity-focused organizations peer into the exceptions to these processes looking for incremental improvement opportunities. But incremental improvements tend to deliver only incremental results. Even as they jump on the outsourcing bandwagon to reduce costs, quantity-focused organizations are merely handing off an already predictable process to a similarly-skilled team that will repeat the process cheaper. Mind you, the results—the cost savings—may be significant, but the way business is conducted remains the same.

Quality-focused organizations, by contrast, creatively seek new ways to better execute strategic processes that have a high impact on the business, such as new product development, business buyout reviews, budgetary projects, M&A due diligence, and so forth. They are focused on the quality of such processes— how the goals are achieved—rather than on merely the results of operational processes. Strategic processes may be understood and modeled at a high level, but underlying them is a complex orchestration of research, analysis, applied knowledge, and decision-making tasks conducted by highly skilled, educated workers. Collaboration and individual expertise are of greater importance than task completion and role assignment; as such, these processes can be only minimally automated, if at all. The quality of the outcome is dependent upon the expertise, culture, and dynamics of the process participants.

Quantity-focused operational processes, whether automated or manual, typically involve a standard set of forms and well-documented procedures. Work moves from one participant to the next; exceptions are handled by a manager one level up. With throughput and cycle time as indicators of performance, the processes are designed to minimize the need for participant interaction.

Quality-focused processes, on the other hand, rely on the ad hoc collaboration of the "best minds." Work doesn't move forward until discussions have occurred, meetings have been held, brainstorming has been conducted, project plans created, and so forth. These are collaborative activities with nonstandardized outputs: spreadsheets, whiteboard printouts, emails, meeting minutes, and so forth. Progress is tracked at key milestones, but there is very little insight into the activities or tasks that occur daily to reach those milestones. These are your best and brightest people; your most expensive resources. You trust their judgment and their work ethic. They continuously deliver on time and within budget, and the impact of their work is felt throughout the organization.

So as long as your best and brightest people achieve their goals (e.g., on-time delivery of product to market, execution of the acquisition, and winning proposals), the results justify any means that they might employ, right? A quality-focused organization would counter this question with another: how can we challenge and enable our best and brightest assets to improve the way they work to achieve even greater results?

Today, high-impact strategic processes are neither transparent nor predictable. Deliverables are nonstandardized. The processes occur differently every time, with expertise engaged nonuniformly and uniquely to fit the nuances of each process instance. We might call them "emergent" processes in comparison with "structured" processes where tasks move forward in a predictable, well-defined manner.

Quantity-focused managers will accept unpredictability in the execution of processes—they don't care about how predictable, repeatable, or optimizable the activities are—so long as the end results are favorably predictable (i.e., always end up on time and within budget).

Quality-focused managers are uncomfortable with randomness and lack of predictability, regardless of the results. Finding such an environment unacceptable, they seek to empower their highly skilled knowledge workers to analyze the way they are working to discover predictable patterns of interaction that can be formalized, optimized, standardized, and repeated. By making core-function processes leaner and more efficient, they are able to execute them more often. The results of high-impact processes executing more often and with greater predictability are multiplied exponentially in comparison with incremental improvement of operational processes.

Quality-focused organizations are exemplifying the next evolution in process optimization and competitive differentiation. While they may continue to drive incremental improvements through automation and outsourcing of low-skilled jobs, they are also capitalizing on more lucrative efficiency improvements from their high-value teams and high-value work.

The remainder of this chapter will describe the way process optimization efforts can be shifted toward the knowledge worker and the improvement of emergent processes. The interactive manner in which knowledge workers collaborate to conduct business can be captured, measured, analyzed, improved, and optimized using the latest advancements in dynamic business process management software (BPMS) capabilities.

KNOWLEDGE WORK IN NEW PRODUCT DEVELOPMENT

Let's examine just how quickly the web of people involved in a high-value process can extend outward across departments and even corporate boundaries in unstructured and informal ways. We'll use just one phase of an overall product development process to illustrate. In our example, it's been decided that "our product offering needs to include X." We now need to determine if we're going to build X in-house or buy the functionality from an external source. The high-level process flow might look something like the following and as depicted in FIGURE 12-1.

◆ **Key Milestone 1**—Assess build/buy options. If buy, then...

◆ **Key Milestone 2**—Engineering integration plan formulated.

◆ **Key Milestone 3**—Legal contracts finalized.

◆ **Key Milestone 4**—Pricing and packaging models defined and systems updated.

◆ **Key Milestone 5**—Billing system configured to pay vendor royalties.

◆ **Key Milestone 6**—Series of communication and training sessions throughout the organization.

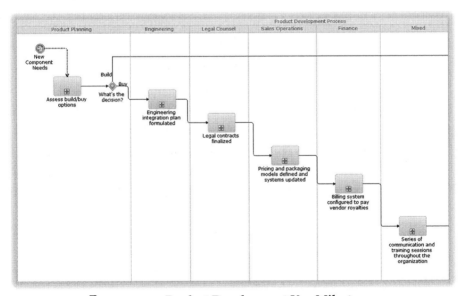

FIGURE 12-1: Product Development Key Milestones

From this list of key milestones, one can get a sense of the key coordinators accountable at each milestone and maybe even obtain some appreciation for the relative time it will take to move the process from milestone to milestone.

For sure, we know that this process will take months to execute, but we can't predict the cost and we have no visibility into the actual work being conducted.

Let's take a closer look at Key Milestone 1 to map out retrospectively the actual interactions of the people involved in the build-versus-buy assessment. In general, at each interaction point, information is repeated to new participants, requests must be worked into planned schedules, nonstakeholders must be enticed to shuffle their priorities to accommodate unexpected participation, and a host of other latencies accumulate. Throughout the network of interaction, documents are exchanged, new information is discovered and relayed, and a collection of artifacts accumulate.

1. **Key Milestone 1**—Assess build/buy options (R&D, Product Management, and Finance).

   A. R&D to estimate build time and cost.

      (i) Consultations with in-house engineers, each of whom is assigned research tasks to work into existing development activities.

         (a) Schedules for current projects reconfigured by forty man-hours to accommodate research tasks.

         (b) Research reports written and emailed to the R&D Manager.

      (ii) Consultation call with an engineer who left the company with discreet knowledge of a key system that will be impacted. He was on a week-long vacation, delaying the information exchange.

         (a) The R&D Manager sends an email to the engineers with additional information he acquired from the conversation. The email references a few documents posted in a shared folder location.

         (b) The former employee sends a few documents related to the system (architectural diagrams and an old development specification) to the R&D Manager, who forwards them to his team.

      (iii) Brief meeting with the quality team to review their schedule. They already have a backlog of projects and are understaffed following the departure of two interns and a full-time employee.

    (a) Consultation calls with a couple of QA contractors to determine availability and pricing.

    (b) Contractors send emails to the R&D Manager with quote attachments, which he forwards to the QA Manager.

B. Product Management to determine OEM candidate from a pool of at least three vendors.

  (i) Consultation call with industry analyst for vendor recommendations.

    (a) Analyst follows up call with an email and recommends several reports the Product Manager should consider purchasing.

    (b) The Product Manager initiates a purchasing process to procure the reports, each costing in excess of $1,000.

    (c) The Product Manager receives a login and downloads the reports to her laptop.

  (ii) Consultation calls with three vendors, requiring a series of phone-tag sessions before live conversation occurs. Follow-up emails occur with each party and product demonstrations scheduled.

  (iii) Three web conferences to view product demonstrations. Scheduling conflicts make a six-hour activity take three working weeks.

    (a) Engineers are invited to each meeting, requiring rounds of schedule refactoring; which impacts current projects.

    (b) Presentations are emailed, along with other supporting documentation, unique to each vendor.

  (iv) Lunch meeting with a friend at another company who's currently using one vendor's products. Discussions about best practices occur but are never documented.

  (v) Another meeting with a former colleague who replaced one of the vendor's products with another vendor on the OEM list. Discussions about lessons learned occur but are never documented.

C. Finance to assess budget and assist with project costing.

  (i) Accounting department runs a budget report for each of the cost centers involved. This report was delayed a week because of month-end closings and a planned IT system upgrade.

(ii) Report is printed and given to a financial analyst in hard-copy format.

(iii) Analyst determines the total pool of money available and sends an instant chat message to the Product Manager with the rolled-up figure.

D. R&D, Product Management, and Finance reconvene to discuss options, budgets, cost and time estimates, and so forth. Output from Key Milestone 1 defines the remaining process milestones. In this case, the output of Key Milestone 1 is the decision to embed another vendor's product.

Just like Key Milestone 1, within each of the follow-on milestones is another network of players, both internal and external to the organization, interacting, exchanging documents, sharing information, and collaborating toward the common goal of delivering X product functionality to market. (See FIGURE 12-2.)

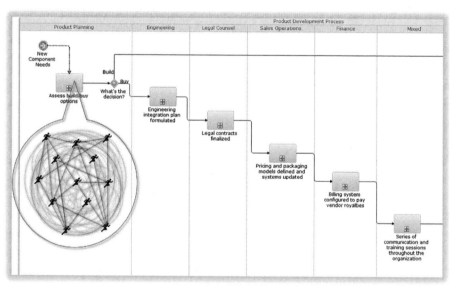

FIGURE 12-2: Milestones and Chaos

Each time the build/buy assessment portion of the entire product development process is executed, there is a similar pattern of structured and unstructured interaction, a similar exchange of documents and information, and the same types of latencies introduced. Naturally, the details of the process will change— for example, the vendors and technology being assessed will be different. But whoever occupies the Product Manager role, as just one example, during the next execution of the process will still likely reach out to an analyst, discuss with friends, coordinate product demonstrations, and so forth. (See Figure 12-3.)

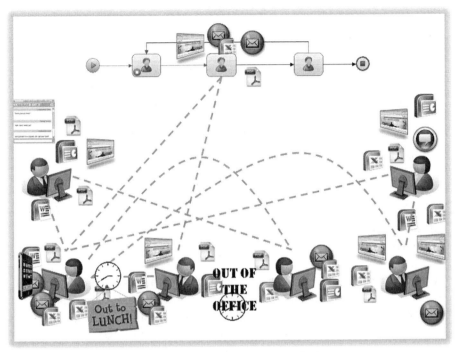

Figure 12-3: Chaotic Collaboration

Rarely do the participants in high-value, emergent processes take a step back to review how the process might be improved next time. For example, the Product Manager has a pattern of speaking separately with each vendor to discuss the business opportunity and then scheduling a live web demonstration with each vendor and inviting several costly engineers, who are already tasked on other projects, to be present through these three sessions. If she were to analyze her process from an objective, macroscopic point of view, perhaps she might improve the process next time by holding a single phone conference with all vendors during which she discusses the opportunity and then makes a request that each vendor record a demonstration showing how they'd solve the problems discussed. The recordings could be posted and available for the Product Manager and the engineers to review when convenient. Because the process she performs is not structured or formalized, it's not subject to review. So long as the end result is favorable (new functionality is delivered to market on time and within budget), she is allowed to continue performing an inefficient process again and again.

A quality-focused organization would not be satisfied with merely the results of a high-value process. Such an organization recognizes that understanding how well the process executes and taking steps to structure and optimize that process will produce substantial long-term gains for the organization. Remember, the resources involved in these processes are your most expensive, and as such, they should be optimized.

Breakdowns in emergent processes are often the sum of minor inefficiencies that accumulate throughout the course of the process. In quantity-focused environments, even when an emergent process does not produce a favorable outcome, there is typically little effort to determine the root cause. Because there is little insight into the activities that occurred, it's difficult to determine exactly where the process broke down or whose fault it was. A likely response to a process failure having a high impact on the business is to replace the process participants next time. The organization then continues full-speed ahead to the next project, where the same inefficient process patterns will repeat with a different cast of participants.

As the participants in the process change due to staff replacements, attrition, promotional advancements, and so forth, the inefficiencies multiply as the new entrants come into a process with little context. They'll execute a now-familiar pattern of events often replicating work previously done because they enter the process with no history to draw upon.

Consider, for example, the increased inefficiencies that occur when the Product Manager leaves the company during the process in course. She'll leave with her own knowledge of best practices and lessons learned from her associates, as well as the budgetary numbers for the project. She may take with her the analyst-recommended reports that cost the company several thousands of dollars. When the new Product Manager enters the process, he'll likely repeat a similar pattern of events that have already occurred. He'll want to know the budget numbers, so he'll contact the Finance team. He'll want some insight regarding the chosen vendor, so he'll contact the analyst. He may re-order the reports that walked out the door. He may also consult with friends or former colleagues. There is a time and cost associated with the duplication of these activities that is rarely quantified.

Without context—some insight into what's been done in the past—emergent processes are doomed to a repetitive cycle of inefficiency wherein technology acts as an inhibitor rather than an accelerator. Emails, instant messages, spreadsheets, reports, and documents are generated and scattered throughout personal and corporate storage facilities and beyond corporate boundaries through email and the Internet. When discovered, they lack the context of where, when, why, and how they are relevant. The artifacts of your most expensive knowledge workers—in whom an organization may have invested hundreds of thousands of dollars during their tenure—morph into nothing more useful than litter upon their departure. The next time the process executes, new emails inquiring about previously discussed information will be generated; instant messages asking already-asked questions will be sent; reports already generated will be run again. These are your best, brightest, most expensive assets (i.e., people and technology) allowed to continue operating far from peak levels of performance. Quality-focused organizations recognize the opportunities that lie within this complex web of interactions and have begun utilizing technology—adaptive case management (ACM) enabling tools—to enable continuous improvement.

ADAPTIVE CASE MANAGEMENT FOR CONTINUOUS IMPROVEMENT

Imagine the experience of a new process participant who has full access to the context of a process in-progress, as well as insight into how the process has occurred in the past. Let's continue using our Product Manager example. It's her first day and she logs in to a system through which she can view all of the interactions that have occurred during this process instance. She can see who the former Product Manager contacted and can review the associated documentation. She can quickly see interaction patterns among various teams and bring herself up to speed on decisions made and the rationale behind them. Within just a matter of minutes or a few hours spent navigating through the history of a business process, she can bring herself up to speed and avoid a lot of the latencies and duplication that occur when a new participant enters a process in motion.

From an executive viewpoint, ACM provides insight into knowledge-worker activities that were formerly a "black box." Managers can see the interactions occurring between people, measure the time and cost of various milestones, maintain control of the documents created within the context of a process, and begin to analyze the process for optimization opportunities.

This is the promise of ACM: the ability to dynamically "spawn" and document ad hoc subprocesses from a high-level definition, recording a macrolevel view of the complex web of interactions that occur and artifacts generated and shared. ACM offers its users the ability to do the following:

◆ Bring people into a process as needed.

◆ Visualize those ad hoc steps that have already occurred and are occurring within in a nonformalized, emergent process.

◆ View the interactions of the participants within that process, including those external to the organization.

◆ Govern and maintain ownership of the documentation generated by knowledge workers.

◆ Gain context regarding the electronic documents generated to support the process.

◆ Analyze completed processes to determine cost, time, and potential areas of improvement.

◆ Copy and reuse the process to develop best practices.

Unstructured processes cannot be entirely modeled in advance because some parts of them are unpredictable. Key milestones can be defined, but the steps occurring within them are ad hoc, unplanned, and a natural progression of the creative process. Let's return to our product development process as an example. Within the build/buy assessment, we know that at least three people are involved: someone from R&D, Product Management, and Finance. What we don't know is how those people will interact with others to achieve their goal.

ACM capabilities allow a participant to spawn a new process and include people as needed. These tasks do not have to be modeled in advance or assigned participants prior to their execution. Where these collaboration activities occur today in an ad hoc manner using various technologies (typically through email, instant messages, and voice messages) isolated from the original context, ACM offers a framework to initiate and record these activities in a visually rich, interactive format that lends itself well to analysis (see FIGURE 12-4).

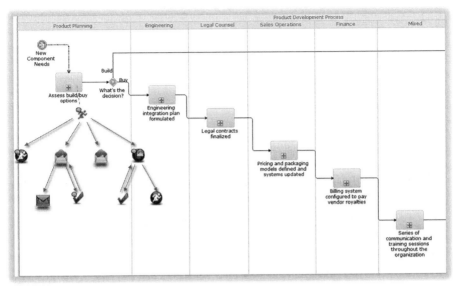

FIGURE 12-4: Dynamic Construction of Interaction Tree

The ad hoc interactions that occur may surprise a nonparticipatory observer. Take the step where the R&D person contacts a former employee outside the company. This person controls valuable information about a particular system; information that is not available within the walls of the company. Each time this person is contacted, he is provided with confidential information about future development plans. As he fits these (for him) low-priority requests for information into his schedule, he introduces latencies into the process. Finally, risk enters the process as he sends confidential architectural and system documents via open information systems (e.g., email). In the normal execution of this interaction, there is no corporate oversight of this collaboration activity, subjecting the organization to repeated latencies and an unacceptable level of risk.

ACM technology provides a framework through which the process activities are modeled as they occur. When a process is executed within the confines of this framework, one can see who is involved, how they were involved, why they were involved, and when they were involved. Furthermore, the documents exchanged during collaboration are accessible from within the system and in their proper context. Chaos is tamed and risk is managed.

Once recorded, these dynamically generated processes can be referenced by new process participants attempting to assimilate smoothly into a process, or they can be reviewed later to analyze the performance of the process measuring the following:

◆ Duration of tasks and overall process.

◆ Cost incurred based on who's involved and duration of participation.

◆ Team dynamics, particularly interactions occurring externally.

Through this analysis, organizations may likewise uncover training needs or areas of risk that need to be controlled. There may even be areas where business activity monitoring could reduce knowledge-gathering tasks by proactively delivering certain information to participants. Recorded processes can be optimized, copied, and then pasted into new processes, ensuring that the next time these activities occur, they execute faster or at less cost than before. (See FIGURE 12-5.)

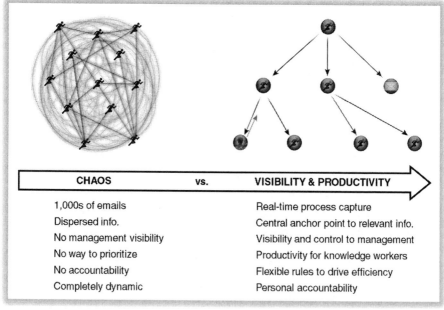

CHAOS	vs.	VISIBILITY & PRODUCTIVITY
1,000s of emails		Real-time process capture
Dispersed info.		Central anchor point to relevant info.
No management visibility		Visibility and control to management
No way to prioritize		Productivity for knowledge workers
No accountability		Flexible rules to drive efficiency
Completely dynamic		Personal accountability

FIGURE 12-5: Convert Noise into Value

ACM enabling technologies offer an exciting frontier upon which competitive differentiation can occur, enabling an organization to extend its process-optimization initiatives beyond tactical operations to include strategic processes. The impact of lean, high-value processes executing more often and with greater predictability are multiplied exponentially in comparison with incremental improvement of operational processes. Furthermore, ACM enables organizations to empower highly skilled, expensive knowledge workers with tools to objectively assess and measure how they conduct work. Through these tools, team dynamics can be explored to discover predictable patterns of interaction that can be formalized, optimized, standardized, and repeated as best practices that can be governed.

Quality-focused organizations are exemplifying the next evolution in process optimization and competitive differentiation (see FIGURE 12-6). While they may continue to drive incremental improvements through automation and outsourcing of low-skilled jobs, they are also leveraging ACM with increasing frequency to capitalize on more lucrative efficiency improvements within their high-value teams and strategic processes.

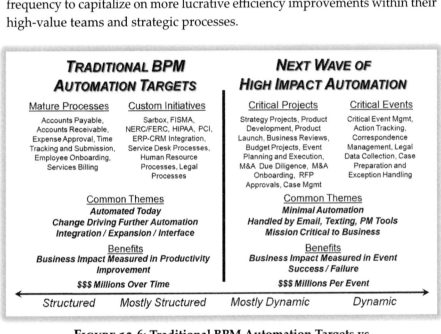

FIGURE 12-6: Traditional BPM Automation Targets vs.
Next Wave of High-Impact Automation

Chapter 13

Historical Perspective

Keith D. Swenson

This chapter presents a brief summary of the technical trends of organization support technology from the 1970s to today. While not a requirement for understanding adaptive case management (ACM), this summary is useful for those in the field to see how the other technologies fit into and ultimately helped the development of ACM. A mapping of terms used in various trends is provided to clarify how those trends fit into the status quo.

It is not necessary to read this chapter to understand the nature of adaptive case management (ACM)—where the ideas came from and where ACM fits relative to other process technologies that exist—but both those who have been involved in the field for a while and those new to the field should find this discussion interesting and useful.

RESEARCH IN THE EARLY YEARS

Efforts to make workers and organizations more effective through IT began in the late 1970s. Until that time, the information communication potential of information systems had not been readily recognized. Computers were highly specialized machines tended to by a cadre of trained specialists in white lab coats. Computer time cost thousands of dollars per second. A large company might have a single computer and used it to make business-related runs of programs to produce reports. The idea to use a computer to coordinate the tasks of everyday workers was simply inconceivable.

In the late 1970s, there was interest in a field called office automation (OA). Email was a technology largely unknown to most people. The first email message was sent in 1969. Doug Englebart was demonstrating his experimental collaboration system, Augment, in 1968. Still, by 1979, the only people with regular access to an email system were researchers in computer science departments. Copy machines were expensive. Word processors were rare. At that time, important letters were typed, reviewed, marked up, and retyped multiple times before sending. Those researchers, however, started to wonder if offices could be entirely automated, essentially removing the drudgery from daily tasks.

Some of the earliest published work in the area of business process was that of Michael Zisman at the Wharton Business School, University of Pennsylvania, in his 1977 doctoral thesis called "Representation, Specification, and Automation of Office Procedures." His system for computerization of office procedures (SCOOP) offered a user access to email, a filing system, a meeting scheduler, and a document generator. It offered computer representations of business processes (called "office procedures"), and it maintained data structures to support running instances of processes. These early systems were clumsy by today's usability standards: they required the user to be quite adept at using a command-line interface. The results of this research formed the foundations of the systems we use today.

Another notable system in around 1979 was Clarence (Skip) Ellis' OfficeTalk D system, an experimental office information system developed at Xerox PARC, which used a forms-based analogy to structure business processes. Xerox's advanced environment could represent a process graphically because of their graphical user interface, something not available to general business users until well after the launch of the Macintosh in 1984.

THE FIRST TREND: EMAIL

These early research systems were anticipating a day when LANs would connect the desktop computers that were starting to be used in offices. The early versions of email became available to business users in the 1980s but usage was limited: LANs were rarely connected to every computer in the office and not all office workers had a computer to work with. Distribution of email between offices was a haphazard affair requiring nonstandard email addresses that included a "path" that described how to get from one system to another. As primitive as it was, email represented the first of five major trends in supporting business work. Email had the capability to replace the paper "memo," and it essentially had eliminated paper memos by the late 1990s, when a typical office worker could be assumed to have access to a computer for email use.

Email and document-sharing technologies do not really represent automation of a process. Instead, they can be considered communications tools. Since a work process involves multiple people, communications is a key ingredient, but it is not sufficient to call this automation. Instead, the work process can be implemented manually. Each participant in the process still has to know what to do, when to do it, and who to forward it to next. Often, there is a high overhead, with multiple back and forth exchanges in some cases, and multiple people being copied on messages just so they can manually track the progress. It has been the focus of the following trends to eliminate this waste.

Today, there are many other ways to communicate and share information between people: instant messaging, texting, bulletin boards, forums, social networking software such as Facebook and Twitter, and information-sharing systems such as blogs and wikis, to name a few. All of these are included in the same trend with email because they allow ad hoc communication without an explicit representation of the process. In cases where the process is unpredictable or unknown, this sort of simple ad hoc communication remains the technology that people use to get the job done.

THE SECOND TREND: WORKFLOW

The mid-1980s brought the first commercial workflow systems such as Action Technologies' Coordinator, Staffware, FileNet, ViewStar, Wang, and Xerox InConcert. These early systems often included their own email or message capability within them because there was no common way to connect between email systems. Since the World Wide Web (WWW) browsers did not exist, each such system had to offer some sort of custom client installed on a user's computer to interact with the process itself.

The term "workflow" came to refer to a number of different approaches to automating office work. Some were essentially smart documents that knew how to forward themselves by email to the next person in the chain. Others, such as Fujitsu's TeamWARE Flow, were centralized transactional systems that offered shared processes to any number of participants simultaneously. Still others were simply extensions to programming languages to allow a programmer to easily design workflow applications. The variety of different approaches reflects how unclear it was at that time as to the proper way to represent and execute business processes (see FIGURE 13-1). The workflow wave represents the second major trend in automation of office procedures. Not all approaches were found to be actually useful in real-world situations, and those approaches started to disappear from the market by the late 1990s. This had the effect of focusing products that call themselves "workflow" on what we know it to be today: being useful somewhere in the middle between entirely predictable processes and unpredictable work (which is still handled using email).

The Workflow Management Coalition (WfMC) was founded in 1993 to educate the market about this emerging technology and to help develop standards that would allow such systems to exchange process information. The Workflow Reference Model was introduced in 1995 which defined the five key types of interconnections that you could expect a process system to need. Standards in these five main areas would allow vendors to make products that would work together. The WfMC has succeeded in developing, or working together with other organizations to develop, and gaining adoption of a number of important standards including XPDL, BPMN (business process modeling notation), Wf-XML (an XML-based protocol for runtime integration of process engines), BPAF (business process analytics format), and most recently, WorkCast Protocol.

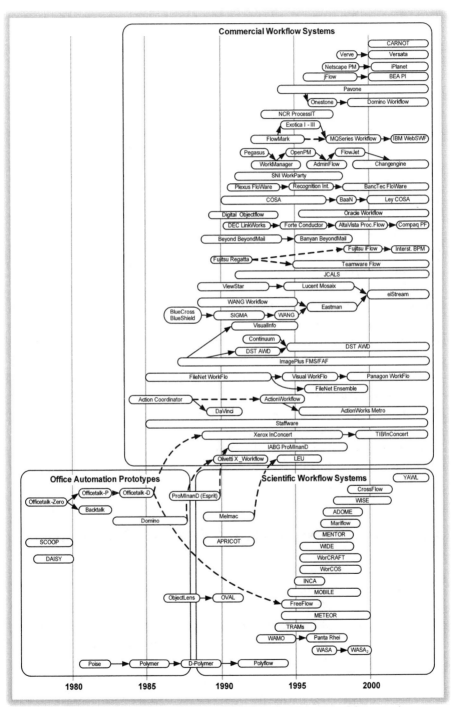

FIGURE 13-1: Historical Workflow Products (zur Muehlen 2004)

The Third Trend: Straight-Through Processing

The late 1990s saw networks and the number of business systems increase dramatically. Instead of a single mainframe with all of the software on it, an IT department might have many servers, each loaded with different specialized software for different particular functions. One challenge was to reduce the tedious job of moving data between systems to accomplish a complete job. This area of expertise was known as enterprise application integration (EAI) in some parts of the industry and straight-through processing (STP) in other parts. This was the third trend in the automation of office procedures, and it was focused on rigorous system-to-system processes.

The end of the 1990s brought widespread experience with the WWW and one critical design principle. The WWW demonstrated that it is far easier to move the information that you need on demand than it is to store information at all the places that you are likely to need it. Information became location independent: you could be anywhere in the world and access information from anyplace else. Software is not so easy to move—there are difficulties in installing, configuring, and maintaining software. Since it does not matter where the information is located, then it becomes possible to install software in a single place and use it to process information from anywhere. This was the origin of service-oriented architecture (SOA), which is simply a way of thinking about software as a resource (service) that can be used remotely when needed and designing systems to leverage this instead of requiring software to be installed in many locations. Products that appear in this space are notably from IBM with their FlowMark server, Microsoft, and integration companies like TIBCO.

The Fourth Trend: Business Process Management

By 2000, the experience with representing and executing process was starting to be widespread, and companies that had adopted the approach were starting to see a secondary effect. The business itself was changing to meet the new demands of their particular marketplace, and this required the ongoing maintenance of the business process itself. The idea that you would design and implement a process once and for all was found to be naive. The world is changing, companies are constantly changing, and you need to put in place a practice of managing your business processes over the long term. Thus, BPM became a new trend that combined several functions to help in the design, implementation, monitoring, analysis, and optimization of business processes in a continuing cycle of process improvement.

Like workflow, the term "BPM" was initially used to mean a wide variety of different approaches to this task. Some products allowed for simplified, easy-to-use modeling tools for business users to be directly involved in the drawing of human processes. Others focused exclusively on SOA and the invocation of what became known as web services. By 2005, the term became associated with business process execution language (BPEL), which is also widely misunderstood. Eventually, a consensus emerged that BPEL is useful for web-service orchestration, and for the most part, BPM has come to mean "what BPEL does." BPEL4People is an attempt to stretch the coverage upward into less predictable realms, but in general, BPM as a category has converged to mean something that is more flexible than STP and not quite as loose as document-routing-style workflow.

If you plot these trends out and use the value of predictability for the work being performed as the vertical dimension, they can be depicted as shown in FIGURE 13-2.

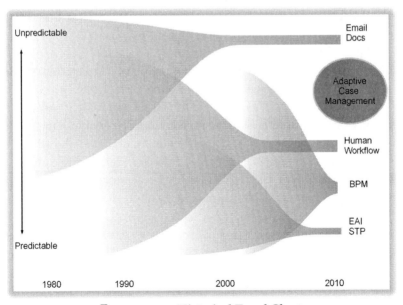

FIGURE 13-2: Historical Trend Chart

In the 1980s, email and ad hoc information sharing was the only technology to support any kind of process. As workflow appeared in the 1990s, it displaced some of what had been done with email before, in order to pick up some of the more predictable processes. By 2000, highly predictable server-to-server processes went to STP technology, while workflow remained dominant in the middle range with human processes that required flexibility. Email has not disappeared and remains the only solution for unpredictable processes. The middle of the decade was dominated by discussions of BPM, which many assumed might pick up the full spectrum from highly predictable processes to completely unstructured processes, but by the end of the decade, we see that BPM has become something between human workflow and STP.

THE FIFTH TREND: ADAPTIVE CASE MANAGEMENT

ACM becomes the fifth in a succession of trends for the support of business processes. It fills a gap in the spectrum from predictable to unpredictable processes with a fundamentally different approach from previous process-technology trends.

FIGURE 13-2 shows why there is interest in ACM at this time, and why it is so important. It makes sense that inventions of new technology focus on predictable processes first. A predictable process is repeatable, and thus, a single definition can be used many times. Just like mass production of physical goods makes it worth investing in a factory, if it takes a lot of effort to define a process, then that effort can be paid back through the use of the process definition many times over. Well-defined, predictable processes were the focus of early process technology. In fact, it was widely assumed that most processes would ultimately be predictable. The goal was the complete automation of the office and the complete elimination of all the ad hoc style email interactions. Experience shows that processes are far more complex than anyone had previously suspected and many processes are emergent, making them essentially unpredictable. The challenge now is to better handle the less predictable processes.

FIGURE 13-2 is not meant to imply that a given product would be constrained to one of these categories. The more advanced products will cover more than one category. In recent years, we have seen product expand steadily from the very predictable, to greater and greater flexibility in being able to handle less predictable processes. Also, we have seen email and other ad hoc sharing approaches get a better capability to handle simple processes. Thus the gap has been encroached from both directions, but it is important to note that the authors do not expect current process technology to expand and cover this area.

A fundamentally different approach is needed for unpredictable processes. At the top end of the spectrum, the unpredictable end, is knowledge work as described elsewhere in this book. At the low end of the spectrum, the predictable and repeatable end, is routine work. When the process is predictable, then the process itself can serve as the central theme around which everything is organized. Thus applying for a bank account can be a process that is fairly fixed, and the data is brought to and retrieved from the process. When the process is unpredictable, then the dominant organizing theme must be based on the case information alone. Thus, a criminal prosecution may go through many legal processes, but it is the crime and the information about the crime that is the focal point for organizing the work. A patient may be admitted to a hospital for care, and it is the patient record, not the procedures being done, that remains the persistent handle to the case.

The differences between these approaches may seem subtle, but the organizing principle of a system has a profound effect on the system as a whole, and how it is used. FIGURE 13-3 depicts the organization of a BPM system (BPMS) on the left and an ACM system on the right.

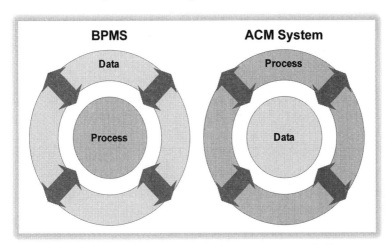

FIGURE 13-3: Organization of a BPM System (left) and an ACM System (right)

Both approaches involve process and both involve information, but the way they approach the solution is different. In the BPMS, the process is the central theme, which accesses data from various places and sends data to various destinations, but the process remains the persistent aspect. In the ACM system, the case data is known first, and it remains persistent along with information that is collected over the life of the case. In an ACM system, processes are brought into the case to handle work as needed.

Epilogue

Now we arrive at the end of our journey. If we look back down the trail that we came along, we see that we have covered a lot of ground. Here is a quick recap:

◆ **Keith** examines the nature of knowledge work through the following questions: what is it? how is it special? and why is this important?

◆ **Jacob** questions the unquestionable: can work be modeled in all cases? and what can we do when it can't be modeled ahead of time?

◆ **Tom** shows how the shifting patterns of knowledge work never stop changing. Using an example from the insurance industry, he shows that agility is needed for any organization to keep up with the changing knowledge work.

◆ **John** presents an overview of case management as it has been in recent years and shows how U.S. courts need something more than what is currently available.

◆ **Max** introduces and outlines the elements of ACM as something that builds on case management but offers new capabilities borrowed from the business process management (BPM), content management, and business analytics spaces.

◆ **Dana** points out the first of two important differences between an ACM approach and a BPM approach: an ACM approach uses a data model as the organizing scheme, while a BPM approach uses the process itself.

◆ **Dana and Keith** point out the second of two important differences between an ACM approach and a BPM approach: ACM solutions consist of templates that are adapted on the fly (an ACM template must be designed so that the case manager can pick and choose elements— analogous to how a diner picks and chooses food at a buffet table—and adapt them to the use at hand, including combining the elements in novel ways), while BPM solutions are programmed.

◆ **DAVID** takes you into the field of healthcare to see how the capabilities of ACM would support the kinds of knowledge work found there.

◆ **FRANK** gets you inside the mind of a help-desk professional to show the kinds of decisions and tradeoffs that must be made in real time as work unfolds, and he shows how this can be supported by an ACM system.

◆ **HENK** explores how organizations that innovate need ACM capabilities and how these organizations might leverage them.

◆ **DERMOT** discusses organizational agility and explores how an agile organization's needs can be met with ACM.

◆ **CAFFREY** gives you a concrete picture of how things in new product development don't simply go as preplanned, and the situation requires active participation of the case manager along the way.

◆ **KEITH** provides a historical perspective for ACM: where the ideas came from and where ACM fits relative to other process technologies that exist.

Where will this go in the future? How will things develop? Next year at this time will everyone be talking about adaptive case management (ACM) and how the different vendors stack up? You have stayed with the book this far, so surely you recognize that the development of the latest technology is knowledge work at its best and most unpredictable. It would be ironic for a book on unpredictability to pretend to be able to foretell the future.

Some things, like the trends above, can point to a direction that the world is going. As questions in the business process management (BPM) space are answered and that field becomes clear, it opens up new areas of inquiry to be explored. As the levels of routine work get more and more supported by process technology, it frees us up to attack the problem of supporting unpredictable knowledge work. This remains, as Drucker (1999) pointed out, "the biggest of the 21st century management challenges."

The authors of *Mastering the Unpredictable* humbly admit to being unable to predict how these events will unfold. We know that there are good tools available to help in this important and worthy goal. We are confident that fast-moving, agile organizations will see the opportunity and use these tools to outpace their competition. But we don't need to predict the future precisely.

Mastering the unpredictable is not eliminating the unpredictable. Mastering the unpredictable is not about committing to an immutable plan. Instead, we will use an ACM approach that gives us the tools to be able to adapt our course, respond quickly as things unfold, and take advantage of the best opportunities as they appear.

ABBREVIATIONS

ABC	activity-based costing
AC	authority collection
ACM	adaptive case management
ADT	admission, discharge, transfer
AIIM	Association for Information and Image Management
API	application programming interface
BAM	business activity monitoring
BEI	Business Ecology Initiative
BMM	business motivation model
BOP	business operations platform
BPAF	business process analytics format
BPEL	business process execution language
BPM	business process management
BPMM	business process maturity model
BPMN	business process modeling notation
BPMS	business process management suite/software/system
BPO	business process orientation
BRE	business rules engine
CAD	computer aided design
CAM	computer-aided manufacturing
CAPA	corrective and preventative action
CEDP	Court Executive Development Program
CMIS	Content Management Interoperability Services
COBOL	Common Business-Oriented Language
COE	center of excellence
COTS	commercial off-the-shelf
CPU	central processing unit
CRM	customer relationship management
CSCW	computer supported collaborative work
DBMS	database management system
DMAIC	define, measure, analyze, improve, control

DoD	Department of Defense
EAI	enterprise application integration
ECM	enterprise content management
EHR	electronic health repository
EMEA	Europe, Middle East, and Africa
EMR	electronic medical record
ERP	enterprise resource planning
Evo	evolutionary project management
FERC	Federal Energy Regulatory Commission
FF	finish-finish
FISMA	Federal Information Security Management Act
FS	finish-start
GPS	global positioning system
GUI	graphical user interface
HIPAA	Health Insurance Portability and Accountability Act
HL7	Health Level Seven International
HR	human resources
HTML	Hypertext Markup Language
ID	identification
IDE	integrated design environment
IE	impact estimation
ISO	International Organization for Standardization
IT	information technology
IVR	interactive voice response
JAD	joint application development
JIT	just-in-time
KPI	key performance indicator
KYC	know your customer
LAN	local area network
LDAP	Lightweight Directory Access Protocol
M&A	mergers and acquisitions
MBA	Master of Business Administration
MBO	management by objectives
MEBA	multi-enterprise business application
MES	manufacturing execution system
NBA	North American National Basketball Association

NERC	North American Electric Reliability Corporation
NIEM	National Information Exchange Model
NIST	National Institute of Standards and Technology
NL	natural language
NLR	natural language rule
OA	office automation
OASIS	Organization for the Advancement of Structured Information Standards
OCR	optical character recognition
OECD	Organisation for Economic Co-operation and Development
OEM	original equipment manufacturer
OLTP	online transaction processing
OMG	Object Management Group
PARC	Palo Alto Research Center
PAS	patient administration system
PC	personal computer
PCI DSS	Payment Card Industry Data Security Standard
PDF	portable document format
PDVSM	product development value stream maps
PE	process execution
PGE	Pacific Gas & Electric
PIN	personal identification number
PKI	public key infrastructure
PLM	product lifecycle management
PM	project management
PP	process planning
PPM	project portfolio management
QA	quality assurance
QFD	quality function deployment
R&D	research and development
RFID	radio frequency identification
RFP	request for proposal
RIA	rich Internet application
ROI	return on investment
RPG	Report Program Generator
RSS	really simple syndication

SaaS	software as a service
Sarbox	Sarbanes–Oxley Act
SCM	supply chain management
SCOOP	system for computerization of office procedures
SF	start-finish
SLA	service-level agreement
SMART	specific, measurable, achievable, realistic, and time constrained
SME	small- and medium-sized enterprise
SOA	service-oriented architecture
SPEM	Software and Systems Process Engineering Meta-Model
SS	start-start
STP	straight-through processing
TPS	testing procedure specification
TPS	Toyota production system
UI	user interface
UML	Unified Modeling Language
URL	Uniform Resource Locator
VOC	voice of the customer
VOM	voice of the market
WfMC	Workflow Management Coalition
Wf-XML	XML-based protocol for runtime integration of process engines
WWW	World Wide Web
WYSIWYG	what you see is what you get
XML	Extensible Markup Language
XPDL	XML Process Definition Language
XSD	extensible schema definition

GLOSSARY

ACM solution—A collection of templates created on adaptive case management (ACM) technology designed to meet the needs of a particular business unit. You can think of this as an "application" to meet a particular need.

activity—A description of a piece of work that forms one logical step within a process. It is the basic unit of work within a process. Presumably, work could be subdivided into units smaller than a given activity, but it is not meaningful for the organization to track the work to that level of detail. Synonyms include node, step, and task.

adaptive case management (ACM)—A productive system that deploys not only the organization and process structure, but it becomes the system of record for the business data entities and content involved. All processes are completely transparent, as per access authorization, and fully auditable. It enables nontechnical business users in virtual organizations to seamlessly create/consolidate structured and unstructured processes from basic predefined business entities, content, social interactions, and business rules. It moves the process knowledge gathering from the template analysis/modeling/simulation phase into the process execution phase in the lifecycle. It collects actionable knowledge—without an intermediate analysis phase—based on process patterns created by business users. ACM differs from business process management (BPM) in that the case information is the focus and the thing around which the other artifacts are organized. And it is the case information that persists for the long term.

ad hoc process—*See* emergent process.

agile methodology—To move quickly and lightly. In reference to solution development, it is a method where many short iterations are used, with many quick (internal) releases, so that the nontechnical customer of a solution can be more actively involved in guiding the course of development. The agile approach to development is known to produce solutions that better meet the needs of the customer, and it also allows for greater responsiveness to external changes in requirements.

analytics—A mechanism for collecting and processing statistics. Process analytics will gather and process statistics about the running of processes in such a way that it is useful for evaluating how well the process is running.

best practice—An approach to achieving a particular outcome that is believed to be more effective than any other approach in a particular condition or circumstance.

business operations platform (BOP)—A next-generation technology platform oriented toward continuously designing, executing, monitoring, changing, and optimizing critical business processes; proposed by Fingar (2009).

business process—A set of one or more linked activities that collectively realize a business objective or policy goal, normally within the context of an organizational structure defining functional roles and relationships.

business process execution language (BPEL)—A standard executable language, based on XML, for describing a process that uses web service calls to communicate with the outside world.

business process management (BPM)—The practice of developing, running, performance measuring, and simulating business processes to effect the continued improvement of those processes. Business process management is concerned with the lifecycle of the process definition. BPM differs from adaptive case management (ACM) in that its focus is the process, and it uses the process as an organizing paradigm around which data, roles, and communication are organized. Process models are prepared in advance for particular situations, and the performance can be measured and monitored so that over time the process will be improved.

business process management suite/software/system (BPMS)—A software system designed to support business process management. The acronym BPMS is used to distinguish the technology product from the management practice of BPM.

business process modeling notation (BPMN)—A standard set of graphical shapes and conventions with associated meanings that can be used in modeling a business process.

business process orientation (BPO)—A concept that suggests that organizations could enhance their overall performance by viewing all the activities as linked together into a process that ultimately produces a good or service.

business rules engine (BRE)—A software system for managing and evaluating a complex set of rules in a business processing environment. A business rule is a small piece of logic that is separated from the application logic so that it may be managed separately from the application code. Rules are often expressed in a language that is more accessible to nonprogrammers.

case—The name given to the specific situation, set of circumstances, or initiative that requires a set of actions to achieve an acceptable outcome or objective. Each case has a subject that is the focus of the actions—such as a person, a lawsuit, or an insurance claim—and is driven by the evolving circumstances of the subject.

case file—Contains all of the case information and processes, and it coordinates communications necessary to accomplish the goal for a particular case. A case file can contain information of any type including documents, images, video, etc.

case management—A method or practice of coordinating work by organizing all of the relevant information into one place—called a case. The case becomes the focal point for assessing the situation, initiating activities and processes, as well as keeping a history record of what has transpired. Beyond this generic definition, case management has specific meanings in the medical care, legal, and social services fields. For this book, we see case management as a technique that could be used in any field of human endeavor.

case owner—A person (or group of people) who is responsible for the outcome of a case. The case owner can change any aspect of a case and is actively involved in achieving the goals of the case.

commercial off-the-shelf (COTS)—Describes software or hardware products that are ready-made and available for sale to the general public. This term is used to distinguish such product from custom software and hardware made specifically for a purpose that are presumed to be more expensive to produce and maintain.

customer relationship management (CRM)—Technology to manage a company's interactions with customers and sales prospects.

emergent process—A process that is not predictable. Emergent processes have a sensitive dependence upon external factors outside of the control of the process context, which is why they cannot be fixed according to their internal state. Workers involved in an emergent process will experience it as planning and working alternately or at the same time, such that the plan is evolved as the work evolves. Synonyms include ad hoc process and unstructured process.

enterprise content management (ECM)—Strategies, methods, and tools used to capture, manage, store, preserve, and deliver content and documents related to organizational processes. ECM strategies and tools allow the management of an organization's unstructured information, wherever that information exists.

enterprise resource planning (ERP)—Computer system used to manage resources including tangible assets, financial resources, materials, and human resources.

knowledge work—A type of work where the course of events is decided on a case-by-case basis. It normally requires a person with detailed knowledge who can weigh many factors and anticipate potential outcomes to determine the course for a specific case. Knowledge work almost always involves an emergent process.

knowledge workers—People who have a high degree of expertise, education, or experience and the primary purpose of their job involves the creation, distribution, or application of knowledge. Knowledge workers do not necessarily work in knowledge-intensive industries.

lifecycle—This book uses lifecycle only in regard to the work of creating a solution. The development lifecycle of a solution might start with definition of requirements, development of a process definition, development of forms, testing, deployment of the solution into production, use of the solution by many people, and finally the shutting down of the solution. The lifecycle of a solution may involve monitoring the running process instances and improving those process definitions over time. Note: A solution has a lifecycle that takes it from start to finish; a case has a process or processes that take it from start to finish.

model—A simplified summary of reality designed to aid further study. In the business process field, a process model is a simplified or complete process definition created to study the proposed process before execution time.

node—*See* activity.

online transaction processing (OLTP)—A class of systems where time-sensitive, transaction-related data are processed immediately and are always kept current.

organizational agility—That quality of an organization associated with sensing opportunity or threat, prioritizing its potential responses, and acting efficiently and effectively.

predictable process—A process that is repeatable and is run the same way a number of times. Synonyms include definable process, repeatable process, and structured process.

process definition—A representation of a business process in a form that supports automated manipulation, such as modeling or enactment by a process management system. The process definition consists of a network of activities and their relationships, criteria to indicate the start and termination of the process, and information about the individual activities, such as participants, associated IT applications, and data. Synonyms include process diagram and workflow.

process diagram—A visual explanation of a process definition. Synonyms include process definition, process model, and process flowchart.

process flowchart—*See* process diagram.

process instance—A data structure that represents a particular instance of running of a process. It has associated context information that can be used and manipulated by the process. A process instance plays a role in a business process management system (BPMS) that is very similar to but not exactly the same as a case in a case management system. A particular case may have more than one process instance associated with it.

process model—A simplified or complete process definition created to study the proposed process before execution time. Synonyms include process diagram.

project portfolio management (PPM)—Balancing a set of proposed initiatives to achieve an organization's goals and objectives.

records management—Management of the information created, received, and maintained as evidence and information by an organization in pursuance of legal obligations or in the transaction of business.

role—An association of particular a user, or users, with a particular set of responsibilities in a particular context. In this case, responsibility means the expectation to perform particular activities for that context.

routine work—Work that is predictable and usually repeatable. Its predictability allows routine work to be planned to a large extent before the work is started. As the name implies, routine work is considered normal, regular, and it is not exceptional.

scientific management—An early twentieth century school of management that aimed to improve the physical efficiency of an individual worker by carefully recording precisely what must be done for a particular task, and then training workers to replicate that precisely. It is based on the work of Frederick Winslow Taylor (1856–1915).

Scrum—An agile software development methodology emphasizing iteration and incremental development.

service-oriented architecture (SOA)—An approach to system design where the software functionality is deployed to a specific logical location (a service) and programs requiring that software functionality make use of communications protocols to access the service remotely. SOA has often been discussed together with business process management (BPM), but this connection is coincidental. While BPM might benefit from SOA the way that any program/system would, there is no inherent connection between managing business processes and the system architecture that supports them.

social software—A class of software systems that allows users to communicate, collaborate, and interact in many flexible ways. Generally, such software allows users to form their own relationships with other users and then exchange messages, write notes, and share media in different ways.

solution—A package of artifacts (configurations, forms, process definitions, templates, and information) that have been prepared in advance to help users address particular kinds of recurring situations. A solution may embody best practices for a particular kind of situation.

step—*See* activity.

straight-through processing (STP)—The practice of completely automating a process and eliminating all manual human tasks. This term is typically used in the financial industry.

subject (of a case)—An entity that is the focus of actions performed in the context of a case. For example, a person, a lawsuit, or an insurance claim.

task—*See* activity.

template—The general concept of something that is prepared in advance approximately for a particular purpose with the anticipation that it will be modified during use to more exactly fit the situation. A process template does not define a process in the way that a process definition does.

unstructured process—*See* emergent process.

work—Exertion or effort directed to produce or accomplish something. Organizations exist to achieve goals and work is the means to achieve those goals. The smallest recorded unit of work is an activity. Activities are combined into procedures and processes.

workflow—The automation of a business process, in whole or part, during which documents, information, or tasks are passed from one participant to another for action according to a set of procedural rules. Synonyms include process definition.

Bibliography

(ABA 2010) American Bar Association. *"Digital Signature Guidelines Tutorial."* Section of Science and Technology Information Security Committee. (2010), http://www.abanet.org/scitech/ec/isc/dsg-tutorial.html/.

(Accenture 2009) Accenture. *"Innovation: A Priority for Growth in the Aftermath of the Downturn—Management Shortcomings Hinder Results; Research Summary."* (2009), http://www.accenture.com/NR/rdonlyres/B59FCFD8-E67D-453D-A145-9BFD2E87D34E/0/Accenture_Innovation_a_Priority_for_Growth_in_the_Aftermath_of_the_Downturn.pdf/.

(Ackoff 1999) Russell L. Ackoff. *Ackoff's Best: His Classic Writings on Management.* New York: John Wiley & Sons, 1999.

(AIIM 2009) AIIM. *"What is ECM?"* (2009) http://www.aiim.org/What-is-ECM-Enterprise-Content-Management.aspx/.

(AMP 2008) Object Management Group. *"Agent Metamodel and Profile, Request for Proposal."* (September 29, 2008), http://www.omg.org/cgi-bin/doc?ad/2008-9-5/.

(Anderson 1988) Philip W. Anderson, Kenneth J. Arrow, and David Pines, eds. *The Economy as an Evolving Complex System.* Boulder, CO: Westview Press, 1988.

(Atlassian 2010) Atlassian. Vendor of software development management product JIRA. (2010) http://www.atlassian.com/software/jira/.

(Ballé 2009) Michael Ballé and Freddy Ballé. *The Lean Manager: A Novel of Lean Transformation.* Cambridge, MA: Lean Enterprise Institute, 2009.

(Bartels 2009) Andrew H. Bartels. *"Smart Computing Drives the New Era of IT Growth: A New Tech Investment Cycle Holds Seismic Promise—and Challenges."* Forrester Research (December 4, 2009), http://www.forrester.com/rb/Research/smart_computing_drives_new_era_of_it/q/id/55157/t/2/.

(BEI 2009) Object Management Group. *"OMG's Business Ecology™ Initiative."* (May 4, 2009), http://www.business-ecology.org/Business_Ecology.pdf/.

(Blanchard 2001) Ken Blanchard, John P. Carlos, and Alan Randolph. *The 3 Keys to Empowerment: Release the Power Within People for Astonishing Results.* San Francisco: Berrett-Koehler Publishers, 2001.

(BMM 2008) Object Management Group. *"Business Motivation Model, Version 1.0."* (August 2, 2008), http://www.omg.org/spec/BMM/1.0/PDF/.

(Bohm 2002) David Bohm. *Wholeness and the Implicate Order.* Reissue, New York: Routledge, 2002.

(BPMM 2008) Object Management Group. *"Business Process Maturity Model (BPMM), Version 1.0."* (June 1, 2008), http://www.omg.org/spec/BPMM/1.0/PDF/.

(BPMN 2009) Object Management Group. *"Business Process Model and Notation (BPMN), Version 1.2."* (January 3, 2009), http://www.omg.org/spec/BPMN/1.2/PDF/.

(Brown 2008) Tim Brown. *"Design Thinking."* Harvard Business Review (June 1, 2008), http://hbr.org/product/design-thinking/an/R0806E-PDF-ENG/.

(Bugzilla 2010) Bugzilla. Open source community that provides the defect-tracking product Bugzilla. (2010) http://www.bugzilla.org/.

(Cal-Fire 2009) California Department of Forestry and Fire Protection, *"CAL FIRE Firefighters Receive Medal of Valor from Governor,"* News Release, December 10, 2009. http:/ www.fire.ca.gov/fire_protection/fire_protection_valor2009.php/.

(Carr 2004) Nicholas G. Carr. *Does IT Matter?: Information Technology and the Corrosion of Competitive Advantage.* Boston: Harvard Business Press, 2004.

(CDO 2010) Computer Dictionary Online. (2010) http://www.computer-dictionary-online. org/.

(Chesbrough 2003) Henry W. Chesbrough. *"The Era of Open Innovation."* MIT Sloan Management Review (April 15, 2003), http://sloanreview.mit.edu/the-magazine/articles/2003/spring/4435/the-era-of-open-innovation/.

(CMPM 2009) Object Management Group. *"Case Management Process Modeling (CMPM), Request For Proposal."* (September 23, 2009), http://www.omg.org/cgi-bin/doc?bmi/2009-9-23/.

(Collins 2001) Jim Collins. *Good to Great: Why Some Companies Make the Leap... and Others Don't.* New York: HarperCollins, 2001.

(Cortada 1998) James W. Cortada. *"Where Did Knowledge Workers Come From?"* In Rise of the Knowledge Worker. Woburn, MA: Butterworth-Heinemann, 1998.

(Dai 2008) Weihui Dai, Mingqi Chen, and Nan Ye. *"Research on the Formation of Innovation Ecosystem in Software Industry and Its Development Strategy,"* In The Sixth Wuhan International Conference on E-Business. Management School of Fudan University: Shanghai, China, 2008. http://it.swufe.edu.cn/UploadFile/other/xsjl/sixwuhan/Paper/IM305.pdf/.

(Damiani 2007) Ernesto Damiani, Alberto Colombo, Fulvio Frati, and Carlo Bellettini. *"A Metamodel for Modeling and Measuring Scrum Development Process."* Milan, Italy: Department of Information Technology, University of Milan, 2007. http://www.springerlink.com/content/544342304704x475/.

(Davenport 2005) Thomas H. Davenport. *Thinking for a Living: How to Get Better Performances and Results from Knowledge Workers.* Boston: Harvard Business School Publishing, 2005.

(Doar 2005) Matthew B. Doar. *Practical Development Environments.* Sebastopol, CA: O'Reilly Media, 2005.

(Drucker 1959) Peter F. Drucker. *Landmarks of Tomorrow: A Report on the New "Post-Modern" World.* New York: Harper Colophon Books, 1959.

(Drucker 1969) Peter F. Drucker. *The Age of Discontinuity: Guidelines to Our Changing Society.* New York: Harper and Row, 1969.

(Drucker 1992) Peter F. Drucker. *"Drucker on Management: Planning for Uncertainty."* The Wall Street Journal, July 22, 1992, Section A.

(Drucker 1998) Peter F. Drucker. *"The Future That Has Already Happened."* The Futurist 32, no. 8 (November 1, 1998), http://pqasb.pqarchiver.com/futurist/access/35379083. html?FMT=ABS&FMTS=ABS:FT:TG:PAGE&type=current&date=Nov+1998& author=Peter+Drucker&pub=The+Futurist&edition=&startpage=16&desc=The+ future+that+has+already+happened/.

(Drucker 1999) Peter F. Drucker. *Management Challenges for the 21ˢᵗ Century.* New York: HarperCollins, 1999.

(FCSO 2008) Fresno County Sheriff's Office. *"Update on Rescue of Boy Scout,"* News Release, June 26, 2008.

(Fingar 2009) Peter Fingar. *Dot.Cloud: The 21ˢᵗ Century Business Platform Built on Cloud Computing.* Tampa: Meghan-Kiffer Press, 2009.

(Friedman 2006) Thomas L. Friedman. *The World Is Flat: A Brief History of the Twenty-First Century.* New York: Farrar, Straus & Giroux, 2006.

(Galliers 2009) Robert Galliers. *"Ignore Technology at Your Peril."* Financial Times (December 1, 2009), http://discussions.ft.com/bused/forums/soapboxforum/ ignore-technology-at-your-peril/.

(Galvan 2008) Louis Galvan. *"Rescuers Save Boy Trapped by Boulder."* The Fresno Bee, June 28, 2008.

(Gilb 2004) Tom Gilb. *"Adding Stakeholder Metrics to Agile Projects."* Cutter IT Journal 17, no. 1 (July 1, 2004), http://www.cutter.com/content/itjournal/fulltext/2004/07/ itj0407f.html/.

(Gilb 2005) Tom Gilb. *Competitive Engineering: A Handbook for Systems Engineering, Requirements Engineering, and Software Engineering Using Planguage.* Burlington, MA: Elsevier Butterworth Heinemann, 2005.

(Gogek 2007) Jim Gogek. University of California, San Diego, *"UC San Diego's High-tech Tools Helped Combat Wildfires: Emergency Advancements Can Aid Disaster Worldwide,"* News Release, November 5, 2007. http://ucsdnews.ucsd.edu/newsrel/ general/11-07HighTechToolsCombatFiresJG-L.asp/.

(Harmon 2007) Paul Harmon. *Business Process Change: A Guide for Business Managers and BPM and Six Sigma Professionals.* Burlington, MA: Morgan Kaufmann, 2007.

(Harry 2006) Mikel Harry and Don R. Linsenmann. *The Six Sigma Fieldbook: How DuPont Successfully Implemented the Six Sigma Breakthrough Management Strategy.* Random House, 2006.

(Havenstein 2007) Heather Havenstein. *"LA Fire Department all 'aTwitter' over Web 2.0."* Computerworld (August 3, 2007). http://www.pcworld.com/article/135518/ la_fire_department_all_atwitter_over_web_20.html/.

(Heffner 2005) Randy Heffner. *"Digital Business Architecture: IT Foundation For Business Flexibility."* Forrester Research (November 7, 2005). http://www.forrester.com/rb/Research/digital_business_architecture_it_foundation_for_business/q/id/36927/t/2/.

(Hertle 2007) Jochen Hertle. *"The Dimensions of Innovation and Its Dynamics."* Munich University of Applied Sciences (May 23, 2007). http://w3-0.cs.hm.edu/~hertle/veranstaltungen/Innovation.pdf/.

(Hertwig 2009) Ralph Hertwig and Ido Erev. *"The Description-Experience Gap in Risky Choice."* Trends in Cognitive Sciences 13, 12 (October 15, 2009). http://www.cell.com/trends/cognitive-sciences/abstract/S1364-6613(09)00212-5/.

(Hutchins 2008) David Hutchins and Hoshin Kanri. *The Strategic Approach to Continuous Improvement.* Burlington VT: Gower, 2008.

(ISO 2001) ISO 15489-1:2001. (http://www.iso.org/iso/iso_catalogue/catalogue_tc/catalogue_detail.htm?csnumber=31908&commid=48750)/.

(Iver 2009) Robbie Mac Iver. *"Scrum Is Not Just for Software: A Real-Life Application of Scrum Outside IT."* Scrum Alliance (February 9, 2009). http://www.scrumalliance.org/resource_download/548/.

(Janner 2008) T. Janner, C. Schroth, and B. Schmid. *"Modeling Service Systems for Collaborative Innovation in the Enterprise Software Industry: The St. Gallen Media Reference Model Applied."* Paper presented at the IEEE International Conference on Services Computing, Honolulu, Hawaii, July 7–11, 2008.

(Jeston 2008) John Jeston and Johan Nelis. *Business Process Management: Practical Guidelines to Successful Implementations.* 2nd ed. Burlington, MA: Butterworth-Heinemann, 2008.

(Jeston 2009) John C. Jeston. *Beyond Business Process Improvement, On To Business Transformation: A Manager's Guide.* Tampa: Meghan-Kiffer Press, 2009.

(Karel 2009) Rob Karel and Clay Richardson. *"Warning: Don't Assume Your Business Processes Use Master Data: Synchronize Your Business Process and Master Data Strategies."* Forrester Research (September 21, 2009). http://www.forrester.com/rb/Research/warning_dont_assume_business_processes_use_master/q/id/46559/t/2/.

(Kasten 2006) Vince Kasten and Gary Wolfe. *"Moving Courts into the Future—The Organizational Agility Imperative."* 2006. https://www.unisys.com/public_sector/insights/white__papers/index.htm/.

(Kemsley 2006) Sandy Kemsley. *"A Short History of BPM, Part 8: The Current State of BPM."* (June 15, 2006). http://www.column2.com/category/bpmhistory/.

(Kerremans 2008) Marc Kerremans. *"Case Management Is a Challenging Use Case for BPM."* Gartner (December 8, 2008).

(Liker 2004) Jeffrey K. Liker. *The Toyota Way: 14 Management Principles from the World's Greatest Manufacturer.* New York: McGraw-Hill, 2004.

(Manyika 2006) James Manyika. *"The Coming Imperative for the World's Knowledge Economy."* *Financial Times* (May 16, 2006). http://www.mckinsey.com/aboutus/mckinseynews/knowledge_economy.asp/.

(March 1958) James G. March and Herbert A. Simon. *Organizations.* New York: John Wiley & Sons, 1958.

(Marín 2008) César A. Marín, Iain Stalker, and Nikolay Mehandjiev. *"Engineering Business Ecosystems Using Environment-Mediated Interactions."* School of Informatics, University of Manchester (2008). http://distrinet.cs.kuleuven.be/events/eemmas/2007/contents/papers/eemmas_06_ready.pdf/.

(McAfee 2006) Andrew McAfee's Blog, comment on *"Enterprise 2.0, Version 2.0,"* comment posted May 27, 2006, http://andrewmcafee.org/2006/05/enterprise_20_version_20/.

(McDonald 2009) Lawrence G. McDonald. *A Colossal Failure of Common Sense: The Inside Story of the Collapse of Lehman Brothers.* With Patrick Robinson. New York: Crown Publishing Group, 2009.

(Meadows 2008) Donella H. Meadows. *Thinking in Systems: A Primer.* Edited by Diana Wright. White River Junction, VT: Chelsea Green Publishing Company, 2008.

(Miers 2007) Derek Miers. *"Process Innovation and Corporate Agility: Balancing Efficiency and Adaptability in a Knowledge-Centric World."* BPTrends, February 2007. http://www.bptrends.com/deliver_file.cfm?fileType=publication&fileName=02-07-ART-ProcessInnovationand%20CorporateAgility-Miers-Final.pdf/.

(Moore 2009) Connie Moore and Craig Le Clair. "Dynamic Case Management— An Old Idea Catches New Fire." Forrester Research (December 28, 2009). http://www.forrester.com/rb/Research/dynamic_case_management_%26%238212%3B_old_idea_catches/q/id/55755/t/2/.

(Morgan 2006) James M. Morgan and Jeffrey K. Liker. *The Toyota Product Development System: Integrating People, Process, and Technology.* New York: Productivity Press, 2006.

(Morris 2004) Peter Morris and Ashley Jamieson. *Translating Corporate Strategy into Project Strategy: Realizing Corporate Strategy Through Project Management.* Newtown Square, PA: Project Management Institute, 2004.

(zur Muehlen 2004) Michael zur Muehlen. *Workflow-based Process Controlling: Foundation, Design, and Application of Workflow-driven Process Information Systems.* Advances in Information Systems and Management Science. 6. Berlin: Logos, 2004.

(NCSC 2001) National Center for State Courts. *"Introduction to Functional Standards (Draft)."* (February 2, 2001). http://www.ncsconline.org/d_tech/standards/Documents/pdfdocs/IntroductionToFunctionalStandards3_1_01.pdf/.

(NCSC 2005) National Center for State Courts. *"Consolidated Case Management System Functional Standards Vo.10 (Exposure Draft)."* (November 11, 2005). http://www. ncsconline.org/d_tech/jtc/meeting/CMS%20Report%20Draft%20vo.10.pdf/.

(NCSC 2006) National Center for State Courts. *"Consolidated Case Management System Functional Standards* Vo.20 *(Exposure Draft)."* (June 26, 2006). http://www. ncsconline.org/d_tech/standards/Documents/Consolidated_CMS_Functional_ Standards_v_0_20.pdf/.

(Nelson 1982) Richard R. Nelson and Sidney G. Winter. *An Evolutionary Theory of Economic Change.* Cambridge, MA: Belknap, 1982.

(OECD 2009) Organisation for Economic Co-operation and Development. *"OECD Health Data 2009: Statistics and Indicators for 30 Countries."* (July 1, 2009). http://www.oecd. org/document/16/0,2340,en_2649_34631_2085200_1_1_1_1,00.html/.

(Palmer 2010) Nathaniel Palmer. *"2009 BPM — State of the Market Report,"* Transformation & Innovation, 2010. http://www.bpm.com/component/option,com_docman/ Itemid,54/gid,77/task,doc_download/.

(Popper 2002) Karl Popper. *The Logic of Scientific Discovery.* New York: Routledge Classics, 2002.

(Pucher 2007) Max J. Pucher's Blog, *"Welcome to the Real (IT) World."* http://isismjpucher. wordpress.com/, (2007-10)/.

(Pucher 2009) Max J. Pucher's Blog, comment on *"Adaptive Process Defined!"* Comment posted on December 4, 2009, http://isismjpucher.wordpress.com/2009/12/04/ adaptive-process-defined/.

(Rogers 2003) Everett M. Rogers. *Diffusion of Innovations.* 5th ed. New York: Free Press, 2003.

(Rogers 2005) Everett M. Rogers, Una E. Medina, Mario A. Rivera, and Cody J. Wiley. *"Complex Adaptive Systems and the Diffusion of Innovations."* The Innovation Journal 10, no. 3 (December 23, 2005), http://www.innovation.cc/volumes-issues/ rogers-adaptivesystem7final.pdf/.

(Sawhney 2006) Mohanbir Sawhney, Robert C. Wolcott, and Inigo Arroniz. *"The 12 Different Ways for Companies to Innovate,"* MIT Sloan Management Review 47, no. 3 (April 1, 2006), http://sloanreview.mit.edu/the-magazine/articles/2006/spring/47314/ the-different-ways-for-companies-to-innovate/.

(Schadler 2009) Ted Schadler. *"Harness the Power of Workforce Personas: Survey and Segment Your Workforce to Understand What They Truly Need."* Forrester Research (December 9, 2009). http://www.forrester.com/rb/Research/harness_power_of_ workforce_personas/q/id/46408/t/2/.

(Schlenoff 1996) Craig Schlenoff, Amy Knutilla, and Steven Ray. *"Unified Process Specification Language: Requirements for Modeling Process."* NIST (September 1996). http://www.mel.nist.gov/msidlibrary/doc/schlen96/req-paper.pdf/.

(Senge 1990) Peter M. Senge. *The Fifth Discipline: The Art & Practice of the Learning Organization*. New York: Doubleday, 1990.

(Spear 2009) Steven J. Spear. *Chasing the Rabbit: How Market Leaders Outdistance the Competition and How Great Companies Can Catch Up and Win*. New York: McGraw-Hill, 2009.

(SPEM 2008) Object Management Group. *"Software & Systems Process Engineering Meta-Model Specification Version 2.0."* (April 1, 2008). http://www.omg.org/spec/SPEM/2.0/PDF/.

(Standish 2009) The Standish Group, *"New Standish Group Report Shows More Project Failing and Less Successful Projects,"* News Release, April 23, 2009. http://standishgroup.com/newsroom/chaos_2009.php/.

(Sutherland 2007) Jeff Sutherland and Ken Schwaber. *"The Scrum Papers: Nuts, Bolts, and Origins of an Agile Process."* October 14, 2007. http://scrumtraininginstitute.com/home/stream_download/scrumpapers/.

(Sutherland 2009) Jeff Sutherland and Igor Altman. *"Take No Prisoners: How a Venture Capital Group Does Scrum."* December 2009. http://jeffsutherland.com/SutherlandTakeNoPrisonersAgile2009.pdf/.

(Swenson 1993a) Keith D. Swenson. *"A Visual Language to Describe Collaborative Work."* Paper presented at the Proceedings of the International Workshop for Visual Languages, Bergen, Norway, August 24–27, 1993. http://kswenson.workcast.org/1993/199308_VL93/VL93.pdf/.

(Swenson 1993b) Keith D. Swenson. *"Visual Support for Reengineering Work Processes."* Paper presented at the Proceedings of the Conference on Organizational Computing Systems, Milpitas, CA, November 1–4, 1993. http://kswenson.workcast.org/1993/199309_COOCS/Coocs93.pdf/.

(Swenson 1994) Keith D. Swenson et al. *"A Business Process Environment Supporting Collaborative Planning,"* *The Journal of Collaborative Computing* 1, no. 1 (April 27, 1994), http://kswenson.workcast.org/1994/199405_Journal CC/JournalCC.pdf/.

(Swenson 2001) Keith D. Swenson. *"Workflow for the Information Worker,"* in Workflow Handbook 2001, edited by Layna Fischer, 39–49. Lighthouse Point, FL: Future Strategies, 2000. http://kswenson.workcast.org/2001/Workflow for the Information Worker.pdf/.

(Taleb 2007) Nassim Nicholas Taleb. *The Black Swan: The Impact of the Highly Improbable*. New York: Random House, 2007.

(TX-OCA 2008) Texas Office Of Court Administration. *"Data Dictionary Data Field Diagram for the OCA TexDECK Project Case Management Functional Requirements 04/24/08."* TexDECK Functional Requirements: Data Diagram. http://www.courts.state.tx.us/oca/texdeck/frd/TexDECK%20Data%20Diagram%20PDF.pdf/.

(VDM 2009) Object Management Group. *"Value Delivery Metamodel (VDM), Request for Proposal."* (March 9, 2009). http://www.omg.org/cgi-bin/doc?bmi/2009-3-9/.

(Wagner 2006) Ferdinand Wagner, Ruedi Schmuki, Thomas Wagner, and Peter Wolstenholme. *Modeling Software with Finite State Machines: A Practical Approach.* Boca Raton, FL: Auerbach Publications, 2006.

(Webster 1996) Lawrence P. Webster. *Automating Court Systems.* Court Management Library Series. Williamsburg, VA: National Center for State Courts, 1996. http://contentdm. ncsconline.org/cgi-bin/showfile.exe?CISOROOT=/tech&CISOPTR=157/.

(Womack 2008) Jim Womack. *"The Power of Purpose, Process, People."* Lean Enterprise Institute (2008), http://www.lean.org/events/may_2008_webinar_womack_slides_ postpresentation.pdf/.

(Zisman 1977) Michael Zisman. *"Representation, Specification, and Automation of Office Procedures,"* Doctoral Thesis, Wharton Business School, University of Pennsylvania, 1977.

Author Biographies

David Hollingsworth

David Hollingsworth is a Managing Architect working with the Fujitsu Services global healthcare unit. He has been actively involved in business transformation programs for twenty years, contributing both to industry standards work through the Workflow Management Coalition (WfMC) as well as developing business solutions for major customer implementation projects for Fujitsu. Since 2003, David has led the architecture work on healthcare systems delivery in the U.K., bringing together healthcare and business automation experience.

Dana Khoyi

Dana Khoyi is Vice President of Development at Global 360, and he is responsible for the development of its case management products. He has been working on case management, business process management (BPM), and content management products for the past ten years with a focus on providing powerful and flexible platforms to enable knowledge work. Dana has been working in the software industry for thirty years in a variety of areas including operating systems, programming languages, office applications, and imaging and email systems, and he holds a number of patents in related technology.

Frank Michael Kraft

Frank Michael Kraft has nineteen years of experience as a systems analyst and software architect for custom and standard software for business processes. In his last role at SAP AG, he defined the architecture for the model-driven development of the business processes of two hundred business objects as part of the business process platform that is the foundation for SAP Business ByDesign. These business objects cover the application areas of supplier relationship management, customer relationship management, logistics planning and execution, production, project management, human resources, and financials. Frank was responsible for the governance process for the business process management (BPM) models, and he conducted many thousands of model reviews, which included the design of many thousands of service operations as part of the service-oriented architecture. A special focus of Frank's work was the flexibility and adaptability of the modeled business processes, for which he developed innovative concepts. He is an inventor with various patents in the area of business process integration and design and flexibility. Recently, he was member of the BPMN 2.0 specification team and contributed in the area of choreography modeling, where he also published scientific articles.

Frank's new role is founder of a company that will offer adaptive case management (ACM) software as a service (SaaS) including community library content, as well as knowledge products and coaching services in the area of business process design. Frank holds a Diplom. Inform. degree from the Technical University of Berlin. Visit www.adapro.eu for more information.

CAFFREY LEE

Caffrey H. J. Lee is Vice President of Product Management at HandySoft Global Corporation, and he has over fifteen years of experience in workflow and business process management (BPM). Caffrey has held a variety of positions throughout his career—from systems integrator and developer to project lead and product management—giving him extensive experience solving complex business challenges of diverse organizations. Examples of process improvement initiatives that Caffrey has successfully completed for federal government entities and consumer product companies include capital acquisition, correspondence management, investigative case tracking, new employee onboarding, recruitment, and customer relationship management processes. Caffrey holds a BA in Business Administration from Hanshin University in Korea.

As Vice President of Product Management at HandySoft, Caffrey focuses on delivering continuous innovation and thought leadership evidenced by his drive behind the vision and product strategy for BizFlow® and BizFlow® OfficeEngine™: dynamic BPM products that he believes have the potential to enable adaptive case management. Since 1991, HandySoft has specialized in BPM offering a powerful BPM lifecycle solution and a full range of consulting/training services. BizFlow® Plus Suite offers complete business process lifecycle management. Through powerful new innovations in forms development and data integration, BizFlow® Plus achieves a 15%–20% decrease in development time, faster process performance, and improved process quality through advanced process execution collaboration and superior analytics/reporting. HandySoft works closely with customers and partners around the globe to deliver process automation ranging from complex integration initiatives to dynamic case management and action tracking systems. Visit www.handysoft.com for more information.

HENK DE MAN

Ir. Henk de Man MTD is Research Director at Cordys. His main focus is to further expand Cordys' technology capabilities to support transformation and management of business operations in (networked) enterprises. Henk represents Cordys in the Object Management Group (OMG), participating in standardization in the fields of business architecture and business modeling. He serves on the board of directors of the Value Chain Group. Henk has over fifteen years of experience in IT, working for Baan Company and Cordys. Henk holds an MS in Mathematics from Delft Technical University, and a post-masters degree in Designing Logistic Control Systems from Eindhoven Technical University.

Cordys is a global provider of software for business process innovation. It is Cordys' mission to improve customers' business operations with world-class software that allows organizations to change and innovate the way they do business with greater speed and flexibility. Cordys delivers a single platform that allows organizations to design, execute, monitor, change, and continuously optimize their critical business processes and operations. The unique combination of BPMS and cloud technology in the Cordys platform complements existing enterprise software while adding agility to business operations. Global 2000 companies worldwide have selected Cordys to achieve performance improvements in their business operations, such as increased productivity, reduced time to market, and faster response to ever-changing market demands. Headquartered in the Netherlands, Cordys has offices in the Americas, EMEA, and Asia-Pacific. Visit www.cordys.com for more information.

JOHN T. MATTHIAS

John T. Matthias, J.D., is a Principal Court Management Consultant, National Center for State Courts. He has twenty years of experience as a management consultant and business analyst in courts of forty states and countries and ten years of law practice that includes five years of experience as a city prosecutor. As a consultant, John has directed or participated in over seventy requirements-gathering and process/technology evaluation projects. His domains of expertise include court performance metrics, information integration, and many aspects of courts, prosecution/defense, and adult/juvenile probation. He is certified to use the Justice Information Exchange Model (JIEM) tool and was active in development of Case Management Functional Standards for criminal and juvenile case types.

John holds a BA from the University of Iowa, an MA from Seton Hall University, and a law degree from New York Law School. John practiced law for ten years in Texas and Iowa, managing cases of all types and conducting investigations, bench trials, and jury trials. He is a Fellow of the Institute for Court Management's Court Executive Development Program (CEDP).

Dermot McCauley

Dermot McCauley is Director of Corporate Development at Singularity. Previous to joining Singularity in 2003, he held President and General Manager roles in publicly quoted, high-growth technology companies in the U.S. and Europe, including Cambridge Technology Partners (CTP) and Rare Medium Group. An executive in his own successful start-up that was purchased by CTP in 1995, Dermot has previously worked for JPMorgan Chase, Dun & Bradstreet, and Sema. Dermot holds a Mathematics degree from Imperial College, London.

Singularity increases the performance and agility of business processes by the rapid implementation of its industry-leading business process management (BPM) and case management products. From offices in London, New York, Singapore, Ireland, and India, the company provides software products and professional services to increase the agility of organizations across the globe. Visit www.singularitylive.com for more information.

Nathaniel Palmer

Nathaniel Palmer is a Principal and Chief BPM Strategist with SRA International, Inc., a $1.5 billion system integrator based in Washington, D.C., as well as Editor-in-Chief of BPM.com, and Executive Director of the Workflow Management Coalition (WfMC). Previously, he was Director, Business Consulting for Perot Systems, working under business process guru Jim Champy, and prior to that, he spent over a decade with Delphi Group as Vice President and Chief Analyst. Over the last two decades, Nathaniel has published several dozen articles on many topics surrounding business process management, and in 1998, he was the first individual to be awarded the distinction of Laureate in Workflow. Nathaniel is co-author of *The X-Economy: Profiting from Instant Commerce*, as well as contributing author to *The BPM and Workflow Handbook, BPM in Practice*, and *The Encyclopedia of Database Systems*. He has been featured in publications ranging from *Fortune* to *The New York Times*, and he has had over one hundred bylined articles in IT publications such as *CIO* and *InformationWeek*. He has also been featured as a guest expert on National Public Radio and World Business Review.

SHIVA PRASAD

Shiva Prasad KHK is a Product Manager at Cordys responsible for the product management of the Business Operations Platform (BOP)—Cordys' flagship product offering. Shiva has fourteen years of professional experience in software—in both service consulting and new product innovation and development. As a business consultant, Shiva has executed enterprise resource planning (ERP) assignments, worked on large-scale knowledge management programs, and customer relationship management (CRM) projects spanning a range of verticals including manufacturing, travel and travel services, and government.

MAX J. PUCHER

In 1988, Max Pucher founded what is today the ISIS Papyrus Group: a medium-sized but global software business—present in fifty countries through subsidiaries or partners—with Fortune 1000 clients. Max guides ISIS Papyrus software development as its Chief Architect. Prior to ISIS Papyrus, he worked for IBM from 1973 to 1988 in Austria, U.K., and Saudi Arabia as a hardware engineer, systems consultant, and finally in sales.

Max has long been innovating content and process management software. For example, before PDF became popular, he was the first to propose the "electronic original" for formatted outbound business documents when others still created line-mode printstreams. He invented the PrintPool—a spooling database for "electronic originals"—used to sort/bundle/consolidate documents from various applications for printing, enveloping, and archiving. He designed the core technology for the Papyrus Platform with its business architecture repository, distributed object-oriented transaction engine, and embedded object relational database. He holds several software patents in the area of artificial intelligence for the so-called user-trained agent, a machine learning component for auto-discovery of process knowledge.

Max has been a driving force behind the creation of the adaptive case management (ACM) concept and proposes an extension into adaptive process, which makes orthodox business process management (BPM) obsolete as it covers all kinds of processes without preemptive analysis and modeling. Max is an advocate for placing human aspects before cost optimization aspects in process management. Empowerment utilizes intrinsic motivation to increase cost/quality ratios rather than using monetary motivation to target key performance indicators.

Max speaks and writes frequently on IT, and he has written two novels on artificial intelligence and its religious/political consequences.

Founded in 1988, ISIS Papyrus Software offers a consolidated business solution platform that can be configured to cover a consolidated spectrum from customer relationship management, to inbound and outbound content management, rich Internet applications, dynamic business applications, process management, business intelligence, and business rules. More than 2,000 well-known enterprise clients use Papyrus Software for high-volume (50 million pages per day) content generation (such as bank statements), interactive correspondence generation for thin-clients for up to 25,000 users, high-volume (500,000 scans per day) distributed inbound content capture, classification, data extraction, and validation all seamlessly linked into case and process management. ISIS Papyrus is committed to furthering standards and is a foundational sponsor of OASIS. Visit www.isis-papyrus.com for more information.

TOM SHEPHERD

Tom Shepherd is Director of Case Management for Global 360. In addition to driving product strategy for Global 360's industry-leading case management solutions, his work at Global 360 involves helping customers realize significant business benefits through the adoption of case management solutions. Tom's career spans fifteen years as a software solution provider in the business process management (BPM), enterprise content management (ECM), and business rules industries. His experience includes working with some of the largest companies worldwide on a variety of business process improvement projects.

KEITH D. SWENSON

Keith Swenson is Vice President of Research and Development at Fujitsu America, Inc. and the Chief Software Architect for its Interstage family of products. He is known for having been a pioneer in collaboration software and web services, and he has contributed to the development of workflow and business process management (BPM) standards. Keith is the Chairman of the Technical Committee of the Workflow Management Coalition (WfMC). In the past, he led development of collaboration software at MS2, Netscape, Ashton Tate, and Fujitsu. In 2004, he was awarded the Marvin L. Manheim Award for outstanding contributions in the field of workflow. Visit Keith's blog at http://kswenson.wordpress.com.

Fujitsu produces the Interstage family of middleware products, including Interstage Business Process Manager, a full-featured BPM suite (BPMS) supporting server-to-server integration, human routine process automation, dynamic process capability, and a collaboration platform for knowledge workers. The suite is rounded out with a process analytics server and a unique automated process discovery capability that can mine the process out of existing application log files to be exported onto the suite platform to streamline and automate the business processes. Visit www.fujitsu.com/interstage for more information.

THEODOOR VAN DONGE

Theodoor van Donge has more than twenty-five years of experience in IT innovation and leadership in the software sector. Together with Jan Baan, Theodoor is recognized for pioneering disruptive technologies focused on process innovation. Theodoor is the key architect behind Cordys' Business Operations Platform (BOP), and he is responsible for the company's technology architecture and software development.

JACOB P. UKELSON

Jacob P. Ukelson, D.Sc. is Chief Technology Officer at ActionBase. Jacob has a proven track record in discovering and developing innovative solutions to real-world customer problems, and then developing those solutions into products. Jacob has fostered innovation in many different environments, including both research and business settings. Until recently, Jacob served as CTO of Itemfield, the leader in next generation data transformation, where Jacob oversaw Itemfield's innovation, vision, and strategy until its acquisition by Informatica. Previously, Jacob was CTO and Business Development Executive for IBM's Global Technology Unit. Prior to that role, he was a department general manager at the IBM Thomas J. Watson Research Lab, managing a group of one hundred thirty cross-disciplinary researchers. Jacob received his Doctorate of Science in computer science from the Technion University in Israel. Visit www.actionbase.com for more information.

Index

Companion Book
www.mkpress.com/hi

How people really work
and how they can be helped to work better

HUMAN INTERACTIONS

The Heart and Soul of
Business Process Management

Keith Harrison-Broninski

Innovation at the Intersection of Business and Technology
www.mkpress.com